Understanding Youth

Adolescent Development for Educators

Understanding Youth

Adolescent Development for Educators

Michael J. Nakkula

and

Eric Toshalis

HARVARD EDUCATION PRESS
Cambridge, Massachusetts

Fourth Printing, 2013

Library of Congress Control Number 2006930074

ISBN 978-1-891792-31-1
ISBN 978-1-891792-32-8

Published by Harvard Education Press,
an imprint of the Harvard Education Publishing Group

Harvard Education Press
8 Story Street
Cambridge, MA 02138

Cover Design: Alyssa Morris

The typefaces used in this book are Galliard and RotisSemiSans.

Dedicated to the students we've taught and counseled

Contents

Preface

Understanding Youth is a book for educators of adolescents. By educators we mean teachers; school-based counselors, psychologists, and social workers; school administrators; future professionals in training as well as seasoned veterans; and youth developmentalists educating young people and promoting their development in community recreation centers and elsewhere. Our definition of educators also includes parents, guardians, mentors, and other caring adults who play significant roles in the education and development of young people. The impetus for writing this book stems from three primary sources:

- The lack, in our opinion, of a broad book on adolescent development devoted specifically to educators and their particular needs for developmental knowledge;

- Our years of educating teachers, counselors, and other school-based professionals, and gaining a sense of the information and skills they need for working with adolescents from the transition to middle school through the transition to work and/or college;

- Our convictions from our work as teachers and counselors regarding what it takes to educate adolescents effectively and to promote their development optimally.

In this book, we have drawn extensively from all three of these sources of inspiration in an effort to impart developmental understanding to those invested in its promotion: educators of the types described above. In that vein, we have embedded a broad range of practical, theoretical, and empirical information on adolescent development into what we call *threaded case studies.* Our threaded case-study approach introduces specific developmental issues within the context of particular adolescent lives in particular educational and relational scenarios. We then follow those issues as they evolve in conjunction with new challenges and new educational and developmental demands. In each chapter we introduce one or more characters—students and educators—who manifest, or bring to life, the developmental themes presented. In subsequent chapters we see how the issues become part of larger developmental and educational challenges. Our hope is that the wedding of thematic content within situations already somewhat familiar to educators, or educators-in-training, will help bring development to life and, in that sense, give the concepts educational utility.

A word about the phrasing of the main title, "understanding youth": from our perspective, to understand youth is not to arrive at a destination (i.e., when you finish this book, you will not be able to claim you "understand youth") but to commit to an approach that seeks insights from multiple sources about what *might* be going on for our students. We have attempted to adopt an orientation toward our students that suggests a posture of humility, advocacy, and ongoing learning about how adolescents see things and what they may need to grow. We emphasize humility as an antidote to "professionalism" or "expertise," given how little we can actually know about the complexities of any individual life. To assume knowledge or genuine understanding is likely to foreclose on the additional learning necessary to making us better educators. To throw up our hands and claim ignorance, however, is just as problematic; we need to find a balance that provides the space needed to explore *with* our students in order to be effective educators and advocates *for* them.

As we describe more fully in chapter 1, we endorse a *constructionist perspective* in this work, meaning that we emphasize the role of creating development through the generation of lived experience rather than focusing on "objective" descriptions of developmental processes, whether biological, psychological, or otherwise. A constructionist perspective argues that people work with one another in creating development. Rather than being a purely individual phenomenon, then, development is conceived of as fundamentally relational: it occurs within relationships of all types. This approach is intended to empower educators in recognizing the roles they play in helping construct the development of their students. Similarly, it is intended to help educators recognize how their own development, professional and personal, is affected by their relationships with students, including the sense of self-efficacy, or lack thereof, experienced through those relationships. From this perspective, the core meaning of adolescent development lies fundamentally in the interpretations adolescents make of themselves and their worlds. It argues that the meaning they make of their experiences is theirs, and that we as educators can play key roles in the meaning youth make of their lives, just as they can play that role in the meaning we make of ours.

The constructionist perspective also argues that adolescence itself is a social construction rather than an objective reality. As we argue in the book, that perspective does not diminish the importance of understanding adolescence as a reality within our time and culture. Our school system and other social institutions are designed according to particular interpretations of childhood, adolescence, and adulthood. Consistent with this social construction, we define adolescence roughly as the period of transition to middle school (starting in the sixth grade) through high school and the transition to work or college. For the purposes of our audience, we have selected educational markers rather than ages, but there is a close parallel, of course. Middle school begins when students are approximately 12, and the transition from high school to work and college typically occurs when students are approximately 18 or 19. Adolescence, then, is defined approximately as the teen years. Although new theoretical arguments are being made to extend the definition into the early twenties at least, given the structure of contemporary Western society, there is other literature that argues for a new developmental era called early adulthood to capture this time frame. Given that our primary audience is middle- and high-school educators, we have opted for a socially constructed definition fitting that educational period.

Although we anchor much of this book in theories of identity development, starting with Erik Erikson's classic contribution to the topic, we incorporate more contemporary notions of relational development into our conceptions of identity. While we find much of identity theory useful to understanding adolescence, we argue, along with others, that identity is less an individual endeavor than a collective one. Because we grow into who we are in and through relationships with others, we devote a good deal of this book to explicating relationship-based identity development processes, including those that involve student-educator relationships.

Our stance on the developmental importance of student-educator relationships extends beyond the theoretical. We believe there is an ethical imperative to approaching our work with youth relationally. To distance ourselves from our students is to put us and our work dangerously out of touch. This is a particular risk in our current era of high-stakes testing, in which students who pose particularly demanding developmental challenges are all too often sacrificed in the name of improved school-wide test scores. We hear time and again in our work that inordinate amounts of energy cannot be invested in a few "tough students" at the cost of educational quality for the larger whole. While this orientation holds an obvious logic, it puts us on a slippery slope: Who are the tough students? Where do we draw the line? And what happens to those who don't make it under the current "standards"? These are tough questions, and they are by no means rare. Our belief is that the adoption of a relational approach to education reduces the chances of writing students off as test-score risks or impediments to the greater good. At the end of the day, our work is not only about what we teach or counsel but also about how we relate to our students and the possibilities that open up for youth through these relationships.

The ethical imperative of taking a relational approach to education applies beyond the individual to the greater ecology of adolescent development. By expanding our attention to include the familial, cultural, institutional, and societal forces that shape who and how we become, we are able to read the subtleties of adolescent development with greater acuity. While we accept the notion that educators "can't do it all"—we can't be teachers, counselors, parents, and friends with all of our students—it is incumbent upon us to try to comprehend our students within the larger contexts of their lives. To view them as decontextualized learners virtually assures that we will reach many of them ineffectually. Throughout this book we provide examples of strategies for understanding youth within the contexts of their lives, at least from the limited perspective of those contexts available to us.

Teaching and counseling relationally means educating *to* care and educating *through* care. We attempt to educate our students to care about the world, to play a meaningful role in it; we are most effective in these efforts, we argue, when we make such attempts through caring about who our students are as people, through our curiosity regarding their ambitions, and through our empathy with their trials and challenges. Such caring brings us into *developmental alliance* with our students; we join them in their developmental processes and, in doing so, not only contribute to their growth but grow as educators through that experience as well. Forging developmental alliances means more than unilaterally advocating for our students; it means listening and adapting to the meaning they make of their lives and of our work with them. Education of this sort is more reciprocal than unilateral. It means accompanying youth rather than directing them, listening to them as much as we speak to them, and being open to the changes they inspire in us just as we hope they'll be open to the changes we may inspire in them.

This is not a "how to" book. It is more of a "to understand and engage" book. Our hope is that educators who read this book will be encouraged in their efforts to engage with their students to build greater reciprocal understanding and, through that process, come to learn more about themselves. As we learn more about how we engage with students, we are placed in the best position to have the impact that brought us to our work in the first place. To be optimal agents of change through education, we must learn and grow through our students. To understand youth is to understand ourselves in relationship with them. As we stated at the outset, understanding isn't an endpoint; it's a process. We hope to share in our understanding with you by depicting developmental change in the students' lives portrayed in the pages ahead.

Acknowledgments

A book like this one, which covers a wide range of topics in a broad area like adolescent development, clearly owes a great deal of gratitude to a host of people. As coauthors, we extend a collective thanks to those who have been instrumental to both of us, followed by individual acknowledgments to the key people who allowed our ideas to become the reality presented here.

Our first order of thanks go to the middle-school, high-school, college, and graduate students we have taught and counseled over the past many years. Consistent with our views on education and human development presented here, it goes without saying that we have learned and grown a great deal through our opportunities to teach and counsel you. The approach to this book congealed through our work together in the Harvard Graduate School of Education's course on adolescent development (H-236). To the hundreds of students who have taken this course over the years, we express our deep appreciation for helping us figure out what school-based professionals need to know about adolescent development and how to promote it. On the editorial side, we thank Caroline Chauncey for her enthusiastic support, unyielding patience, and eye for the big picture in the construction of this book, Doug Clayton for his original and lasting faith in the project, Daniel Simon for his thoughtful editing when it came to making the pieces fit and the narrative flow, and Dody Riggs for helping us get the whole thing right.

I (Mike) extend individual thanks to Steve, Mark, and Ron, who were there at the beginning of adolescence and remain extraordinary friends to this day, with a special thanks to Steve and his 18-year-old son, Jared, for hanging in there with me as I finished my work on this book while we tackled the relentless developmental task of reroofing Bessie's Place. Our cycles of hearty laughter and intense arguments capture the best of adolescence as it continues on into middle age. I am also grateful to my brothers—Tim, Greg, and Shawn—who joined me in making adolescence a particular challenge for our parents, Arvid and Joyce Nakkula, whose teaching and counsel laid the foundation for all I do. Intellectually, I am gratefully indebted to Bob Selman, whose contributions to human development generally—and to my work and life specifically—are woven throughout this book. For the past eight years I have had the pleasure of teaching adolescent development with an immensely talented and fun group of teaching fellows: I cannot thank you enough for the contributions you have made to this work. In that vein, I am particularly indebted to you, Eric, my coauthor, for your unyielding support for my approach to this work, and for your ability to blend it with your unique talents and insights; you both allowed and made this book happen as it did. Finally, to my wife, Caroline, and my sons, Lukas and Sam: my most profound gratitude for your love and sacrifice as we fit this book into our already rich and challenging lives. It's midsummer now, and a Red Sox–Tigers playoff run seems like an ideal, if strangely unimaginable, way to relax and have fun. I'm ready if you are!

For me (Eric), this book exists because so many people have been willing to teach me (or let themselves be taught by me), and for that I am humbled and grateful. First and foremost among those I must thank are all my students at Jonata School, Goleta Valley Junior High, and Cambridge Rindge and Latin. You have taught me more about adolescent development in our day-to-day classroom interactions than all other sources and scholars combined. Likewise, I am grateful to all the students of H-236, H-210A, and the interns of the Harvard Teacher Education Program over the years who have provided me with invaluable insights into the myriad ways in which educators move back and forth between theory and practice. I owe much to Dave Cash, my first principal, who gave me and all his teachers the autonomy we needed to experiment and grow. To Kay Merseth, I am grateful for the innumerable opportunities you've given me to train teachers, test assumptions, and stay rooted in classrooms. I am indebted to Ann and Irwin Sentilles for generously providing the lofty and quiet retreat that enabled me to work in peace and with clarity. To my teacher, advisor, counselor, and friend, Mike Nakkula, I am forever grateful for the knowledge, trust, levity, and coauthoring genius you have shared with me; a greater mentor I have never had. To Sarah, who believes in my work and what I have to say even when I don't, I will always be thankful for and in awe of your brilliance, radicalism, and gentle companionship; I couldn't do what I do without you. Finally, I thank the original applied adolescent developmentalists in my life— my parents. You taught me to think and work with reverence and care for those struggling to become who they are, and this book stands as a testament to the value of that approach.

CHAPTER ONE

The Construction of Adolescence

Four months into her fifth year of teaching, Danielle Petersen's third-period tenth-grade world literature class is progressing fairly well.[1] Most are passing and many have earned A's, which is a source of pride for those students, given Ms. Petersen's reputation for high standards. She gets along pretty well with most of the class and seems to handle the occasional disruption or defiance in a manner acceptable to the majority of her students. But her relationship with Antwon Saladin has been rough as of late. Although Antwon was cordial, if not eager to please, back in September, Danielle has experienced him as rude, disrespectful, and downright hostile for most of the last several weeks. Antwon, likewise, feels like Ms. Petersen is also rude, disrespectful, and hostile toward him. Each can cite specific instances where they were made to feel unappreciated, maligned, ignored, or spitefully treated, but neither has confronted the other about the growing discontent fomented by these experiences.

Unknown to Ms. Petersen, Antwon has been struggling with competing peer groups and the difficult decisions that come with negotiating allegiances to different friends. Concerned about his reading and writing abilities and the fact that his recent test scores indicate the possibility of failing the state-mandated graduation exam, Antwon has been inventing ways to avoid having to demonstrate his lack of competency: he neglects homework, remains off-task during group-work time, claims he doesn't know the answer or refuses to offer his ideas when called upon by Ms. Petersen, and generally looks for opportunities to derail the class into tangential discussions about current events. Although increasingly annoyed and even offended by this behavior, Ms. Petersen does her best to hide the fact that she is uncomfortable with confrontation and therefore tries to ignore problem areas in her classroom in hopes that they will go away on their own. To compound matters, she is afraid of urban African American students like Antwon who do not communicate with one another or with her in the way she is accustomed by virtue of her middle-class European American upbringing. Antwon's louder tone and tougher, streetwise demeanor are particularly frightening for Danielle since it exposes what she feels is the lack of credibility or cultural capital she needs to interact with him in a way that feels comfortable.

ADOLESCENT DEVELOPMENT AS SOCIAL CONSTRUCTION

Interpretation is central to adolescence on a host of different levels. Because cognitive development, roughly defined as the increasing capacity for rational and complex thinking, is relatively advanced by the beginning of the teen years, most adolescents possess the skills necessary to interpret their worlds in new and interesting ways. Children are magnificent interpreters of their worlds as well, but their thinking is simultaneously more concrete and less indebted to "reality"; young children's fantasy play, for example, is unburdened by reality checks on how ordinary humans can transform themselves into extraordinary superheroes. To mark the distinction between the child and adolescent minds, developmental psychologists often refer to adolescent thought as *theoretical thinking;* it is thought rooted in assumptions about the way things work—assumptions that are then tested through real-world, trial-and-error experimentation.[2]

In Antwon's case, he has been testing Ms. Petersen for weeks, trying to determine whether she is an ally or an impediment to his success. Unwilling or unable to simply talk to her about his fears regarding the upcoming graduation exam and his relationships with peers, he resorts to various forms of disruption to provide interactions in which his theory can be built and tested. Antwon's assumption, based on previous experiences with other teachers, is that she will let him down and respond more with measures of control rather than a deeper engagement built on a negotiation of the terms of the relationship. The red flags he sends up in class are interpreted by Ms. Petersen as defiance, rudeness, and disrespect, which is why she responds with sanctions, discipline, and disappointment. Antwon, believing that his theory has been proven true, begins to reject Ms. Petersen as an ally and orients himself as her adversary. Ms. Petersen begins to write Antwon off as another one of her students who is choosing to fail and begins to construct an explanation for his increasingly lackluster performance that hinges on Antwon's apparent preference for misbehavior.

When middle- and high-school students disrupt class routines by defying their teachers' attempts at classroom control as in the case above, they are testing the nature and boundaries of their relationships and the learning environments in which these relationships are created. By testing in this way, they are constructing implicit theories about their classroom, the adults in their lives, their peers, and, by extension, forming theories about themselves. The accumulation of such *tested knowledge* comes to define adolescents' beliefs about how the world works and how they should position themselves within it. Understood in this way, the very testing behaviors that historically have been either pathologized or dismissed as mere "adolescent rebelliousness" are, rather, integral to an ongoing construction and interpretation of the developing self-in-the-world. As adolescents test limits through experimentation with their behavior and the responses it elicits, and as adults help shape and label that behavior, adolescence itself is being constructed.

As school-based professionals, we are active contributors to the co-construction of adolescents (and adolescence) in our work. Possessing decades of experience in which we have engaged the world imaginatively and theoretically within the confines of our own capacities, we as educators are well positioned to mentor youth to adopt these new modes of thinking. When adolescents implicitly ask what kind of person they should be, who their friends ought to be, in what or whom they should place trust, or what kind of world they should make, the answers we construe and imagine with them help co-construct who they become and the way they approach the world, even if those answers are patently rejected. Whether working with us collaboratively on the questions that hold critical meaning for them or working hard to reject our efforts to help shape their world, adolescents join with educators on a day-to-day basis to build the theoretically imaginative thinking skills necessary for an interesting and productive life. If we are skilled enough to witness it, adolescents' theoretical imaginations offer some of the richest, most critical, and deeply hopeful worldviews we might find.

Building upon the emergent capacity for theoretical thinking, the *theoretical imagination* requires holding onto and pulling together a history of information gleaned from multiple contexts and transforming that knowledge into possibilities for what might be. Envisioning the possible based on lessons from the past and experiences in the present constitutes the core of the theoretical imagination. Adolescents engage in this activity exceptionally well. Think, for example, of the prototypical questions adults either ask adolescents or expect them to be asking of themselves: What do you hope to study in college? What kind of career would you like to pursue? What is most important to you in an intimate relationship? Where do you stand on religion or the practice of your faith? All these questions require drawing on past experience, connecting it with present interests, and projecting forward toward future possibilities. In Antwon's case, these questions are a source of significant anxiety, and the ways in which he is theorizing his past experiences with teachers and projecting them into his relationship with Ms. Petersen seem to make the situation even worse. Likewise, Ms. Petersen's anxiety is borne of her past experiences and shaped by the reality she is co-constructing with Antwon each day during third period. Their relationship demonstrates how the skill of connecting life experiences across time in personally meaningful ways is precisely the work of constructing reality for oneself and of co-constructing it with others. Rather than simply recalling facts and connecting the historical dots of past experience, the theoretical imagination allows for the unique creation of historical meaning as a foundation for building and supporting future possibilities.

These same questions posed above might, in a developmentally different form, be asked of children, but the expected answers would be far different. Adolescents are expected to have thought through the interests, values, and related characteristics required for answering abstract questions in an informed way. They are asked to think ahead, and to do so with a firm grounding in past experience. But they also are asked to do so with little systematic experience in actually testing many of the key beliefs and assumptions required to answer their most abstract questions. In this sense, adolescents are, by necessity, experimenters. They not only experiment with risky behavior but also with the everyday questions that hold deep implications for shaping the rest of their lives. They are theoreticians precisely because they lack many of the necessary facts. They do not know, for example, how college will be experienced, even if they know people who have attended. Most do not know what role children will play in their future decisionmaking or the feeling of being promoted within or fired from a valued job. Therefore, they must imagine. They must imagine who and what they might become, based on who they are or hope to be, and in doing so they must experiment with getting there.

In short, adolescents are in a near-constant state of constructing their lives. Far from assuming or growing into a particular stage of development or simply adapting to an environment that determines developmental possibilities for them, adolescents are actively creating development itself. It is largely this process of creating themselves and the worlds they inhabit that we call the *construction of adolescence.* In many respects our notion of adolescent construction work is similar to postmodern literary positions on the true meaning of texts. We maintain that the core meaning of adolescent development lies fundamentally in the interpretations adolescents make of themselves and their worlds. As adults in their lives, we may have an enormous impact on those interpretations; ultimately, however, the meaning they make of their experiences is theirs, regardless of how it may match or conflict with ours. It is meaning rooted in their theoretical experiments, in the varied forms of adolescent experimentation that yield the results around which life is built, understood, and, at times, ended. Given the magnitude of the consequences involved in adolescent self-construction, especially as they come to be realized in schools, the constructionist perspective is anything but academic or abstract.[3] It is, rather, the real-life heart and soul of adolescence itself.

How then do we, as professional educators, support our teenage students in the productive imagination of themselves and their worlds? How can we best encourage and even join them in their experiments in possibility development? Are our pedagogies, curricula, counseling approaches, and even disciplinary practices aligned with these efforts, or do they get in the way? Questions such as these must be kept central in our work with adolescents, and we will revisit them time and again throughout the chapters ahead.

AUTHORING LIFE STORIES

As adolescents construct their lives through experimentation, testing, and theorizing possibilities, how do they hold it all together? Which experiments become instrumental in shaping who they are and who they will become?

Which theories of self-conception and future possibilities ultimately become tried-and-true realities? Research ranging from a wide variety of studies suggests that people build guiding stories for their lives. These stories serve to integrate experience across time, and like literary fiction or accounts of world history, they become marked by core themes. The construction of one's life, from this perspective, occurs through and gets held together by the evolving stories we tell ourselves and the ways in which these stories become internal guideposts for ongoing decisionmaking, everyday behavior, and self-understanding. In this sense, the construction of one's life is a matter of authorship. We take authority over the interpretation of what we have experienced and who we are as a result. Being human requires the authoring of one's life, of one's life story. Having a coherent, functional sense of one's self requires ongoing, active engagement in this authoring process.

In the chapters that follow, we discuss the role of identity development in relationship to the task of constructing or authoring one's life. In many respects, our identities capture the stories of who we are; that is, they represent the core themes around which we construct the meaning of our lives. Because adolescence ushers in so many new experiences, accompanied by advanced thinking skills, the processes of identity development are highlighted during this time. But although identity development and self-construction are sometimes viewed as individual endeavors, they are thoroughly interpersonal or interrelational processes. We do not construct our life stories on our own. We are, rather, in a constant state of cocreating who we are with the people with whom we are in closest connection and within those contexts that hold the most meaning for our day-to-day existence.

Children's self-understanding is strongly influenced by parental support and experiences with siblings, friends, and other important caretakers. Early life experiences weigh heavily in the shaping of subsequent behavior and self-understanding. We build upon, try to escape from, and attempt to rectify the childhood markers that begin our life stories. By adolescence, the opening chapters have been written, setting in place fairly clear parameters for the construction of new experiences and the interpretive possibilities for making sense of them.

Just as children require near-constant support from others to access the material from which they will start building their lives, adolescents and adults likewise depend on ongoing support to construct their realities and the internalized stories of those realities. In this sense, no one is a solo author. All life stories are multiauthored. The adolescents with whom we work as educators are cowriting our narratives just as we are cowriting theirs. The material that comprises our life stories comes from all directions, contributed by people who care about, are indifferent to, and feel antagonistic toward the person whose life they are helping to shape. But contributions to this constructive process are anything but random. The order and magnitude of coauthorship are critically important, even if the particular authors and their evolving roles cannot always be determined in a convenient manner.

This is clear in Antwon and Ms. Petersen's relationship. Each has co-constructed the other based on what they imagine from past experiences and how they interpret the theories they test in each interaction. Antwon's behavior and self-understanding are being coauthored by Ms. Petersen's actions toward him just as Ms. Petersen's identity and effectiveness are being cocreated by Antwon's decisions. The fact that Antwon orients himself differently toward other teachers and that Ms. Petersen acts differently toward other students underscores how necessary it is to view adolescent development (and teacher development) from a co-constructive perspective.

During adolescence, coauthoring possibilities become more complex as the venues for accessing life experiences grow more varied and the implications for selecting and interpreting organizing themes take on exceeding weight. In the educational realm, for example, the meaning of "school" often becomes dramatically revised. During childhood, school largely is used to build academic and life skills that have strong personal meaning for the present. If a third-grade student succeeds or fails, those outcomes have important implications for status among one's peers and can bring either favor or negative consequences at home. But implications for "one's future," with the exception of concern about passing into the fourth grade, tend to be vaguely felt or understood. By early adolescence, however, students clearly associate their school performance with possibilities for the future. And by middle high school—tenth or eleventh grade—school performance is strongly associated with life opportunities and plans for early adulthood. During adolescence, then, the theme of education is critical to one's developing life story, in whatever form that theme takes.

Just as the larger constructed self-narrative is multiauthored, so too is the more specific educational self-story. Who then are the educational coauthors, and what roles are they playing? This question ought to be asked by all educators, parents, and friends of adolescents. In the larger scheme of adolescent development, this question carries particular weight for educators. Given how important education is to the life prospects of young people in American society, how do we as educators (which we understand to include teachers, administrators, support personnel, counselors, psychologists, and social workers) assume an instrumental role in the construction of our students' educational identities? For example, should teachers' roles be prescribed largely by the subject matter and state-mandated curricula of their classrooms and the standardized tests to which they and their students are held accountable? Or should they and their fellow educators reach out beyond the curriculum or beyond their specific formal roles? In short, should we as educators think of our work with youth in more relational terms? If so, how do we do this? How do we form those relationships? With which students? All of them? Every day? Is this possible? If not, how do we choose?

Most conscientious educators ask a litany of such questions. Fortunately, there are no absolute answers. Unfortunately, many of the answers contribute to poor educational outcomes and constructions of self that are forged from negative associations with formal schooling. By assuming the role of educator, teachers, counselors, school psychologists, social workers, and school administrators have taken a highly privileged position within the lives of their students. The special access we have accepted brings both opportunity and responsibility. The renowned Russian developmentalist Lev Vygotsky initiated an influential line of study which shows that children's cognitive development is shaped by the access they have to the thinking of others. That is, it is not enough just to give children books and lessons; development requires providing children with the workings of other people's minds. The same holds for adolescents but in an even more complex way, given their increased capacity for multiplicity, abstraction, and theory construction. Adolescents learn to think with more sophistication in all areas, based largely on their access to the complex thinking processes of others.

Educators of adolescents, then, must go beyond merely transmitting curricula if they hope to influence their students' thinking more deeply; they must share how they themselves think about or make sense of this content. In short, there must be a *meeting of the minds* if educators are to play an influential role in the development of their adolescent students. This meeting can occur around formal academic content as well as less formal social interactions, depending on the goals for the "meeting." The key is that the educators' thinking be made as transparent as possible in order for students to access and connect with it or for them to contest and reject it in an informed manner. To state the obvious, any such meeting cannot happen on a one-way street. More precisely, the impact of any such meeting is reduced if the transparency is one-sided. Think, for example, how differently Antwon and Ms. Petersen's relationship would be unfolding were Ms. Petersen to become more transparent about her motivations, interpretations, and even her fears and expectations, depending, of course, on how such information was shared. Moreover, consider how differently Ms. Petersen might respond if Antwon were able to talk about his fear of failing, feeling incompetent, finding the right friends, and being disappointed by his teachers. The fact that no meeting of the minds has yet occurred places each in a less than optimal state of co-construction, if you will. Fortunately for them, the possibility always exists for new interpretations to take root and new co-constructions to drive more favorable development.

To share their thinking in an optimal way, educators must understand the approximate level or nature of their students' thinking. In other words, to meaningfully coauthor their students' educational self-stories, educators must constantly read their students' minds. The reading might prove difficult and inaccurate, but without a concerted effort to learn how our students think, it is virtually impossible to optimally share our thinking with them. In short, we too often miss the mark and waste time and effort when we co-construct or coauthor ideas independently; optimal coauthorship can only occur through collaborative mental engagement and the open, transparent negotiation of meaning.

MIND-TO-MIND LEARNING

Vygotsky referred to this collaborative learning process as *interpsychological development*. This concept implies that individual psychological development is inherently a relational process. Each individual mind develops within the context of other minds by which it can be influenced. This notion should not be confused with interpersonal development, the more popular concept that refers specifically to how individuals learn to become healthy social beings. Interpsychological development includes the interpersonal domain, but in its classical definition refers to the interconnected means by which the individual mind develops.[4]

Two widely used concepts from Vygotsky's work help turn interpsychological theory into a practical education model: *scaffolding* and the *zone of proximal development.*[5] Scaffolding refers to the specific strategies or structures that help people move along in their development. The concept of scaffolding rests on the assumption that everyone comes to their learning already in possession of knowledge and the implicit theories that organize it, and it is on those mental structures that new learning is built. For example, when teachers try to establish classroom norms for behavior based on the maintenance of a "safe space," every student participating in the construction of that space already has a notion of what "safe" feels, looks, and sounds like. To adequately co-construct a safe space, the teacher must be transparent about the assumptions she already has about "safe" and then find out from the students what they understand the term to mean. Only after such basic knowledge is made mutually transparent can the teacher and students negotiate new co-constructed ways of interacting with one another in a safe manner, scaffolding their new learning and ways of interacting on the content and structures they already possess.

Consistent with the constructionist metaphor, scaffolding supports the building of new learning, new skills, new insights. Developmental scaffolds help us reach new levels of understanding. As discussed above, although tools of all types can be provided, optimal scaffolding requires a mental connection or a mental bridge that helps students use the available tools to connect with the skills that may be just out of their individual reach. In this sense, scaffolding refers to the intellectual support needed to reach new levels of understanding built on those already obtained. Outside the academic realm, social and emotional supports are required to achieve more advanced levels of development in these areas as well. The important idea to remember here is that adolescents (like the adults who work with them) never approach new learning with a blank slate. They/we are always and ever building new knowledge and behaviors onto what we possessed before, and this is as true for such academic concepts as quadratic equations, the War of 1812, Shakespearean sonnets, and photosynthesis as it is for our emotions, relationships, motivations, and identities.

Related to Vygotsky's notion of scaffolding is his *zone of proximal development* (ZPD). It refers to the relative level of one's development in particular areas and is expressed as the difference between what a child can do without guidance and what he or she can do with assistance (fig. 1.1). The area of potential learning between these two parameters is where the most possibility for growth occurs. This concept has proven to be invaluable to educators who strive to maximize the learning of their students. Vygotsky and subsequent researchers have found that optimal learning occurs when lessons are targeted toward the higher edge of one's ZPD or educational comfort zone. It is important to realize that an in-depth consideration of the students' already existing scaffolds of understanding is necessary if one hopes to effectively teach or counsel adolescents within their ZPD. In short, we must know where they are coming from before we can hope to take them where we want to go. If lessons are too repetitive of what one already knows (indicating that the teacher did not assess or consider the students' preexisting knowledge and understanding before proceeding with the lesson), students tend to become bored and little new learning is likely to occur. If lessons are made too challenging—too far beyond what one knows or one's current skill level—they become frustrating and too difficult to master (fig. 1.2).

The ideal lesson or developmental challenge is situated at the edge of one's knowledge or skill level, thereby requiring the student to stretch her mind. In this model, as with any other, no one size fits all. Some students learn best with challenges that require exceptional stretching, whereas others prefer a stronger dose of familiarity with certain aspects of the subject matter in order to strengthen their resolve to reach out toward that which is newer or more complicated.

It would be a mistake, however, to assess a student's ZPD or her preference for educational challenges on the order of an individual trait. Students often have varying skill levels across different learning contexts and may prefer highly challenging experiences in one class but not in another. For exam-

FIGURES 1.1 and 1.2

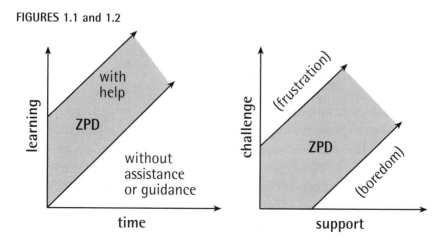

ple, a student for whom English is a second language may relish tough mathematical challenges in her morning algebra class but be reticent to take on challenging material in her English class later that day. Like adults, adolescents want to feel competent and powerful, and the formal learning process can compromise such feelings. The ZPD suggests how critical it is to match student learning demands with the requisite supports if we hope to cultivate competent, powerful learners who are motivated to take on the next level of challenge in the educational process.

Whatever the students' skill-level preferences for learning challenges, effective education from a Vygotskian perspective requires that educators constantly assess the level of their students' learning or development in order to construct the appropriate scaffolding helpful to their growth. The same holds true for counseling situations. Such assessment processes are rooted in intellectual engagement and relational connection rather than formal tests or diagnostics. Unlike the scaffolding required to construct a building, educational scaffolding is more fluid and flexible. It is constructed and reconstructed through every meaningful engagement with students in response to the needs presented by the immediate learning opportunity. The intellectual scaffold is adjusted each time an educator consciously reaches out in an effort to connect her thinking on a particular topic with that of her students. Without the effort to create this mental bridge, one leaves the learning to the student and the subject matter, thereby weakening the potential support structure. While such an individualistic approach to education can work for some students, to some degree, every missed opportunity to connect teacher and student minds expands the potential for students to connect in other areas, some of which may be unhealthy, if not dangerous. And there is ample research to show that weakened learning bridges open the floodgates to waves of experience that progressively render school less meaningful, less relevant to the developing storylines of the young person's life.

RECIPROCAL COAUTHORSHIP

Just as educators play critical roles in the construction of their students' life texts, so too are students critical to the life texts of their teachers, principals, and counselors. The professional narratives of educators and their sense of self-efficacy are grounded in experiences with their clientele. How I experience myself as a teacher, for example, is very much rooted in the connections I feel with my students and their relative levels of achievement. As with any meaningful profession, moreover, how I experience myself as a teacher influences my self-assessment as a person. The researcher Mary Haywood Metz observes that because teaching is a vocation that suffers from a lack of extrinsic rewards relative to higher-paying and higher-prestige professions, teachers depend on intrinsic rewards to make their work feel worthwhile. This leaves teachers dependent on and vulnerable to their students since they "can confirm or destroy . . . teachers' pride of craft." Metz goes on to explain the dependency this way:

> Because teachers' work consists of affecting their students, they are dependent on their students both for the actual success of their work and for evidence of that success. Even in the best of circumstances, this inescapable characteristic of the work makes teachers dependent on people whose status is inferior to theirs because of younger age and lesser knowledge. It also makes them dependent on people they are charged to direct and control. Their situation is always paradoxical, even when students are eager and able to learn and the teacher is effective.[6]

Any experienced teacher, if being honest, will tell you how much it can hurt to confront student resistance, distrust, or hostility after devoting hours, days, or even weeks to the preparation of the perfect lesson that was supposed to thrill a grateful classroom. While it is common for teachers to exalt the power they possess to shape their students' self-understandings, the reverse is equally true. Students shape teachers' self-understandings as well.

When teacher-student relationships become less than optimal for either party, it is natural for those involved to look for ways to disengage or resist. Adolescents do this in a variety of ways, as do teachers. Metz observed teachers struggling to make sense of "students' heads going down on their desks during a carefully prepared presentation, a whole class failing a test on material that had been faithfully taught . . . students turning their back on the teacher's lecture to gossip with friends, or even small violent confrontations and a nagging sense of a lack of safety." The ways in which teachers internalize these actions depend on how well they know the students and what their drives and needs may be. Regardless of the source of student disengagement or resistance, such interactions exist within and are exacerbated by the dominant professional narrative that teachers "should be in charge and responsible for all that happens in their relations with children." According to Metz, this is further underscored by the commonly espoused belief that "the art of teaching is supposed to lie in persuading the unwilling learner to learn."[7] Given the importance of professional narratives to personal self-concept in our society, students play a significant role in coauthoring the life stories of the educators they encounter. As such, authentic mind-to-mind connections forged through interactive learning processes not only create the cognitive linkages essential to student development but also nurture the personal and professional identity of educators. By engaging with their students, educators ingest the nutrients for their own professional growth and, in turn, their own personal gratification.

In their book *Matters of Interpretation*, Nakkula and Ravitch use the term *reciprocal transformation* to capture the processes through which youth and the adults who work with them promote each other's development.[8] Through case studies of interns being trained to promote youth development via a range of modalities—teaching, counseling, mentoring, and prevention programming—the authors depict the unique role of children and adolescents as influential teachers. Educators and other *applied developmentalists*, as Nakkula and Ravitch call them, are shaped in their own professional development through the nature of their connections with the young people they teach and support. Based on the cases they present, the authors argue that transformative learning, and development more broadly, is best understood as a reciprocal experience, at least as it applies to the teacher-student or developmentalist-youth relationship. Growing and learning through relationships brings change in both directions.

Reciprocal transformation runs throughout Antwon and Ms. Petersen's relationship. Each is affecting the other's development through the influence of interactions and the meaning-making that results. Antwon is teaching Ms. Petersen how to (or not to) think about, relate to, and ultimately *be* in relationship with him and others like him. Ms. Petersen then develops as a teacher in response to Antwon's lessons, interpreting his actions based on the scaffolds she already possesses. She uses that information and the impressions gleaned from it to craft an assessment of his ZPD and try to teach to it, even though in this case hers is largely a misreading of Antwon's capacity and needs. That her efforts of late have been less than successful has everything to do with how little she knows about the meaning Antwon is making about his experience as an African American male student working with a White[9] female teacher, and how his relationships with competing peer groups and his worries about the graduation exam are influencing his self-understanding and decisions. Likewise, Antwon is being transformed and co-constructed by the ways in which Ms. Petersen relates to him and the assumptions she reveals when she interacts with him. Ms. Petersen is teaching much more than world literature—she is coauthoring Antwon's self-understanding and co-constructing the meaning he makes of his relationship with her. All this illustrates how the relationship is indeed reciprocally transformative, even though the transformation process is less than optimal at the moment. The fragility of this relationship and either the peril or possibility tied to its outcomes highlight how vital it is that educators understand their work as a co-constructive, reciprocally transformative process. To promote the development of one's students and safeguard the development of one's own craft as an educator demands that we stay connected to the ways in which adolescents are interpreting and constructing their lives and, in turn, ours.

As veteran teachers know all too well, the ideal of remaining connected over the course of a career is difficult to actualize. The day-to-day, year-to-year demands—of large class sizes, new restructuring efforts, national reform movements, not to mention personal challenges—can lead to distancing in teacher-student relationships or a denial of the relational component altogether. In many respects, distancing between educators and students has less to do with the participants themselves and more to do with the logistical or social demands placed on the learning relationships, but this fact does not absolve educators from the ethical responsibility of approaching their work relationally. While such distancing may seem necessary for survival, it takes a heavy toll developmentally, both for the educator and his students, and the consequences of this are rarely overestimated. A distancing from one's work or one's relationships constitutes a distancing from one's self in important and dangerous ways. And a distancing from one's professional self leaves educators fundamentally absent from their coauthoring role in the development of students' life texts. The remainder of this book can be read largely as an attempt to preclude that possibility.

CHAPTER TWO

Identity in Context

Most theories of adolescent development address the contributions of context, or environment, to the growth of young people. Rarely, however, do they address the ways in which adults in those contexts are growing with the youth and, as such, the opportunities afforded them to promote development interactively. In this chapter, we present influential theories of adolescent identity development, grounded in the work of educators and other school-based professionals. Our goal is to help educators move beyond a mere understanding of adolescent identity development and toward constructive ideas for promoting such development through their everyday interactions.

Like our students, we as educators wake up each morning as complex, ever-evolving people. Upon entering school, we encounter a fractured landscape of content specializations, differentiated responsibilities, and tracks of proficiency that compartmentalize our roles and reduce our selves in ways that sometimes miss the totality of who we are and what we bring to our work. When teachers deliver a lesson, they are interacting with more than their students' intellects; when school counselors talk with students, they address more than feelings; when administrators discipline students, they deal with more than behavior; when coaches teach athletes how to play a zone defense, they are affecting more than physical skills. The applied development work of adults in schools is never as one-dimensional as our compartmentalized roles might suggest. Whether or not we are aware of it, when educators work with adolescents in school spaces, we are engaging the interplay of intellect, feelings, behaviors, and bodies—both ours and our students'—which makes it a complex undertaking. Perhaps the most effective way to understand what is at stake in these interactions is to view them as manifestations of identity. To that end, this chapter begins with a simple assertion: *our work in schools is identity work.*

As adolescents adjust to a changing body, develop abstract thought, acquire more complex interpersonal skills, negotiate new relationships with caretakers and significant others, reformulate a value system, and set goals for future achievement,[1] they are forming an identity. Because so much is in flux in adolescence, the question "Who am I?" is asked with great passion and urgency. It is not a stretch to claim that forming the core of an identity is *the* pivotal task of adolescence, particularly in a culture as fixated on individual and unique representations of selfhood as ours. In fact, much of what adolescents choose to do, whom they relate to, and how they spend their time is contingent upon the self they are seeking to create, test, and revise.

The contemporary history of identity theory begins most coherently in the work of Erik Erikson in the 1940s.[2] To trace the evolution of this concept and to build a foundation for later investigations into how identity is shaped by categories of race, ethnicity, gender, and sexual orientation, we begin here by briefly outlining several theories in the Eriksonian tradition. This outline presents the dominant themes through which identity has come to be understood developmentally. As we show toward the end of the chapter, there may be more value to practitioners in leaving open the multiple and competing interpretations of identity than there is in fixing it arbitrarily according to one theorist's perspective. As with much of our work in schools and with adolescents, the capacity to hold multiple perspectives on an issue, especially one as weighty as identity, is critical, even though it might be more comforting to secure a single definitive answer.

ERIKSON'S INFLUENTIAL MODEL

Erikson framed identity as a developmental concept, with roots in early childhood and implications extending throughout adulthood unto death. The comprehensiveness of the model extended its influence throughout the modern West within the applied fields of education, psychology, and social work and across the social sciences. The field of guidance counseling, for example, was strongly influenced by Eriksonian notions of identity, which were then linked to career aspirations and developmentally appropriate strategies for supporting youth in their transitions into adulthood.[3]

Erikson's theory begins in the classic Freudian vein of *psychosexual* development, which argues that psychological well-being requires an ongoing negotiation between the individual's innate biological drives (sexual and otherwise) and the normative expectations of the family and society. Our psychological selves—our thoughts, feelings, habits, and behaviors—develop, according to this psychosexual perspective, in response to the ways in which we experience our sexuality, including the sublimation (transformation) of our sexual energy into productive work and other constructive activity. In short, all energy is sexual energy in this model. Whereas Freudian theory articulated a host of complex psychological defenses for transforming impulsive expression of the sexual and other biological drives into societally acceptable behavior, Erikson emphasized the social side of the equation. He placed less emphasis on understanding the inner workings of the self as a discrete being and more on the emerging fit (or misfit) between the individual self and the larger society. In this sense, Erikson serves as a bridge between individual development and social psychology.

Building on Freud's psychosexual model, Erikson articulated a theory of (mis)fit between the evolving individual and the social contexts within which we live.[4] His model was designed to explain how people progress through various stages of life from birth to death and was one of the first coherently articulated models of lifelong development. The model is fundamentally psycho*social* in that we are forever facing incongruities between our internally defined selves and those selves that are defined, confirmed, or denied by others. He identified eight stages in all, each organized around a specific crisis that must be resolved in order to increase the likelihood of healthy development in subsequent stages. Each stage is linked with physiological maturation and framed as an either/or dichotomy, with the primary task listed first and the threat posed if resolution is not obtained presented second:

1. Basic Trust vs. Basic Mistrust—the task in infancy of developing a sense of basic trust that one's parents or primary caretakers will be adequately nurturing

2. Autonomy vs. Shame and Doubt—the toddler's task of establishing first steps toward self-sufficiency and the sense of competence that accompanies it

3. Initiative vs. Guilt—the early childhood task of building on one's budding autonomy to initiate constructive activities and begin to take leadership roles within the family and friendship groups

4. Industry vs. Inferiority—the middle to late childhood task of consolidating a sense of efficacy as a skilled contributor within school and family contexts

5. Identity vs. Role Confusion—building on the experiences of late childhood, the adolescent task of organizing skills, interests, and values into a core sense of self and applying it to present and future pursuits

6. Intimacy vs. Isolation—the early adulthood task of bringing one's sense of self into intimate relationships with others, typically for the purpose of building a lifelong partnership

7. Generativity vs. Stagnation—the middle adulthood task of utilizing one's social and vocational/professional attributes to make a lasting contribution to one's family and larger community

8. Ego Integrity vs. Despair—the late-adulthood task of accepting one's lifelong contributions and moving toward death with a sense of integrity and peace

The ways in which each stage is confronted and resolved (or not) has profound effects on subsequent stages. This is especially true for Erikson's fifth stage, identity vs. role confusion, the one most closely associated with adolescence.

To capture the essential importance of identity, Erikson contended that "in the social jungle of human existence there is no feeling of being alive without a sense of identity."[5] He described identity as the "person in personality," as the property of the ego that organizes our experience of self-in-the-world. Identity formation, then, is the dynamic process of testing, selecting, and integrating self-images and personal ideologies into an integrated and consistent whole. For Erikson, identity had a "claim to recognition as the adolescent ego's most important accomplishment,"[6] a cohesive sense of self formed within a period he called the "psychosocial moratorium"—the developmental pause between the intense psychosocial growth of childhood and the awaiting demands of adulthood. In this period, the adolescent attempts to find "the real me" by playing many roles, by experimenting with possible selves, and by shifting back and forth between potential identities in different contexts. Whereas a child may have had difficulty resolving the differences between the identities of, for example, "me-with-grandma" and "me-with-friends," the adolescent engages such differences in order to derive meaning about the "me-I-am" and the "me-I-want-to-be."

To arrive at an integrated self through the psychosocial moratorium, Erikson posits that adolescents must experience a crisis of sorts. Although this period functions to open space for youth to explore opportunities and entertain possible selves, over time it becomes psychically unsustainable. Facing daily questions about who one is and who one ought to become is not only exhausting, but, as Erikson maintained, it also produces an identity crisis. This crisis results from the pressures placed on adolescents as they attempt to construct an identity that will meet with the support of their friends as well as their family, teachers, and society at large. Anxiety can come to define this process as adolescents struggle to balance the need to be distinct from family/friends/society (i.e., making themselves unique) with the simultaneous need to establish and maintain meaningful relationships with significant others (i.e., feeling a sense of belonging and being known by those who are similar to oneself in some meaningful way). They seek expressions they can call their own yet also invite connection. Thus, the push toward distinctiveness continually vies with the pull toward belonging.

> The competing demands of distinctiveness and belonging were apparent in the last chapter when we met Antwon Saladin and witnessed him struggle with academic competency and his relationships with teachers and different sets of friends. Perhaps his closest friend is Julian Thomas, a fellow tenth-grader born to Haitian immigrant parents. Julian and Antwon were childhood playmates, virtually inseparable for most of their elementary school years, and were always the first two to be picked for any neighborhood games of soccer or basketball. In high school, Julian began to distinguish himself academically, especially when it came to math and science. His interest in sports waned as the encouragement and expectations of his parents drove him to focus on his studies as a means of self-betterment. Consequently, Julian often set the curve on the exams in his algebra and physics classes and was tracked into the more accelerated courses by the end of his freshman year. He even joined the math club and planned to compete in this year's "Math Bowl." These developments made his parents

glow with pride, but they also meant he no longer shared any classes with Antwon and rarely played soccer or basketball with him after school. Not only did this put a strain on Julian's relationship with Antwon; it began to challenge who Julian understood himself to be.

Before high school, being the best friend of Antwon meshed well with being the son of Mr. and Mrs. Thomas, and both of these were congruent with being a good student. Now, however, everything—from what he wears, where he sits at lunch, what he does after school, which music he listens to, and which words he chooses when talking with friends versus talking with teachers—seems to carry enormous weight. Exhausted by the gravity of these decisions, unable to find spaces in which he could experiment with who he wanted to be, and feeling ill-prepared to present an identity that felt authentic, Julian began to retreat from his relationships and make himself invisible in situations where he might be challenged. Racing home to cloister himself in his room, he immersed himself in the interpersonal dynamics and interplanetary disputes of comic book heroes and developed an impressive capacity to draw nearly as well as the illustrators of his favorite series.

Julian's case reminds us that adolescents yearn to be themselves both in relation and reaction to others and that they need spaces and relationships in which identity experimentation will be embraced. Struggling to find a balance between individuation and connection drives adolescent identity experimentation and the fleeting passions that often accompany it. Youth who are unable to meet the challenge of this crisis lapse into what Erikson called a state of *role confusion*, in which they find it difficult to arrive at self-definition and experience decisionmaking and the flexibility required to move across multiple contexts as threatening and conflicting. Frictions between adolescent peers often occur when an individual is observed acting differently with one set of friends relative to another and is then asked to account for those differences. Peers may ask, "Who *are* you if you're like *that* with them and like *this* with us?" Implications of Erikson's identity vs. role confusion stage are evident in such questions. Indeed, who *am* I? How *do* I rectify those differences? Peer pressure can be felt with such intensity in adolescence precisely because allegiances are experienced as indicative of one's true self, as manifestations of a durable identity rather than momentary choices in behavior or relationships. Over time, with the support of environments that encourage healthy social experimentation, adolescents form stable identities that can withstand challenges to their authenticity and are flexible enough to adapt as necessary across the competing demands of multiple social contexts.

For Julian, however, such an environment had not yet materialized, and despite his attempts to retreat from relationships and situations that threatened to expose his fragile sense of self, he found complete withdrawal an untenable option. He prepared well for all of his algebra and physics tests, but nothing prepared him for a chance meeting with Antwon in the boys' bathroom during third period. Antwon had used the bathroom pass in Ms. Petersen's world lit class to avoid having to share his essay with his writing group at the same time that Julian was using Mr. O'Leary's bathroom pass to avoid being labeled a nerd during the obligatory homework-review time. (Julian knew his answers were all correct since he reviewed them with his father the night before, but he had grown sensitive lately to others' comments that he was a "teacher's pet" or "Einstein.") Wanting a reprieve from his peers' teasing, however gentle and complimentary it may have been, he entered the bathroom to find Antwon on his way out. Antwon was glad to see him, they exchanged greetings, and that's when Julian faced his test.

Antwon produced a large-tip permanent marker and asked Julian to guard the door so he could tag the bathroom wall with a nasty comment about Ms. Petersen. When Julian paused to consider what to do, Antwon suggested Julian would likely do it for him if he were one of his "math homeys." Quickly recognizing that his relationship with Antwon was in jeopardy, Julian relented and moved toward the door to look out for adults or distrusted students. A minute later, when Antwon had finished his graffiti, he asked Julian to add a drawing to the wall since he knew Julian had "madd drawing skillz." Realizing it was too late to turn back now and that he was being offered a way to reconnect with a friend he feared he was losing, Julian took the pen and began to draw a caricaturized Ms. Petersen. Just then, Mitch Guillermo, one of the school psychologists, walked in. They were caught. The knowledge that he had passed Antwon's test of their friendship did little to assuage the dread Julian felt when he realized he would have to explain his behavior to his disappointed parents and teachers, further exacerbating the anxiety he felt as he grappled with his evolving sense of identity.

In Julian's behavior, we can see how experimentation forms the foundation of the identity vs. role confusion stage. Likewise, we are able to see the courage he possesses and the support he requires to construct an identity he can call his own. Caught between the demands of his teachers, his parents, and his longtime friend, Julian attempted to be everything to everyone and was reasonably successful as long as all those realms stayed separate. But when those worlds collided that day in the bathroom, he faced the Eriksonian confusion of not knowing which version of Julian was the most authentic. While punishment and/or reconciliation may be appropriate adult responses to a transgression such as graffiti, if Julian's experiment were to be viewed *only* as an infraction, an opportunity for the adults in his life to positively coauthor his development may be squandered. And treating Antwon the same as Julian simply because they were involved in the same event also misses a key developmental opportunity. The two of them approached that event from very different perspectives and present unique needs. The point here is that identity is at stake in Julian's actions, and he desperately needs someone to talk to about it.

Erikson's perspective on situations such as this is that identities are only formed after the threat of role confusion is addressed, after an identity crisis is resolved. When adolescents express unpopular opinions, revolutionary ideas, antiestablishment positions, and stylistic choices that fly in the face of adults' normative expectations, they are trying on possible selves and testing the boundaries of their environment as part of their psychosocial moratorium. Adolescents are conscious of making choices that differ from those that conventional authority figures would choose; in fact, that is part of their developmental job. To dismiss such experimentation and the anxieties associated with it as a mere "phase they'll get through," "raging hormones," or simple "rebelliousness" is to devalue the unique opening this developmental era represents. It takes tremendous courage for an adolescent to become someone he or she can call "myself" and then dare to bring that self into the world. School-based professionals are ideally positioned to support that process. Imagine how our schools would be experienced by adolescents, immersed as they are in meaning-rich identity-searching experimentation, if we were to ask with genuine curiosity and care (rather than judgment and fear) why they chose that shirt, why that music, why that book, why these friends, why this hair, why that movie, why that food. Adolescents want to talk about such things, and if we are fortunate and skilled enough to be trusted by them, such questions can lead us into pivotal conversations in the unfolding drama of crisis and possibility.

Mitch Guillermo knows of identity crises, having faced them as a teen himself years ago. Although now a school psychologist with 12 years of experience under his belt, he has not forgotten what it was like to grow up Filipino on the poorer side of the district, often having to fight his way into respect from his peers while working hard at his studies to keep his mother happy. He knows well the push and pull of role confusion in negotiating multiple contexts, each with its different demands on the individual. To this day, he credits football as the one arena where he was allowed—encouraged, even—to manifest all aspects of his full self: the nerdy academic who wanted to do well in school, the tough lineman who loved to get physical and work as part of a team, and the proud Filipino kid who wouldn't put up with teasing about his family. When he discovered Julian and Antwon in the bathroom tagging the wall, he swallowed his anger and simply escorted the boys to the office, closing and locking the bathroom door behind him so word of the graffiti would not spread.

That afternoon, he spoke with Ms. Petersen and Julian's mother, and both requested that Julian sit down with Mitch for a series of conversations. (Antwon's issues would be addressed by Maggie Lang, a counselor at the school. More on that conversation later.) Julian is understandably guarded and divulges little of what is going on inside him. Mitch lets him know that the purpose of the conversations is not punitive, that the goal is to provide a place where Julian can talk through what is going on for him in school. After 45 minutes of receiving largely monosyllabic responses to his questions, Mitch chooses not to push further that day and instead simply informs Julian when their next meeting will occur, thanks him for being there, and sends him on his way. For the next week, Mitch gathers information about Julian. He peruses his cumulative record, observes him interact with peers in the hallway and cafeteria, speaks to each of his teachers, and has a longer phone conversation with both his parents. During a meeting with the math club leader, Mitch strikes a deal whereby Julian will be disallowed from participation in the next two Math Bowl competitions unless he agrees to complete a few outside assignments to be determined by Mitch. Informed by the multiple perspectives on Julian's behavior and the various demands on his identity, Mitch hatches a plan.

Familiar with Erikson's framing of identity vs. role confusion as the central crisis of adolescence, Mitch plans his counseling approach based on the reality that this era of the life cycle is as expansive as it is perilous. The adolescent expansion of cognitive abilities occasions a heightened awareness of how one's self-concept is linked to such personal characteristics as race, gender, class, and sexuality. These new cognitive abilities also allow for experimentation with the deepest undercurrents of an adolescent's being, including relational connection, faith perspectives, and moral convictions. Just as adolescents seek a "true self," they also yearn for a true orientation, an authentic way to live, for meaning and purpose that inform their developing worldview. This renders adolescents susceptible to charismatic leaders, moral crusades, and cultural fads, particularly for those youth who are ever on the lookout to test the extreme edges of what is and what might be. As Erikson puts it:

> The evidence in young lives of the search for something and somebody to be true to can be seen in a variety of pursuits more or less sanctioned by society. It is often hidden in a bewildering combination of shifting devotion and sudden perversity, sometimes more devotedly perverse, sometimes more perversely devoted. Yet in all youth's seeming shiftiness, a seeking after some durability in change can be detected. . . . This search is easily misunderstood, and often it is only dimly perceived by the individual himself, because youth, always set to grasp both diversity in principle and principle in diversity, must often test extremes before settling on a considered course. These extremes, particularly in times of ideological confusion and widespread marginality of identity, may include not only rebellious but also deviant, delinquent, and self-destructive tendencies. However, all this can be in the nature of a moratorium, a period of delay in which to test the rock-bottom of some truth before committing the powers of body and mind to a segment of the existing (or a coming) order.[7]

As adults working in schools, we have a unique opportunity to participate with young people as they build their selves, to co-construct those selves with them just as they co-construct our ever-evolving professional and personal identities. All of us working in schools were once adolescents facing our own dilemmas and challenges in the building of a self. In working with our students, we are often reminded of our own adolescence, the decisions we made, the challenges we faced, and the crises we resolved as we co-constructed our identities with those youth and adults with whom we were most intimately connected. Erikson helps us to see the crises of adolescence as developmental opportunities common to everyone in one form or another and to engage them with fascination and compassion. Viewed in this way, our own development is reflected in the challenges of our students; if we pause to recognize the images of adolescence reflected back to us, the possibilities for authentic connection are multiplied exponentially. The us-them dichotomy can be reconfigured as an integrated "we," working together, relying on one another, to create possibilities for who we are and what we might become.

> Before Mitch meets with Julian a week after the incident in the bathroom, he first reflects on his own adolescence and the troubles he encountered that were similar to and different from Julian's. To make sure their work together was relevant to Julian's concerns, Mitch asked him to list the various spaces and relationships he must negotiate each day. Sensing his resistance to the task, Mitch reminds him again of the purpose of the conversations and adds the fact that there will be no Math Bowl if he chooses not to participate. After 20 minutes of hemming and hawing, Julian starts to open up, listing home, mom, dad, bus stop, school hallway, each of his five academic classes, the cafeteria, P.E., each of his teachers, his Math Bowl friends, and Antwon. Gently recognizing the breakthrough, Mitch then hands Julian a piece of paper and asks him to write down each of those spaces and people. After Julian complies, Mitch asks him to write down what each of those spaces and people expect of him. "Huh?" Julian replies. "You know, what you think people want from you in those places and relationships." "Oh, you mean like who they expect me to be?" "Precisely," said Mitch. After a half-hour or so of describing the peculiarities and demands of each venue, Mitch asks Julian to complete one more assignment before they meet two days later. "Between now and Thursday, I want you to pay attention to how you feel, and specifically note when you feel safe and when you feel anxious or uneasy. Got it?" Julian agrees, as long as he doesn't have to write it down where someone might see it. "No problem," says Mitch. "As long as you come on Thursday ready to talk about what you noticed."

MARCIA'S EXPANSION OF ERIKSON'S MODEL

In his research with adolescents, James Marcia found that Erikson's notion of a psychosocial moratorium held immense explanatory power.[8] The adolescents he studied frequently described experiences of exploring possible selves, and constructing and deconstructing their identities with regularity in an effort to claim or inhabit an internally consistent and externally valued self. However, Marcia found Erikson's crisis model (where one either achieves an identity or becomes lost in confusion about one's role) to be somewhat limited in its capacity to explain what he saw as a more gradual process of unfolding experiences that inspired conscious decisionmaking. To better explain these developmental phenomena, Marcia underscored the notion of *commitment* in Erikson's crisis-based model. Similar to Erikson's framing of *crisis*, Marcia constructs *commitment* in binary terms: either an individual commits to an identity and devotes oneself to living accordingly or one does not. The graphic below (fig. 2.1) illustrates how commitment and crisis relate, giving rise to four distinct statuses in one's identity development.

Marcia's notion of *identity statuses* differs from the more common usage of *developmental stages* in important ways. A stage typically describes a developmental era bounded by common experiences or life events. Each

FIGURE 2.1: Relationship between Marcia's Commitment and Erikson's Crisis

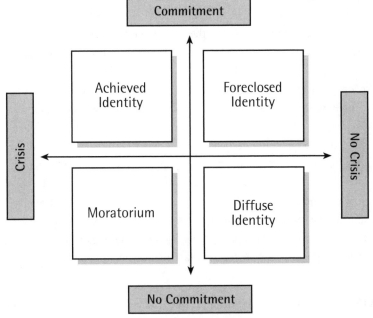

Derived from J. E. Marcia, "Identity in Adolescence," in *Handbook of Adolescent Psychology*, ed. J. Adelson (New York: John Wiley, 1980), 159–87.

stage is part of a sequence, preceded and followed by neighboring stages that also are defined by common experiences and events. Stage models generally are linear, with the assertion being that we move through them sequentially. Erikson's eight developmental crises, for example, mark the core of their respective stages across the life cycle. The crises are taken up and resolved (with varying degrees of success) sequentially as the individual grows from one stage through another.

Statuses, on the other hand, are not necessarily linear. They describe the dominant issues, concerns, or developmental experiences during a particular era in one's life, and they may or may not be preceded or followed by other specific statuses. The status one inhabits depends on the peculiar sets of experiences and support structures available and the ways in which these structures are understood by the individual. Statuses, unlike stages, are not linked specifically with any age group and thus can occur at any time in the life cycle. Whereas stages are represented by an A-B-C-D progression, statuses may show C-B-C-D or A-B-C-A patterns, depending on the individual and the surrounding environment. In fact, statuses are never done, never completed. It is possible and may even be beneficial for people to loop through the statuses multiple times throughout life, revisiting experiences and reconstructing decisions based on changing environments and relationships, possibly vacillating between statuses for years before emerging into a stable identity.

Foreclosed identity

Within Marcia's model a *foreclosed identity* status is one in which an individual has committed to a life direction or way of being without exploring it carefully and without experimenting with alternatives. A foreclosed identity is one that is either thrust upon a person (the need, for example, to assume a particular vocational direction due to limited environmental opportunities) or simply accepted with little reflection. When an individual is not experiencing a crisis wherein she must decide upon key facets of her identity—but rather remains committed to whatever identity she inhabits regardless of its origin or the means by which it was assumed—that person can be said to possess a foreclosed identity. Marcia's theory rests on the assertion that it is possible to inhabit an identity and live fully in/from it without ever having committed to it in a conscious or willful fashion.

When identity expectations from others are accepted without question and then rigidly maintained regardless of setting or relationship, the outcome is foreclosure on alternative ways of being. The foreclosed individual has made a commitment to a particular identity or belief system, often one selected by parents or peers, but has done so without actively considering alternatives or experiencing a crisis that might expose multiple identity-related options. Externally motivated and relatively unconcerned with autonomy, they often repress internal inclinations that conflict with the narrowly defined sense of self they have adopted. At times youth (and adults) with foreclosed identity statuses are actively engaged in defining themselves against other possibilities (possibilities they refuse to explore) and, as a result, tend to be rigidly authoritarian in their response to difference.

To choose a benign example, an adolescent who grows up in a household where a particular sports team, say the Boston Red Sox, is revered, and another team, say the New York Yankees, is despised, may never have made a conscious decision to become a Red Sox fan, wear Red Sox regalia, or instinctively cheer for the Sox and against the Yankees whenever possible. That identity as a Red Sox fan (and a Yankee opponent) was part of the normative air the child breathed in her family, supported by years of watching games on television with trusted adults and friends, being surrounded by images of Red Sox sportswear and decorations, and possibly even momentous visits to Fenway Park to see a game in person and cheer (or jeer) alongside influential adults. The possibility of being anything other than a Red Sox fan does not occur to someone with a foreclosed "baseball identity," but the individual may not be able to describe the reasons and experiences that compelled her to arrive at that identity construction. It's just who she is. In this simple example, foreclosure may be a healthy option. Not all aspects of identity need to be explored. The cumulative effect of nonexploration, however, can lead to passivity and stagnation as well as the inability to challenge the status quo within which every person is born.

Because the individual with a foreclosed identity is basically acting as an extension of other people and is dependent on them for validation, he may be defensive and rigid when confronting situations that require flexibility or adaptability. Closeness to and security in peer and/or family relationships is common, as is an inability to trust those outside one's group. Dichotomous thinking (e.g., "You're either with us or against us") and a lack of tolerance for ambiguity in loyalty are also representative of this status. Over-identification and conformity with peer group or parental norms often occur in this status as a result. Wholesale devotion to styles of dress, modes of speech, musical groups or genres, cultural traditions, hobbies, favorite sports teams, religious beliefs, and career plans are common. At its extreme, the foreclosed identity status can be seen in undying allegiances to charismatic figures, gangs, or even cults.

For these reasons, questions about or challenges to someone's foreclosed identity are rarely experienced as supportive. To introduce doubt into one's unquestioned identity is to destabilize not just who the individual believes herself to be but also to call into question the unquestioned family relationships and peer networks from which the individual springs. The extent to which support structures exist for that individual to sort through and consider such questions and challenges has everything to do with how the individual will make sense of her identity and become comfortable within it.

> This fact is clear in Julian's work with Mitch. When Julian returned on Thursday with an assortment of experiences in which he felt comfortable as himself as well as numerous examples of moments in which he felt anxious, vulnerable, and at risk of being exposed as a phony, Mitch and Julian had a rich conversation about how stressful it can be trying to negotiate who we want to be with different people in varying situations. Mitch shared some of his struggles, which made it easier for Julian to share his. Julian began to revel in the openness with which Mitch spoke to him, feeling like he was being heard, understood, and somehow belonged. These talks did nothing to alter the challenges he faced as he struggled to find an authentic self, but knowing that a space and relationship existed in which he could at least talk about them gave Julian great comfort. Having learned about Julian's talents in drawing and his fascination with comic books, Mitch ended their third session with another assignment, this time asking him to name, draw, and describe the powers a superhero would have to possess to navigate the sort of challenges Julian faces daily. After first making sure no one other than Mitch would see what he creates, Julian agrees.

Seeking to lean into the crises Julian was experiencing and in doing so probe for the commitments that may be emerging, Mitch incorporates Marcia's model into his practice. Perhaps one of the most valuable insights Marcia provides is his recognition that our identities are not always the product of a reasoned weighing of assets and liabilities afforded by various options but instead may often be the unexamined parts of ourselves we have internalized without consideration or critique. Bringing those parts of ourselves to the surface, naming them, and then becoming sensitive to how they operate is part of the identity-construction process. Because challenges to and questions about one's identity are inevitable if the individual is exposed to diversity of any type, and because adolescents apprehend those questions and challenges with newly acquired cognitive sophistication (which means not just a richer appreciation of complexity and possibility but also a deeper experience of the potential pain that comes with changes to the self), it is imperative that we learn to recognize the psychic value of a foreclosed identity so that we can accompany the individual without judgment if he or she chooses to begin questioning it. This is why Mitch first began with the listing assignment, to find out if Julian was even experiencing a crisis at all and to make sure he was not imposing his own adolescent developmental trajectory onto Julian's.

Diffuse identity

If an individual possesses neither a crisis in nor a commitment to one's identity, Marcia labels that status diffuse. A *diffuse identity* status is a state in which there has been little exploration or active consideration of a particular identity and no psychological commitment to one. Individuals in this status are easily influenced by others and often change rapidly from one belief or representation to another to fit into changing contexts. Like a chameleon, an individual in this status matches her surroundings in order to blend in and avoid detection as a differentiated outsider separate from the background. Externally oriented, often quite impulsive, highly sensitive to setting, and vulnerable to the appraisals of others, identity diffuse individuals' self-esteem may fluctuate wildly, depending on how others react. The rapid mood swings often associated with teens may actually be more a manifestation of the status of identity diffusion than of the entire era of adolescence. Social bonds, like moods, may be unsteady and issues of trust foregrounded as the individual moves between different sets of context-dependent expectations and changes with them. With little sense of personal integration, those in the diffuse identity status often live moment to moment, may avoid talking about their past or even their recent behavior, and may indulge in ego-escaping experiences through sex, drugs, travel, or blind adhesion to peer-directed activity. While there is a tendency to pathologize this status, for obvious reasons it is important for educators, as applied developmentalists, to recognize the inconsistencies and fleeting allegiances characteristic of diffuse identities as parts of a critical process. That process can be healthy, if it leads to exploration of multiple alternatives from which one ultimately makes identity-based commitments, and can lead to perpetual flailing if such commitments cannot be made.

As educators we might consider how to accompany adolescents as they struggle with the emotional impact and sheer energy expenditure associated with a diffuse identity status. Imagine what it is like to negotiate, in a single day, family and peer expectations as they are experienced at the home breakfast table, on the school bus, in the school hallway, during six or more different periods of academic classes (each with a different set of cultural expectations and peer relationships), in such after-school environments as team sports or jobs, with one's close peers or romantic interest, and then again at the dinner table at home, possibly with a different parent/guardian than the one present at breakfast. Managing each of these situations would be taxing on any given day for any of us, but the reality is that many adolescents do this five days per week at the same time that their bodies require enormous energy to grow and change. It is no wonder many teens sleep through the weekend and look for mindless escapes in music, movies, video games, hobbies, or devoted and exclusive friendships—they provide safe spaces for them to rest and be just one identity, at least for a while.

Still, as a result of shifting identity performances across various contexts, conflicts may develop between peers, leading to the questions: "Why are you like that with them but like this with me? Which is the *real* you?" When an adolescent within a diffuse identity status comes to us in dismay about how to manage this dilemma, we must think developmentally about how best to co-construct a healthy understanding *with* them, not for them. To tell a student who expresses difficulty in negotiating all these contexts that he should simply "be himself"—when there is no singular self for him to locate—is to demonstrate a lack of understanding and an underestimation of what is faced each day.

Although adolescents will not articulate their identity experiences in Marcia's terms, they will describe what happened in their day and how they are making sense of it. When they do, it is essential that we listen developmentally, not judgmentally. Rather than being unilateral advisers who tell their students what to do or how to act, it would be more effective to ask them about their experiences in these various settings, listen to their struggles and thrills, then help them to hear the moments about which they speak with the most passion. To ask, "What did it feel like to be like that in that setting?" or "What was it like when you were with those people in that place?" is to allow our students to live in their diffuse identity statuses positively and productively. After listening awhile, if we choose to describe our own experiences and perspectives, not as exemplars or directives (which will only be heard as a displacement of theirs) but as empathic possibilities designed to connect with them, we position ourselves as developmental allies in our students' struggles for self-understanding. When we function as an interactive mirror for them rather than a didactic evaluator, we may earn enough trust for them to be vulnerable with us and ask, "What do you think I should do? Who do you think I should be?" If in those moments we can still resist the urge to answer outright and instead open space for them to begin to answer those questions for themselves, they may move from a diffuse identity to a period of moratorium.

> Sensing that Julian was in need of some identity experimentation without any pressure to commit to one particular way of being, Mitch tried to structure their time together around Julian's questions and the ways in which he was making meaning of the various representations of self he was juggling. At their next meeting, Julian tosses his backpack in an empty chair, unzips the top, and pulls out a notebook of his drawings. "Wanna see the character I made up?" he asks, without even pausing to greet Mitch. "You bet," Mitch replies, trying to contain his excitement about Julian's clear engagement with his most recent assignment. Julian then flips through dozens of pages of drawings and plot notes until he gets to his most recent creation: the Chameleon. Appropriating character traits and storylines from years of comic-book consumption, Julian describes how a mild-mannered scientist discovered an extremely durable material that mirrors precisely the color of its surroundings, literally adapting to the colors and subtleties of contrast that shift according to background. Constructing a suit of this material, the scientist realizes that he has found a way to blend seamlessly into any environment and begins using it to come and go from spaces previously hostile to his presence. "The Chameleon can change and adapt and go anywhere, but he can still be himself at the end of the day. Inside the suit, he's just himself, you know?" Nodding in agreement, Mitch replies, "Pretty sweet story, Julian. You did some beautiful work here, and your drawings are

fantastic. Very impressive." Seeking to engage Julian's understanding of how the Chameleon feels, Mitch then asks, "What do you think it must feel like to be in that suit?" After pausing, Julian looks down at his drawings and says, "Uh, I dunno. Chill, I guess. Like, safe."

At this point, with the drawings sitting on the table between them, they begin talking about Antwon and the situation in the bathroom, Julian's math friends, how he acts when he's with his parents versus with this group of friends or that group of friends, and ways he might be supported in dealing with the competing versions of himself he seems to possess. Both refer to the Chameleon repeatedly as a sort of exemplar for how to maintain a consistent sense of self amid multiple changing contexts. Mitch points out the superheroic utility of having such a suit but notes how it renders the true identity of the scientist invisible. "Do you want to be invisible?" Mitch then asks. "Sometimes," admits Julian. This occasions a fruitful and revealing discussion of Julian's desire to be invisible, to possess the power to be present among others—but only as an unnoticed observer—and to use the information gained in those observations to know how to reenter those areas appropriately when one's invisibility is turned off.

Seeing an opening here, Mitch tells Julian how great it is that he is able to be in relationship with all these different people in all these different contexts, how powerful that he is already doing it without the need to be invisible, and that occasional misunderstandings about who we "really are" and who others think we're supposed to be is an inevitable byproduct of being so adaptable. Encouraging him to resist the temptation to conform to one particular version of himself, Mitch lets Julian know that experimentation, reflection, and dialogue with others could become his Chameleon suit. "You know how people are always saying, 'I was just playin'? Well, that's a pretty good indicator of when they are trying on an identity and seeing how it plays with others. People all around you are doing it all the time. All of us are playing with and experimenting with identities, trying to be a sort of Chameleon, but one that people can actually see and like. We all want that. And you, Julian, are doing a pretty sweet job at figuring it out for yourself. Keep at it. And let me know if I can help." As he leads him to the door, Mitch shakes Julian's hand firmly and adds, "But if you tag the bathroom again, the playin' part's over. Got it?" "I got you, Mr. G.," Julian replies with a grin. "I got you."

Identity moratorium

When an individual like Julian experiences a crisis of identity with no commitment, Marcia termed that status a *moratorium*, consistent with Erikson's concept described above. This is a developmental state in which one actively explores roles and beliefs, behaviors and relationships, but refrains from making a commitment. This stage is often accompanied by a great deal of anxiety due to the competing demands experienced in the exploration of an authentic "me" and the immediacy with which a lack of identity cohesion is felt. Consequently, adolescents in a state of identity moratorium may seek stability, however fleeting it may be, in idealized friends, mentors, relatives, and heroes. An aunt or cousin may become the embodiment of the perfect role model, a rock star an Adonis, a professional basketball player the flawless representation of athletic achievement, a historical figure a larger-than-life archetype. Idealizing these figures is a way of trying on what it would be like to emulate them and chart a life path that might reach similar heights. The emotional and intellectual investments these figures represent are as hopeful as they are fleeting, some being adopted and subsequently abandoned with passionate regularity. What is key to this status is the role of personal research—the adolescent has reasons for choosing this identity or that one and may even be able to express it as purposeful experimentation.

While they may become deeply fascinated by great existential questions, issues of ultimate purpose, and concerns with justice, such individuals become dedicated to right answers often with an infatuation incommensurate with their knowledge of the issue at hand. Multiple tentative commitments are often made by someone in this status as she tries out roles and experiments with them in various settings, but this often leaves little time to examine such commitments in depth. These roles and experiments are experienced differently than the shifting identities one assumes in the diffuse status. The distinction is rooted in the fact that the moratorium is accompanied by the conscious experience of a crisis, whereas the diffuse identity is not. For a student in the diffuse status, there is no conflict between the multiple selves represented across multiple contexts. For the individual in moratorium, however, there is a conflict and an active search for ways to resolve it. Several sports or forms of musical/artistic expression may be sampled, various peer-group memberships may be formed, numerous political viewpoints investigated, and multiple romantic partnerships may be established and ended in this period. Attempts to try on ways of thinking and being are often done not simply to be rebellious but to search for expressions of the self that feel authentic and internally consistent.

As the individual in moratorium struggles to maintain relationships during this active experimentation, conflict and disappointment are inevitable. One cannot be all things to all people. This realization often occurs when the adolescent confronts the fact that he is not being what his parent(s) always want(s) him to be, what his best friend always wants him to be, what his romantic partner always wants him to be, what his teachers always want him to be. With the guilt of disappointing a particular significant figure and the feeling of failure that identity experimentation creates, the adolescent may overcompensate by investing time and energy in the cultivation of one set of relationships at the expense of others. If we express consistent disappointment in and dissatisfaction with the adolescents we know, and if those adolescents are in a moratorium status in which they are experimenting with different possible identities, we should expect them to take their experimentation to contexts where there is some chance of success and some expectation of reward. If we do not provide them with safe spaces and rich experiences in which their fleeting identities can be engaged, adolescents will look for and find confirmation elsewhere. These observations underscore how important it will be for Mitch to check back in with Julian in a few weeks and throughout the school year. To accompany an adolescent in a period of moratorium is to talk with him about his experiences, interpretations, and decisions and to give him a safe space in which to share his experimentations.

> Knowing that there is a fragility to this developmental progression, Mitch makes sure there are multiple possible spaces and relationships in which Julian can take off his Chameleon suit and discuss what it's like to be him. He chats informally with each of Julian's teachers and his parents to let them know Julian is feeling some anxiety about his identity and may need to experiment a little here and there to figure out what works best for him. Realizing that Julian was on the cusp of seeking and finding meaning in risky behaviors, Mitch relays to the adults in Julian's life how important it is to engage him at the level of his meaning-making (while still holding him accountable for the effects of his actions) and to keep him talking about his experiences instead of retreating into solitude or the imaginary worlds of superheroes. With each adult, Mitch repeats a

similar explanation: "My job is to help Julian see his identity as a developmental process—ways of being himself that shift around from time to time as he figures out who he is—instead of something rigid that he feels trapped in. I'm trying to keep the lines of communication open so he feels free to unpack what's happening with himself when he's around different people in different places. So let me know what you think I can do to help Julian work toward the achievement of an identity that makes sense to him."

Achieved identity

As Mitch suggests above, Marcia's fourth status is in fact an *achieved identity*. It occurs when the identity crisis is resolved and the commitment to the selected identity is high. In this status, the individual has successfully integrated his ego-identity needs from the past, within the present, and into the future and can therefore display a certain level of self-acceptance and ego strength across changing contexts. An achieved identity is typically the result of a period of high exploration and experimentation; therefore it usually follows a period of moratorium. With the search for an identity relatively complete (at least for now), youth in the achieved identity status may be less anxious about who they need to become and more settled into who they are. This allows for an elevated level of self-reflexivity and a higher tolerance for criticism of one's behavior and decisions. Expressions of belonging and purpose are common here, as is the durability of personality across different contexts. While still desiring connection and affirmation, an enhanced sense of autonomy and personal control are also common for those in the achieved identity status.

An achieved identity status does not represent the conclusion of the identity construction process; rather, it is a waypoint in the individual's lifelong journey of understanding and constructing the self. If the individual has an experience that disturbs the achieved identity either through a powerful event of joy and wonder or an unsettling incident of pain and suffering, she may cycle back through the other statuses until the crisis has been resolved and a commitment has been formed. Marcia's statuses help us to realize this fact, to see identity as a dynamic process as opposed to a fixed achievement. Even as adults, we are no more "done" forming our identities than the adolescent, given the opportunities for lifelong revision. The formation of identity in adolescence is momentous not because it marks a completed task or process but because it is the first time in which it can be engaged with such sophistication and possibility. Crises in and commitments to sexual orientation, ideological stance, vocational direction, and faith tradition all are unpacked and examined in adolescence with a level of complexity unrealized in childhood and carried throughout adulthood. Each day and each relationship presents challenges to and confirmations of who we have become, and this is as true of a 55-year-old as it is of a teenager. That we have an opportunity to revisit the decisions we made as adolescents as we interact daily with those making them right now—to help co-construct the adolescents as they help co-construct us—does more than just "keep us young"; it keeps us aware of the extent to which we are always in the process of becoming. If we attend to this fact with compassion and persistence, we will be doing our identity work in schools in ways that support the development of our students as well as ourselves.

IDENTITY BEYOND ERIKSON

The constructionist approach we introduced in chapter 1 neither embraces nor is inconsistent with the Eriksonian perspective on identity development. Our emphasis within a developmental framework such as Erikson's, however, is on the coauthoring function of close relationships. Youth do not enter particular identity statuses alone, nor do they negotiate them independently, as we see through Julian's relationships with Antwon and Mitch. As stated in chapter 1 and reiterated throughout the chapters that follow, development from our perspective is promoted interactively within all of the relational and opportunity contexts within which we exist. Our presentation of the Eriksonian tradition here provides a starting point for considering identity development. That starting point will be critiqued and expanded upon in the theoretical and practical depictions that follow.

CHAPTER THREE

Risk Taking and Creativity

Adolescent risk taking has come to represent trouble or *problem behavior* in much of mainstream academic and professional discussion. And, indeed, risk taking can lead to all forms of developmental difficulties for young people. Experimenting with alcohol and other drugs, having sex, and reckless driving, for example, can lead to the host of detrimental outcomes we are so accustomed to hearing about. Similarly, risk taking is, at times, a sign or symptom of such underlying problems as family difficulties or low self-esteem. In these cases, high-risk behavior, such as substance abuse or precocious and unsafe sexual practices, may be a way for youth to salve the pain they feel. Risk-taking behavior, then, can be both a cause of difficulties and a marker of them.[1]

On the other hand, risk taking can be seen as a prototypical phenomenon of adolescence. It is a way of challenging the limits of one's capacities, the power of authority figures who place limits on one's activities, and the norms of one's peer group, which might be experienced as constraining or dull. In other words, risk taking has become the contemporary equivalent, in many respects, of the classic notion of adolescent experimentation. In the original conceptions of such experimentation, the argument was that experimenting with different ways of being, including those that are risky and challenging of authority, was important to healthy identity development. Although not all theorists agreed that adolescent experimentation was necessary to healthy development, they were largely in agreement that such experimentation was not by definition unhealthy or problematic, except in extreme cases.

In this chapter, we explore various forms of risk taking—those that can be precursors to or markers of serious difficulties, and those that serve to build a competent and confident sense of self. In a twist that differs from most depictions of risk taking, we couple it with the concept of creativity. After all, many, if not most, acts of creativity require taking risks or breaking out of the typical ways of seeing and doing things. Drawing on the work of eminent adolescent researchers and theorists, we show how much of adolescent risk taking is an effort toward creative expression, an effort to create an interesting and unique self. Even in cases of dangerous or high-risk behavior, the impulse to create novel or alternative experiences often is at play. We attempt to open up ways for educators to interact with the risk-creativity dialectic, and in that vein to risk creative means of teaching and reaching out to the adolescents whose lives and life experiences we are cocreating every day.

RECASTING RISK

Much of what adults consider high-risk behavior is not perceived as risky to the adolescents themselves. For example, heavy drinking that becomes a chronic, ingrained pattern of weekend behavior might be viewed as dangerous and a clear violation of family norms. Still, for the young person engaged in this repetitive behavior, the action may be experienced as anything but risky. In fact, it may be experienced as "what we do," a way of fitting in. It might not create challenges or novel experiences, although, of course, the inhibitory effects of alcohol consumption can pave the way for experimentation that otherwise might seem unfathomable. In this case, the risks are objective, such as the potential for substance dependency, health problems, or car accidents. They are not subjective or experiential.

Take the same behavior (heavy drinking), change the context, and that behavior can constitute an experiential risk. Teens who drink to excess to "get crazy" or "crunk," to do things they otherwise would not, to experience excitement, fit the experiential definition of risk taking. They are consciously going after new experiences, or altered experiences, even though they may engage in this activity over and over again. For this group of drinkers, though, the risk taking is rooted in the craving of heightened experience. So which group is more "at risk," those who drink heavily to fit in and simply do what they do, or those who use alcohol to be different or to do what they otherwise would or could not do? If such teenage heavy drinking ultimately culminated in alcoholism, we might envision two very different pathways to that potentially lethal problem: passive, habitual behavior turned to dependency versus the active, seemingly unquenchable thirst for new experience turned to insatiable addiction. Although these two portraits of risk are quite different, they each represent a picture of being "at risk."

High-risk behavior, then, is risky whether or not it is perceived as a risk to those engaged in it. In addition to these two forms of risk-taking behavior, there are the classically "positive risks," defined as taking chances on engaging in challenging activities beyond one's comfort zone. Experiential education is built around positive risk taking. Such educators create challenges for young people and teach, through reflective practices, the lessons learned in confronting such challenges. The goal here is to teach youth to take calculated risks and to confront the fears that hold them back. Rock climbing has become an increasingly popular staple in many experiential education programs precisely because it requires a confrontation with the basic human fear of falling. But classroom teachers, school counselors, and psychologists can also create challenges for students that are experienced as risky, as pushing beyond the students' comfort zones. Indeed, powerful learning opportunities exist whenever we move beyond the safe and known.

This third form of risk taking is, of course, the one most educators find consistent with their own practices. It seems logical to create healthy risks in the classroom and to sponsor outdoor, experiential risk-taking activities for our students. But limiting our appreciation of adolescent risk taking exclusively to this third form may place serious limitations on our appreciation of our students. The developmental psychologist Cynthia Lightfoot has conceptualized a comprehensive view of risk taking that argues for full recognition of the nature and benefits of the entire array of risky behavior.[2] Lightfoot conceives of a *culture of adolescent risk taking* that emerges as an interrelated set of complex processes that help structure the adolescent world. Similar to Erikson's notion of experimentation as a means of forging an identity separate from that imposed upon an adolescent by his or her family, Lightfoot argues that adolescents strive to create a world, or sub-universe, that exists apart from adult parameters and demands. It is a world created by adolescents for adolescents. Risk taking—pushing beyond the boundaries endorsed by adult authority figures—is, according to Lightfoot, a primary tool used to build that world. Risk taking signals "non-adult," "my way," or "*our* way versus *their* way." In this sense, risk taking is one avenue toward individuation from adults and adult norms, a task which, according to much of identity theory, is normative for adolescence.

Risk taking, as Lightfoot construes it, is creative by definition. It is all about creating a universe of and for adolescents. And this creative process is, of course, risky and sometimes dangerous. As such, Lightfoot neither endorses nor condones adolescent risk taking; rather, she argues persuasively for its importance and its pervasiveness. It is important to many adolescents; therefore, to ignore it or be fully shut out of it is to be left outside the capacity to understand and appreciate adolescent reality, or at least a key part of it. It is important to note here that Lightfoot does not make the mistake of "universalizing" adolescent risk taking, which was done in some older conceptions of adolescent experimentation. She does not argue that one must take risks to grow up to be healthy. She does not argue that adolescents must challenge adult authority in order to attain ultimately a sense of healthy autonomy or independence. She simply states, and depicts through a modest but insightful study, that high-risk behavior is common and deeply meaningful.[3] Risk-taking activities often provide intense experiences from which adolescents construct stories of themselves and out of which meaningful social bonds are forged. Roller coasters, horror movies, video games, "extreme" sports, and dares all depend on an element of risk taking to elevate the stakes and intensify the meaning of an adolescent's life. Given this, it is easy to see why friendships are often cast and identities formed around the meaning made of these risky events.

Janine Montero is a case in point. A sophomore at Central High, she grew up as a tomboy who took the childhood risks of being a faster runner than her male friends and more interested in them and their worlds than she was in her girlfriends. This didn't seem very risky as a seven-, eight-, and nine-year-old, but by the time she approached middle school that started to change. She was questioned on her sexuality before she really knew what sexuality was. While she initially fought back against the increasing taunts of "dyke" and "butch," she had little idea of what she was fighting for. She was fighting against insults she couldn't relate to, and she was fighting alone. By the middle of seventh grade the name-calling had calmed down. Janine had become more "feminine" and began to relate to "her boys" in a different way. While she wasn't sexually active like some of her eighth-grade friends, she was the focus of a good deal of male attention, and this helped her feel accepted.

In her ninth-grade year at Roosevelt High, Janine put the vast majority of her energy into building on her middle-school foundation of peer acceptance. Although she had long given up on her athletic involvement, she found that she could still compete with and at times beat the boys in other areas, including drinking. She got involved with a group of friends that partied heavily on the weekends. She and a number of her ninth-grade girlfriends started hanging out with some older guys from a neighboring town. It allowed the girls to feel more mature and gave them a "rep" in the school, a reputation that was as much myth as reality, but a rep that conferred status nonetheless. Before her ninth-grade year had ended, Janine had a pregnancy scare, which her parents learned about by overhearing a conversation between Janine and a friend. This led to a number of discussions of Janine's "lifestyle," including her deteriorating school performance. After a good deal of negotiation, Janine agreed to transfer to Central High for her sophomore year to gain "a fresh start."

Understanding adolescents as theoreticians and examining risk taking as meaning-making activity helps us see beyond the rhetoric of "at-risk" youth. It reorients us away from snap judgments about what is a "good risk" or a "bad risk" and toward the ways in which adolescents themselves may be making meaning of their experiences. If we follow Lightfoot's lead in understanding risk in this way, we must ask ourselves: How do we come to understand this subworld of risk taking that is deemed off limits to adults? How do we understand and, if possible, interact with this world, even if we cannot participate in it per se? Perhaps we need to approach it as a tourist or foreigner, attempting to learn what we can get access to by those who reside there. We will want a map for that, and maybe a tourist's guide. But no single map or guide exists, only guidelines and perhaps some local markers. We point out what we hope will be some helpful directions throughout the remainder of this chapter.

COGNITIVE DEVELOPMENT AND THE CALCULATION OF RISK

How calculated, really, are the "calculated risks" taken by adolescents? We hear, for example, of the impulsivity and thoughtlessness of adolescence. Neither of these characterizations meshes well with calculation. Is adolescent risk taking, then, more impulsive than calculated? Or is there something in between, something like *intuitive risk taking* or, perhaps, *spontaneous risk taking*? Intuitive risk taking might be defined as intuitively knowing that the risk can be met successfully. Gamblers take intuitive risks routinely, with mixed results at best. Stock investors refer to "informed intuition" in their risk-taking behavior; they too show mixed results. What about spontaneous risks? They might be defined as acting in the moment, perhaps on impulse, but perhaps through quick calculation as well. Spontaneous intimacy, for example, is not necessarily impulsive intimacy; it is, rather, an effort to take advantage of an unplanned opportunity. Theoretically, healthy spontaneity would not be synonymous with impulsivity. How do we make sense of all these pathways to risk taking, and the relative roles of impulsivity and calculation in the process? Julian's participation in Antwon's graffiti (chapter 2), from the perspective of an adult who may come upon the scene, may indeed look impulsive and qualify as risky behavior. However, to Julian, it was taking advantage of an unplanned opportunity that, while exposing him to the risk of punishment, provided the benefit of a strengthened bond between him and his longtime friend.

Bartsch and Piaget

The cognitive developmentalist Karen Bartsch defines the hallmark of adolescent thinking as *theoretical.*[4] Relative to children, adolescents typically become immersed in constructing theoretical connections and interconnections that pull their worlds together. For example, they become much more active than their younger selves in realistically projecting possible futures. Whereas children can create ingenious magical futures in which reality is transformed or placed on hold, adolescents tend to imagine possible futures—that is, those that they personally might strive to create or become. These possibilities might be marked by idealism, but the ideals are rooted in real possibilities. A good deal of adolescent thinking is invested in figuring out how to create a more ideal world, and a more ideal self, from the opportunities available in the present.

The revered Swiss developmental psychologist, Jean Piaget, was fascinated by how children's knowledge and capacity to theorize expanded as they moved from infancy to adulthood. Primarily observing and experimenting with his own children, Piaget understood the contents of the human mind to be organized into categories of experiences and impressions that he called *schemas*. Thinking, according to Piaget, is the processing of information in terms of the schemas we already possess. If the new information fits within our already-formed schemas, we *assimilate* it. If it does not, we either reject it or fit it into a new schema and adjust the other schemas accordingly. This mental process is called *accommodation*. Exploring the ways in which such schemas evidenced different ways of theorizing oneself and one's world, Piaget discerned four distinct stages characterized by a progressive construction of logic and increasingly sophisticated capacities to apprehend reality and possibility. These four stages, which have become so central to conceptions of cognitive development, he labeled *sensorimotor, preoperational, concrete operational,* and *formal operational.*[5]

The *sensorimotor* stage is primarily what newborns through two-year-olds experience. It is characterized by schemas formed almost exclusively through sensory impressions and locomotion. New experiences or subtle shadings of old experiences are largely rejected if they do not match existing schemas, and this works quite well as long as the environment is buffered by the parent(s). The *preoperational* stage heightens the process of accommodation, and whole new worlds of meaning open up as a result. Language becomes richer, humor emerges, symbols are comprehended and constructed, social behaviors can be understood, and time becomes less immediate. This rapid accommodation (adjusting existing schemas to account for novel experience) keeps the child fairly busy and in equilibrium until approximately age seven (earlier for some, later for others). At this point, situations that require not just the recognition of symbols but the capacity to make symbolic transformations become operative for the child. In Piaget's famous experiment, water is poured from a stout container into a long slender beaker, and although the shape of the water changes, it remains the same in quantity. Piaget observed that children in the *concrete operational* stage will be able to give the correct answer to the question of whether or not the amount of water has changed, whereas children in the preoperational stage will not.

The last stage, *formal operations,* is characterized by the ability to manipulate mentally abstract concepts, figures, and ideologies, not just physical things. The child or adolescent in formal operations can transform ideas and recognize subtleties of logic, such as the irreversibility of the statement "All squares are rectangles." If a young person dwells in a context that encourages it, the early-adolescent years mark the emergence of reflective thought and the capacity to perceive and manipulate abstract systems of meaning independent of the concrete checks that were previously necessary. As a result, entirely new patterns of reality unfold during the transition from concrete operational to formal operational thinking. Adolescents begin to ask "What if?" and can become passionately invested in explorations of the myriad ways in which the world and they themselves might be. When asked to provide explanations of what should and should not be, adolescents often preface their answers with the qualifier "It depends," signaling their new capacity to consider a multitude of valid possibilities.

Parks and Vygotsky

Sharon Parks nicely illustrates the Piagetian shift from concrete to formal operations (fig. 3.1).[6] Through the emergence of formal operations, according to Parks, an adolescent becomes capable of thinking about her thinking, to abstract herself and her perceptions, to begin to locate what is to be considered truth from her own internal apprehension. Formal operational thought also makes possible the capacity for what Parks and other developmental theorists call *third-person perspective-taking*—the ability to hold both one's own perceptions and the perceptions of another at the same time. This is a powerful new mode of awareness that permits much deeper connections with others, with one's self, and with such core concerns as existential meaning, purpose, truth, and identity. Understood as a cognitive awakening of sorts, adolescence ushers in new forms of creativity that involve the imagination of possibility and the projection of oneself into a world that can be changed. The adolescent literally becomes a theorist in search of experiments that test the boundaries of self-understanding, relationships, and social conventions. Risk-taking experiences can serve as some of the most intense developmental experiments youth devise.

Whether expressed in risk-taking experiences or not, adolescent theoretical thinking also strives to make connections across contexts. The adolescent's projection of her self-possibility into the world often takes the form of deeply considered existential questions: How should I be in school relative to home or out with my friends? How do these different ways in which I am go together to create the complete me? How do I, or should I, do things differently in different places, different contexts? Reminiscent of the identity-

FIGURE 3.1: The Shift from Concrete to Formal Operational Thinking

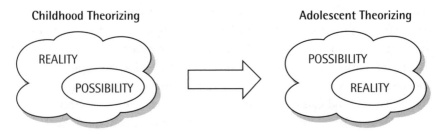

formation processes discussed in chapter 2, these are theoretical questions in search of empirical data. From where are those data gathered? What are the methods for its collection? Adolescent experimentation—risk taking—certainly is one of the methods of choice. Each risk, according to Lightfoot, provides new information that makes up the larger experiment and confirms or denies hypotheses about one's self-in-the-world. Some of these real-life adolescent researchers collect their data slowly and thoughtfully, with careful consideration of a manageable sample size; others collect large-scale batches rapidly, from every available data source, with little consideration given to how the raw data will ever be transformed into coherently interpretable results. Most fall somewhere in between. In all cases, the theoretical understanding that emerges from such experimentation contributes strongly to the young person's evolving conception of how the world works, and the roles he or she might play within it.

Theoretical thinking is abstract thinking. It is about moving from the concrete realities of the here and now to the possible realities of the there and then. It is about projection—projection from the constraining limitations of the current situation to the freeing liberation of future opportunity. As the life data of adolescent experience are collected and accumulate, how are they analyzed? This question is critical, since it is in the analysis of experience that reality is constructed, not in the sheer having or collection of experience.

Bartsch draws heavily on Vygotsky's sociopsychological theory of cognitive development (see chapter 1) in her conception of theoretical thinking. According to Vygotsky, the individual mind grows out of the collective mind. Specifically, an individual's cognitive abilities or thinking skills and strategies are cultivated through connection with other people's thoughts, which can be encountered in close relationships or experienced through culture more generally. Rather than sharing or assimilating already formulated thoughts, we *construct* them interactively, according to this perspective. Theoretical thinking is model building. We build our thoughts from the models of others. Thinking is modeled for us, we connect with it, and we learn from it. That is not to say that we end up with the same model as that thinking which has been modeled for us, but we are guided by it. Because every mind is connected with a multitude of other minds, our thinking models are syntheses of various contributions. This process, by definition, is creative. We create our own thinking through the interconnections we make to others' thinking, each of us creator and cocreator alike.

As explained in chapter 1, Vygotsky refers to the growth of the mind as a matter of *interpsychological development*.[7] As opposed to interpersonal development, which refers to growth in social interaction skills and maturity, interpsychological development refers to the interconnected processes by which individual minds develop in relationship with other minds. Central to the methods by which one mind grows in relation to other minds is the notion of *scaffolding*, which refers to the support needed to build growth-enhancing connections. The theory rests on the observation that there is often a difference between what we can learn by ourselves and what we can learn if helped by others (see figures 1.1 and 1.2 in chapter 1). Teachers, counselors, and school psychologists all work with these sorts of scaffolds, encouraging development in the student/client by working at the limits of their capability and understanding and expanding it from there. Vygotsky's "inter-" in his notion of interpsychological development implies a relational and larger cultural component to learning—that we all learn and grow from the scaffolds we provide one another. For example, what teacher has not learned from her students how to better teach something or someone? Scaffolding, like interpsychological growth, suggests that people do not and cannot grow on their own; rather, they need structured, systematic support—scaffolds. Such support can take a multitude of forms. Common among those forms, however, is the goal of assisting the individual in moving beyond his or her comfort zone within particular cognitive domains—in a nutshell, taking learning risks.

SCAFFOLDED CALCULATIONS

Must intuitive or spontaneous risks, whether social or educational, necessarily occur within one's comfort zone? The notion of intuition suggests a groundedness in what one knows. It suggests practiced experience and a degree of mastery that allows for an informed sense of what is likely to happen or what can be achieved. In this vein, intuition is fairly synonymous with an educated guess. An adolescent taking intuitive risks is acting out of confidence built on a history of prior related experience—experience often constructed through engaged interaction with others. This engagement serves as the developmental scaffolding that leads toward informed intuition. It is not necessarily the case that the particular scaffold would be viewed as positively constructive by adults; nonetheless, the linkages to peers' experiences and their thinking about such experiences help build the cognitive models that lead to intuitive risk taking.

Janine's "fresh start" at Central High provided a new context for enhanced risk taking. Her decision to drive home after having seven beers at her new boyfriend's party might be construed as an intuitively risky decision. It is risky for the obvious reasons that she will have less than optimal control of the car, that she is placing her passengers in harm's way, that she might be stopped by the police, and that she could seriously injure a pedestrian. It is intuitively risky in that she likely has been in similar positions before, perhaps with a couple less beers, or perhaps as a passenger with an older friend driving under similar conditions. As a result, Janine intuitively senses that she can master this risk. While it is possible that she drank excessively and took the car keys without prior experiences leading up to this event, that is not the reality. Janine gradually built her drinking-and-driving experience in relationship with others and expanded her cognitive and behavioral model for this activity over time. In other words, the scaffolding had been built through repeated exposure to modeling in this arena. In this scenario, Janine is operating within her comfort zone, although perhaps at the edge of it, and perhaps moving toward increasingly riskier calculations of the drinking-and-driving experiment.

Just as a gambler's intuition might pay off time and again, only to build false confidence, so too can *intuitive risk taking* lead to devastating consequences. If Janine's intuition suggests to her that she can take a leap well beyond her experienced comfort zone, perhaps by adding other drugs to the mix and continuing to drive under this progressively more intoxicating influence, she may find herself in a realm of experience in which the chances of success or survival are no better than a coin toss. The statistics on teenage substance use and driving fatalities are frightening, and it is likely that the teen victims behind these statistics could be classified as intuitive risk takers— teens taking heightened risks based on earlier experiences of meeting danger and seemingly beating the odds.[8] Because well-developed scaffolding can lead to new heights of experience, the consequences of falling off the edge can be heightened as well.

What about *spontaneous risk taking*? Does it typically occur within or beyond the comfort zone? Many adolescents love spontaneity. It implies freedom from constraint. Rather than planning the night's activities, let's be spontaneous. Let's do what we feel like doing in the moment. There is nonrisky spontaneity, such as deciding to get a game of pick-up basketball going, or going out to see a movie. And there is risky spontaneity, such as deciding to get high on a previously untried drug or to have sex via an unplanned liaison. Although such spontaneous risk taking may be unplanned, the actions typically are built on a scaffolding structure that allows or even prompts the behavior to occur. As with intuitive risk taking, the scaffold is constructed of prior experiences within the risk-taking domain or experiences that serve as a point of comparison or departure. For example, the spontaneous urge to "try something new" typically is built on a foundation of experiences in trying something related to or juxtaposed to the new experience. Even a seemingly spontaneous decision to have sex for the first time usually is built on prior thinking about "the right time" or the conditions under which it might be okay. Spontaneous risk taking, in general, might be viewed as pushing the developmental envelope. It is a move from planned and predictable everyday experience to a leap beyond the ordinary into the novel. Most of the time, however, that leap occurs from a platform of prior related experience, allowing the jumper to at least roughly assess the risks and potential benefits involved.

In Lightfoot's work, risk-taking experiences are understood less as activities that legitimize the labeling of teens as "at risk" and more as experiments providing magnified moments that confirm or deny aspects of a person's identity. Lightfoot points out that when risk-taking experiences are undertaken with others, they often function to secure relational bonds. Groups of adolescents will often take risks with one another, both to add a measure of safety in numbers but also to foment experiences that define them as members of that risk-taking group, as belonging to a peer-set that can say collectively, "I was there" or "I did it too." The power of knowing and testing oneself with another and recording and retelling it narratively as a sort of "Remember that one time when . . ." provides a road-map backward into how we became who we are and who was with us along the way. This is why we understand risk-taking experiences as inherently creative. The two friends who dared each other to dive off a cliff into the lake below, the group of teen hikers who ascended the knife-edge ridgeline to gain the summit, the neighborhood pals who rode their bikes down the steepest hill in their town without using their brakes—these are all examples of risk-taking experiences that provide adolescents with storylines to connect themselves with others. Such storylines mark history, just as they secure the foundation for future intuitive and spontaneous risk taking.

Often romanticized as the adolescent penchant for proof of their invincibility, experiences like the ones above are best understood as constructed, social bond-making, identity-confirming moments that punctuate the mundane and provide opportunities for character development. Smoking cigarettes or marijuana for the first time, "getting to third base," imbibing alcohol, getting in a fight, sneaking out of the house after curfew, stealing, driving too fast or under the influence, snorting crystal meth—these are risk-taking experiences with obvious and dangerous implications. Nonetheless, for the adolescent engaged in such activity, it is important for significant adults to recognize the meaning-making experimentation and relational-bonding intrinsic to whatever risk-taking activity she has constructed. There is a time and place for judgment and even punishment for unsafe behaviors or legal transgressions, but for those of us working with youth in schools, it is imperative that we come to know the meaning *the adolescents themselves* are making of the experience. If we hope to influence that meaning-making, we must first recognize the validity of their understanding of what happened and how it is shaping their life-story. Only then can we co-construct *with* adolescents the forms of creativity they are mustering to project themselves into relationships and the world at large.

THAT'S FRESH!

Creating new experiences—that is what much of adolescent risk taking is about. Because the age itself brings about new possibilities for experiencing the world, including those associated with a maturing body as well as mind, it is natural that the "old ways" of doing things would become boring for many teens. Adolescents will go where the opportunity to create exists, where they can risk novel ways of experiencing and presenting themselves. The goal for educators is to make school a place where learning can be experienced as new, as creative and interesting, or, as the kids put it (through last week, at least . . .), as fresh!

The call to make education enticing to students should not be confused with an approach to making it fun through superficial entertainment. The developmental psychologists Mihaly Csikszentmihalyi and Reed Larson were instrumental in framing the argument that deeply engaging study does not occur through momentary enticements but rather through consistent and challenging activities that build skills and personal investment.[9] Drawing from a physiological model, they describe the experience of disengagement as one of psychological *entropy*, which they define as the blocking of psychological energy that is needed to meet the challenges of complex thinking or behavioral pursuits. The opposite phenomenon is psychological *negentropy*, or the freeing of psychic energy. The goal for educators, from this perspective, is to foster opportunities that open the floodgates of constructive energy. That opening would ultimately lead to what Csikszentmihalyi and Larson call the *flow experience*.[10]

One experiences flow when the stores of pent-up psychic energy are released through highly engaged activity. In *flow states*, self-consciousness largely disappears as one gets lost in the challenge and meaning of the activity at hand. In their study, the authors found that many adolescents rarely experience flow in their daily lives and are frequently bored or engaged in less challenging, less stimulating activities. School is often the chief arena where such entropy is experienced, a fact that has clear and compelling consequences. If school offers little to challenge and excite the adolescent mind, and if flow is experienced exclusively or primarily in such high-risk behaviors as those described in the sections above, adolescents will lose themselves and, at the same time, find themselves in those activities. One will become, will eventually *be*, a fast driver, a heavy drinker, a promiscuous sexual partner, and this may mean turning away from the possibilities inherent in school-based activities. So, we must ask: How do we help our students become, and ultimately be, scholars, musicians, or simply people who are actualizing the range of their talents? How do we build flow in the classroom?

We begin by building scaffolds. We build scaffolds to our own passions and interests and across the passions and interests of the students in our classrooms, computer labs, music halls, and gymnasiums. We begin by building connections, and we progress by helping to deepen those connections. We build scaffolds and we take and promote risks ourselves. In doing so, we work hard to engage the meaning adolescents make of those risks. We make it possible for our students to jump spontaneously off the edge into the realm of new learning challenges, because they have developed the skills of risk taking to make that leap. Schools often do this by providing guided risk-taking experimentation in the form of theater and musical performance, sports, student government, the school newspaper, art classes, and internships with local businesses. In each of these venues, possible selves can be tested, relationships forged, forms of expression investigated, and audiences appraised. Teachers sometimes do this through role-playing activities, simulations, debates, inquiry-based or problem-posing assignments, and performance-based assessments. To get to this level of developmental and pedagogical sophistication in one's teaching requires professional developmental scaffolding for the teacher as well so he can take risks in the classroom, work toward the establishment of negotiable/reciprocal relationships with youth, and remain in dialogue with other professionals facing similar challenges/risks.

As school-based professionals, when we project ourselves into relationships with youth, it is important to be risk takers, not just because it models the sort of risk taking we would like to see in our students but because it helps *us* to secure relationships and project ourselves into possibilities we might not consider otherwise. In fact, the adults who take risks in their work with youth are better positioned to influence youth risk taking than those who do not. As school-based professionals try to encourage students to defend a victim from bullying, step outside the de facto dress code dictated by their peers, voice an unpopular opinion, or raise their hand in class despite being shy, they are most likely to be heard by the youth they are attempting to influence if they have practiced taking the same risks in faculty meetings!

As an example, if Janine's propensity to risk driving herself and her friends home after a night of excessive drinking was accompanied by challenging activities in school that tapped into her creative energy, the likelihood of her becoming more at risk might be reduced. This is particularly true when the constructive school-based activities are linked to relationships with supportive adults. The mentoring and resilience literatures have both been clear in showing how a meaningful relationship with even one nonfamilial adult can have a powerful impact on the life prospects of young people (see more on this topic in chapter 5). Teachers who work supportively with their students on challenging and creative learning tasks often fit the prototype of this caring adult. When their care is accompanied by engaging challenges, teachers are positioned to counter some of the appeal of high-risk, peer-supported risk taking. As we shall see below, Ms. Petersen, whom we met in the first chapter through her struggles with Antwon, positions herself as just such a teacher for Janine.

In their groundbreaking research beginning in the 1970s, sociologists Richard and Shirley Jessor showed how high-risk behavior compounds itself.[11] That is, participation in one risky behavior, such as cigarette smoking, increased the likelihood of participating in other risky behaviors, such as drinking and marijuana use. In essence, every risky behavior enacted increased the likelihood that new risky behaviors would follow. They termed this phenomenon the *problem behavior syndrome*. As their research progressed, the Jessors and their colleagues found that youth alignment with caring adults was critical to preventing the syndrome from mushrooming out of control. Furthermore, the more youth came to share adult values, or what the Jessors termed *adult conventional norms*, the less likely they were to engage in dangerous high-risk behavior.

Building from the Jessors' findings, it seems clear that educators' capacities to connect with students in meaningful activities can serve multiple purposes. They serve to build not only the learning and thinking skills necessary for educational success but also a value system rooted in care, collaboration, and high achievement of various types. The more transparent that value system is, the more clearly school scaffolding is constructed on adult-youth shared values, the more likely it is that educators can foster healthy development and reduce the magnitude and consequences of high-risk behavior.

> Janine entered her tenth-grade year at Central High after nearly failing the ninth grade as well as her pregnancy test. Her parents hoped the new school environment would allow her to make the most of her last years of secondary education before moving on to college. Janine enters Central High not only with a school record of low performance but also with an informal record of high-risk behavior. She had grown deeply connected to her peer subgroup at her former high school and felt valued there. She feels like her parents cannot begin to understand her and that her former teachers made little effort to do so. How can Janine's fresh start become anything other than a repetition of the old ways?

In the Early College High School (Early College) initiative, founded by the Bill and Melinda Gates Foundation, students like Janine are given the opportunity to prepare for college by taking college coursework during their high-school years. The initiative assumes that disengaged students can and will succeed in high school and college if provided with new and challenging activities heavily supported by competent and caring teachers. In a study of this initiative conducted by Michael Nakkula and his colleagues,[12] the researchers have found that some of the students are thriving under this model while others struggle and choose to return to a less challenging, less supportive school environment. What makes the difference?

Students who are thriving in the Early College model tend to report being pushed hard by supportive teachers who not only introduce them to interesting activities but also join them in the skill-building and risk-taking process. In the study by Nakkula et al., students make clear and profound distinctions between those teachers who are committed to them and those who seem interested in the schoolwork only. Teacher commitment to the students as human beings and as learners seems to earn a reciprocal commitment from the students. Such mutual commitment serves as the cornerstone not only for future high-level achievement but also for the construction of a shared value system, one that can counter the peers-only value system that, in turn, can lead to progressively higher-risk behavior.

MADD SKILLZ: FROM MERE COMPETENCE TO SHEER MASTERY

What's fresh is new, is cool, is captivating. But what's captivating ultimately must have deep roots that hold one's attention. "That's deep!" or some hip-hop linguistic variant can be heard with as much frequency in teen culture as references to cool and freshness. The merging of fresh and deep are witnessed in "Madd Skillz!" These are skills that challenge our comprehension. Skills that demand recognition. Madd skillz might be associated most commonly with musical and athletic prowess, but they are referenced in connection with all areas of adolescent performance. The core of madd skillz is the teenage yearning for expression and the endless variations of trying things on that such yearning produces. In fact, the entire youth subculture is mined as a matter of routine by advertising agencies in order to predict and produce the next best thing in popular culture. It is largely teen inventiveness—the creativity of adolescent risk taking—that gives us each new sound, clothing style, game, phrase, fad. Moving such inventiveness from novelty to mastery, however, is required for the development of madd skillz: the skilled person exhibits practiced competence; the "maddly skilled" teen exhibits unique and revered mastery.

Can such mastery be cultivated and displayed in the classroom? The answer, of course, is that it can, hypothetically. In practice, however, scores of students become bored with repetitive learning exercises designed at best to promote "common learning" or the attainment of predetermined standards of competence. The ordinariness implied by common standards is scarcely compelling, which is why No Child Left Behind (NCLB) and related high-stakes testing legislation run the risk of leaving creativity out of the curriculum and losing students in the process.

Ms. Petersen is keenly aware that she is losing Janine in her world litera-ture class. Although she suffers with the potential loss of any of her stu-dents, Ms. Petersen is particularly saddened to see Janine gradually dis-appearing before her very eyes. Janine came into the school year looking for a fresh start after her disappointing ninth-grade experience. She ini-tially was excited to take on whatever content Ms. Petersen introduced. Janine was in Julian's section of world lit, where the two of them engaged in a friendly competition for "topp litt dawgg," as they liked to put it, in order to disguise any hint of being overly studious. They both took a particular liking to Ms. Petersen's approach to the writings of Sophocles, Anne Frank, Chinua Achebe, and Alan Paton, and how she made class discussions relevant to the social-class disparities evident today in our own communities. While Janine didn't have Julian's overall track record of academic success, she could "hang with him" in world lit. She relished this experience, and her enthusiasm in turn sparked Julian's competitive juices and Ms. Petersen's love of teaching.

Unfortunately, two very different factors converged to knock Janine off track and out of her joyful competition with Julian. The tenth-grade trial assessment for the end-of-year high-stakes test, which determines whether students can graduate on time and depicts how the school and school system are performing relative to state norms, showed that Janine was faring quite poorly in language arts. Although she is a highly creative writer and strong critical thinker, her basic writing skills are fairly weak, and her retention of reading material suffers somewhat as well. To ensure that she would pass the upcoming test, Ms. Petersen felt little recourse but to place Janine in a "catch-up" section with some of her peers. While this made sense on the surface, the change proved counter-productive. Janine quickly became bored practicing her technical writing skills and had little interest working on reading comprehension for sub-ject matter that didn't interest her. She missed her literary battles with Julian, and just as importantly, she missed the Ms. Petersen who taught to her higher talents rather than her limitations.

The second experience that contributed to Janine's slide in school was the expertise she was developing as a weekend drinker, an expertise that was finding its way into the school week as well. As school became more boring to her, partying and getting crazy with friends became ever more enticing. Whereas school was routine, drinking and partying created excitement. Sometime around February, Ms. Petersen overheard Janine talking with Julian about her party habits, trying to entice him into a friendly drinking competition, perhaps to replace the connection they had lost in class. Recognizing that the remedial test-prep approach was not working for Janine, Ms. Petersen did an about-face and recruited her former star student back to the content that mattered to Janine. She pulled her aside, had an honest talk about the importance of the graduation test, then said she needed Janine to work with her former competitor on a critique of contemporary society, rooted in the ideas of Sophocles and Achebe and other authors of their choosing. The critique would be featured in the yearbook as the annual contribution from the tenth-grade world lit class.

Feigning ambivalence to hide her obvious excitement over the new plan, Janine approached Julian with the idea:

"You hear about this thing Miss P.'s talkin' about . . . about you and me doin' something for the yearbook?"

"Yeah Dawgg," Julian replied in a welcoming dialect, which he emphasized to counter the embarrassment he knew Janine was feeling over her remedial catch-up work. "We gotta do this. I already got all kindsa ideas for this thing. Whatchyu got?"

"Nothin' . . . nothin' yet," Janine responded in a more reserved tone. "I didn't know if I'd want to do this, if it was even worth it."

"What are you talkin' about, Dawgg?! This gives us a chance to write what we been talkin' about all year. You ain't backin' down are ya, because of that [expletive] test? You'll pass the test, Dawgg . . . and even if you don't you have next year. We don't have next year for this thing. We gotta do it now!"

"Alright, Dawgg, let's do it then. Tell me what you got and I'll start kickin' some ideas around."

Janine and Julian worked diligently on the yearbook piece over the next several months. They produced an outstanding critique of the income disparity in the neighborhood surrounding their school, featuring interviews with homeless people at a local shelter and with owners of a construction company and upscale coffee shop. The article won both students a great deal of praise from teachers and students alike. Ms. Petersen helped the students make contacts with their interviewees and stayed after school with her "topp litt dawgg" pupils to encourage and challenge them to sharpen the project. Janine ended up finishing the year in world lit with even more enthusiasm than she had at the beginning. She risked putting herself out for this project, with the relentless support of Julian and Ms. Petersen, and it paid off for her. She never felt stronger as a student and never felt better about herself in general. Her thinking and writing were displayed for an audience she valued, which allowed her to value herself more fully as well.

But challenging, creative accomplishments like the yearbook project are not panaceas for reducing other risks. Janine did indeed fail her tenth-grade high-stakes test, while Julian and a number of her other friends passed easily. Julian was right, though; the project was worth it to Janine, and she still has at least two more chances to pass the test before graduation. And if Julian wins her over again, the odds of passing might increase. The two litt dawggs have started seeing each other outside of school, which has Julian talking with Janine about her party habits. She's pushed him to back off on "the lectures," but at the same time she has backed off on the partying a bit. Still, it's a long summer. And there are some big parties being planned. "Lots of action to figure out," Janine's thinking. "Lots to figure out . . ."

CHAPTER FOUR

Flow and Possibility Development

There's nothin' like it, man . . . that feeling like you can do no wrong, that feeling like you're really just focused and nothin' can get in the way. I feel that sometimes when I'm rappin'. I feel like, man, the words are just flowin' out of me like someone's back there just pourin' 'em out. And they just come, man, they just keep comin' . . .

—Composite of conversations with various youth

"Just flowin'" is consistent with how Csikszentmihalyi and Larson described the experience of optimal development in their influential book, *Being Adolescent.*[1] But getting to that flow state where the words, or the chords, or the goals "just keep comin'" is something quite different from simply being there and letting it happen. If it were that easy, more adolescents—and people of all ages for that matter—would experience flow in their everyday lives with far greater frequency than is indeed the case.

The experience of optimal development is defined by Csikszentmihalyi and Larson as the high one receives from functioning at the edge of our capacities for a sustained period of time. It is not the quick high that comes from exciting experiences. Rather, it is that contented, deeply gratified feeling that comes from being in the groove, from being deeply focused on a complex task that has taken time and energy to master. According to the authors, the experience of optimal development, or flow, is fairly rare. That finding should come as no surprise, given our culture of sound bites and sensation seeking. We tend to want our information immediately and our gratification now! Quick hits lead to quick highs, but they are not conducive to building complex skills, which requires training our minds to stay on task for sustained periods of time.

Throughout our years of teaching adolescent development to teachers, administrators, and student-support personnel, we have found that flow theory holds particular appeal. Teachers, for example, hope that their students will ultimately learn *for the love of it*, that they will get lost in compelling lessons or challenging physical activities and reach heights of accomplishment that can only be attained through full immersion in the learning process. Teachers also know that this scenario is an ideal seldom reached, particularly with students who struggle academically or who derive little pleasure out of sustained physical exertion. But the enormous developmental benefits that stem from flow experiences make them worth striving for despite their rarity. Like teachers, school counselors also are drawn to flow theory. They would rather counsel students to find their passions, and support them in actualizing their highest aims, than exclusively helping them to uncover the underlying issues that prevent them from succeeding. Like many teachers, however, school counselors often bemoan the fact that they do not have enough time to work at the edge of their students' capacities due to the demands of helping them cope with the pressing struggles that get in their way.

Given the pervasiveness of problems or struggles among our students, particularly those in low-performing schools, how do we integrate experiences of optimal development into our work? How do we help our students feel the sense of gratification that comes with complex task mastery, and how do we help them experience that gratification in both their curricular and extracurricular activities? These are the questions this chapter attempts to answer.

DEVELOPING POSSIBILITIES

"You can't do what ain't possible. . . . I mean, they want us to pass those damn tests without ever even teaching us half a that stuff." These comments by Lorena Chávez, a tenth-grader, describe the challenge of meeting her state's testing requirements. Lorena's sentiments, whether rooted in actual fact or in a personal history of school disengagement, reflect those of many high-school students attending underperforming schools, including Janine, whom we met in the last chapter. Lorena and Janine met briefly in the tenth-grade remedial test-prep catch-up program, and although they came to a similar place academically, they arrived there via fairly different pathways. Lorena was passed on from grade to grade because of her leadership strengths and speaking skills; she didn't realize she was in trouble academically until reaching high school. Janine, on the other hand, started looking for optimal experiences in late middle school and early high school in order to fit in, to feel supported. Academic issues just weren't that important to her by the time she reached the ninth grade. But the two girls share important similarities as well. The No Child Left Behind (NCLB) legislation has left Lorena and Janine, and other students like them, feeling so behind the expectations reflected in their home state's high-stakes achievement tests that catching up is experienced as a sheer impossibility. By the time the high-school assessments come into play, many students have lived through years of low expectations groomed by classroom chaos and pedagogical apathy. If students from such settings are to experience anything approximating academic optimal development—which, in turn, would help them pass their high-stakes achievement tests—the impossible, as Lorena put it, must be transformed into possibility. High goals must be met by realistic hope—hope cultivated by successive, ongoing experiences of accomplishment.

> Lorena's worries regarding her ability to pass the state tests are equally matched by her teacher's concerns about both her academic progress and her behavior of late. She had been a star forward on her seventh-, eighth-, and ninth-grade YWCA basketball team, distinguishing herself as a tenacious rebounder and fierce defensive player. Respected by her teachers and peers in middle school as an articulate and convincing speaker, her writing skills nonetheless languished behind her verbal abilities. She was given passing grades in those years more because she showed promise than because she demonstrated proficiency. In ninth grade, she started exhibiting a more combative attitude, talking back to teachers that demanded more effort or after-school make-up work from her and disrupting nearly every group project in which she was involved. Eventually, Lorena's mouth got her into some trouble, and she ended up starting or finishing (depending on whose story you believed) a series of fights after school in the fall of her sophomore year. When one of those fights broke out in the cafeteria and she verbally threatened the intervening teacher, she received a week-long suspension. Soon after, word spread through the school that the principal was considering her for expulsion. Worried they might lose Lorena to the streets, her English and P.E. teachers intervened. Arguing that "all of Lorena's fighting, defiance,

and negativity are eclipsing what she has to offer," these two teachers contacted her parents and the principal to describe the leadership potential and athletic skill they believed she possessed. When it became clear that recent troubles at home (Lorena's dad had lost his job and her mother had been diagnosed with cancer) may have been contributing to her behavior, all agreed that finding ways to keep her in school and focused on her emerging talents was the best solution. It was then that Maggie, the school counselor, was called in to help.

Maggie began meeting with Lorena during lunch the week after her suspension. It became clear to her early on that Lorena felt like she was learning little to nothing while at school and believed that her teachers were more intent on exposing her poor writing skills and sending her to the office than helping her improve. Trying to convince her that this wasn't the case, Maggie realized that Lorena had come to associate school with punishment, a place where she got in trouble for not learning and for getting mad about it. In hopes that Lorena might import some sort of out-of-school success into her academics, Maggie surveyed a list of after-school clubs for something Lorena might find challenging and rewarding. Since her grades and the suspension made her ineligible for the basketball team, Maggie looked for something that would help Lorena experience the rewards of hard work and the joys of building skills. In consultation with her parents, the principal, and her teachers, Maggie bargained to have the school remove the threat of expulsion as long as she regularly participated in an after-school rowing program for urban girls.

When Maggie told her of the rowing program on the river that runs through the city, all Lorena could think of was that thing she often walked over at the Fifth Street bridge, that slow-moving shimmery ribbon where fancy rich folks drove their boats on hot summer afternoons, that Brown and murky never-to-be-swimmed-in place to be avoided after dark. To be on the river rather than over or next to it sounded kind of cool, though, and it sure beat getting in fights in the park. On Saturday, Lorena met Colby Steinberg, one of the rowing program's coaches, at the boathouse to get to know each other and check things out. She introduced Lorena to the various sculls, the sliding seats, the hollow oars, and the art and power of the rowing stroke. Half paying attention and half not, since she doubted anyone would ever trust her with one of those sleek, shiny wooden boats, Lorena heard herself agreeing to a swimming test and a series of orientation sessions. Within a matter of weeks she found herself in a life jacket seated in front of Colby on a double scull, pushing away from the dock. As Colby rowed behind her, providing guidance on the finer points of the catch, the pull, and the finish of the rowing stroke, Lorena watched parts of her community go by from the middle of the river, momentarily mystified at how much slower and peaceful the city looked from the water.

Impressed with how quickly Lorena adopted the stroke of a more seasoned rower, Colby announced the afternoon's goal. "We're gonna row together, stroke-for-stroke, from the Fifth Street bridge back to the boathouse, and we're gonna see if we can do it in less than twelve minutes." "Alright," Lorena said reluctantly, to which Colby immediately shouted, "Go!" Soon after they'd begun, Lorena felt her body settle into the rhythmic push and pull of her legs and arms as her oars sliced synchronously with Colby's through the water. Even with her quads and biceps burning, Lorena felt like she was flying. When they got to the boathouse dock, Lorena was so exhausted and mesmerized by their speed that she completely forgot about the twelve-minute goal. After showing Lorena how to lift the boat up the ramp and carry it back to its stand in the boathouse, Colby reached out and showed Lorena the reading on her wristband stopwatch—11:38. "Look what we did! We shattered our goal time!" Colby exclaimed. Giggling pridefully, Lorena responded by reaching out and showing Colby the beginning of two red blisters on each of her hands. "Look what I got. I busted my hand!" Grabbing Lorena's right hand and shaking it just firmly enough, Colby commended her effort, saying, "With your skills and strength those blisters will be calluses before long. You have what it takes to be great at this, Lorena. But to really fly, you need to put in the work and develop the skills. Calluses are signs of that commitment. So wear those blisters with pride, girl! They won't last long." Lorena felt the sting of her blisters on the handlebars as she rode home that afternoon, but when she glimpsed pieces of the river through the apartment buildings and trees that lined her route, she remembered what she had done that day. The river would never be the same again, and in some fundamental ways, neither would she.

FROM PREVENTION TO INVENTION

In 1993 Michael Nakkula and his colleagues turned a federally funded school counseling project designed to prevent high-risk behavior into a model that emphasized the development of strengths and interests. They called this transformation "the shift from prevention to invention" and named the new model *Project IF: Inventing the Future*. Project IF was designed explicitly to help middle- and high-school students build a realistic sense of hope for their futures—hope rooted in the interests, strengths, and skills they already possessed, even though they might not be fully aware of them. The project was born from the observation that the majority of students attending the schools where the original prevention project existed were being referred for counseling and prevention services. The students were referred by teachers, parents, or themselves because they were falling behind in school, were in trouble of one form or another, or simply felt depleted by the relentless challenges of urban poverty.

It ultimately became apparent to the project staff that referral of the majority of the schools' students for support services suggested that the problems are not rooted in the students but rather in larger systemic issues. To call the concern a "student problem" to be treated or prevented was to misunderstand the essence of the phenomenon. The more accurate diagnosis was the lack of meaningful opportunities for healthy development available to students; as such, Project IF pursued a course dedicated to cultivating such opportunities, a course of action the project labeled *possibility development*. Pursuing this course required a host of changes from the typical way of doing business in counseling and prevention work. For starters, it required changing intake forms from a format geared toward uncovering clinical or problem-based histories to one that allowed for the assessment of strengths and interests. The shift, which sounds minor in principle, proved challenging in practice.

Counselors and related support staff are trained to help people with their problems, to help relieve the suffering derived from histories of struggle and misfortune. Mental-health workers often come into the field having survived challenging experiences themselves and are determined to dedicate their professional lives to helping others overcome similar difficulties. Working from the matched perspectives of suffering and care, such support staff can find it difficult to radically shift their working lens. For many of them, refocusing on strengths and possibility feels like a turning away from the problems that require professional care. In the language of counseling and psychotherapy, such refocusing can feel like "enabling" or implicitly reinforcing the problems that call out for attention.

Teachers share a similar disposition that can be difficult to shift. Trained to administer diagnostics early in the year in order to assess students' academic capacities and subject-matter preparedness for the content of their course, they are practiced at discerning deficiency and recognizing a lack of aptitude. When teachers see upward of 100 students per day and are expected to assess the progress of each of them and then differentiate instruction to meet the varied needs of each individual child, it is no wonder that standardized diagnostics become necessary. After all, to determine what the student needs, teachers must find out what the student lacks. But there's a downside here. While remediation and skill building are and should be part and parcel of the teacher's job, an overreliance on the identification of student deficits can obscure the many assets or talents they may possess. Grading papers can become an exercise in hunting for mistakes rather than scanning for success, and giving tests can too easily devolve into exposing ignorance rather than displaying knowledge. Such tendencies can be quite durable in the minds of many teachers, deluged as they are with large class sizes and the NCLB requirement that they demonstrate measurable gains in student learning. This is perhaps why many attempts to shift teachers' attention to their students' strengths and possibilities are sometimes dismissed as social promotion, the lowering of expectations, or tacit acceptance of failure.

Whether in the classroom or the counseling office, the shift from prevention and intervention to *invention* (also, at times, called *promotion*) implies a great deal. It implies that prevention work, although critically important and a key step forward from treating problems after they occur, is still a course of action fundamentally oriented toward student difficulties rather than their strengths. Invention also implies that there is not a ready-made future to inherit—not the future that one would want to inherit, in any case—but rather a requirement to create one for oneself with the help of others. This means that to live well, to live fully, is to cocreate, to invent possibilities for living and to work toward actualizing those possibilities collectively.

The Project IF strength and interest assessment, which begins by explicitly asking students to articulate their primary strengths and interests, can prove surprisingly difficult.[2] Students with histories of school failure associated with limited supports at home or in their communities can struggle to identify personal strengths. At the same time, the assessment commonly solicits ambitious dreams from middle- and early-high-school students who hope to become highly skilled professionals such as medical doctors and lawyers. These aspirations are nearly as likely to come from C and D students as from those earning As and Bs. The gap, therefore, between the hoped-for future and current preparation is at times enormous. The future "way out there" and the here-and-now present can be worlds apart. Possibility, however, lives in both places. It serves as the bridge to the most distant future with one end firmly implanted at our feet. But while possibility itself transcends time and context, possibility development is a thoroughly immediate phenomenon. It requires the leap from dreams to reality, from aspiration to application, from tomorrow to today.

BLENDING IMAGINATION AND SKILL DEVELOPMENT

Possibility development, like more traditional forms of invention, blends imagination and skills. Imagination may fuel the vehicle of creativity and learning, but skill building is required to move the vehicle in the intended direction. In other words, while imagination fuels our dreams, the requisite skills are needed to drive them home. Skills are the strengths and aptitudes we possess now. Skill development begins where we are and links our current, stable capacities with those that lie at the edge of our abilities. In this manner, skill development turns our potential into a tangible, personal possession or characteristic. We come to have skills, to be skilled. The developmental psychologist Kurt Fischer and his colleagues have long studied cognitive skill building and have shown how neuropsychological networks are made more complex through intellectual opportunity development.[3] As opportunities for learning are presented through supportive educational and related interactions, networks of neural connections consolidate to capture and hold relevant information. The mind, from this perspective, is an interconnected neural support network, which expands and deepens depending on the nature of learning opportunities presented and the nature and degree of support available for building on those opportunities. Skill development from Fischer's perspective is an important model for envisioning possibility development more broadly.

Possibility development forms a cycle of skill building and imagination. Every acquisition of new skills brings the possibility of new dreams. Finnish psychologist Jari Nurmi has conducted extensive studies on how the future is shaped during adolescence. Through their research, Nurmi and his colleagues articulated the notion of temporal extension, which captures the extent to which adolescents and all people can project future possibilities.[4] That is, some youth are able to vividly project possibilities for themselves into the distant future and articulate clear and realistic plans for getting there. Others can only project into the nearer future because they have not developed the skills needed to make realistic, longer-term projections possible. Drawing on Fischer's cognitive model, that lack of development is likely the result of a limited support network, where connections for future planning, neurological and otherwise, have not been adequately created. Although the individual student represents the outcome or synthesis of developmental opportunities, opportunity development itself is very much a collective endeavor.

SKILL AS A POSSIBILITY LENS

Just as skills represent our present state of competence, they also point toward future states of possibility. In Nakkula and Ravitch's conception of applied development work, they present the hermeneutic notion of a fore-structure of understanding and its importance for interpreting young people's experiences.[5] This forestructure represents the consolidated life history of one's ways of seeing and being in the world. From a hermeneutic perspective, the forestructure is not only a repository of the past but also holds the possibilities for moving forward and anticipating the future. That is, we can only build from the particular foundation that has been laid. The skills we possess are the bricks and mortar of that foundation, the scaffolds, in Vygotskian terms, on which we build new learning. We pursue the next possibilities for our development based largely on the skills developed up to the moment. Therefore, the domains in which we build skills, and the ways in which this building happens, play a large role in the possibilities that follow.

Consider, for example, the national concern over girls and science. Despite the growing evidence that girls are outperforming boys in most academic subject areas across the K–12 years, women tend to be grossly underrepresented in certain higher-education majors and professional careers. The academic skills they build in primary and secondary schools track them away from advanced study and career opportunity in the sciences and various other arenas. When Harvard University president Lawrence Summers speculated that the lack of women within academic leadership roles in the sciences might indicate an innate difference in specific male and female learning capacities, his comments ignited an immediate and intense reaction from scientists and educators concerned about opportunity development for groups underrepresented in particular disciplines. The reactions to Summers's comments were rooted in the reality that girls and women have not been socialized to learn math and science comparably to boys and men. Because girls have been encouraged to focus on reading, writing, and the humanities, young women are far more likely to pursue college majors and career tracks related to those skill and interest areas. This is a concrete example of how early skill development channels the possibilities for subsequent opportunity development.

How then should educators respond to and nurture the range of our students' skills? Should we pay particular attention to areas of high aptitude and encourage further development in those areas, or should we pay equal attention to the weaknesses, to those skills that might lag behind some of the others in order to prevent the foreclosure of possibilities for our students? Most of us would agree that these questions do not call for either/or answers. We must nurture the high-end skills just as we must help students develop in areas of relative weakness. But this simple response does not bail us out quite that easily. There are still matters of degree in question. Educators and students alike have finite amounts of time and energy. How should that precious time and energy be invested?

Focusing the possibility lens

As discussed in chapter 2, part of adolescent identity development requires making commitments to particular directions, including career directions. The moratorium or exploratory phase of identity development suggests that informed exploration should precede investments in committed directions. But how wide should that exploration be? Given that highly successful careers in the sciences, for example, require strong early foundations in math and science coursework, it would seem imperative that girls who ultimately pursue this direction would need intense early focusing in these subjects. Can one invest deeply here while also developing strong skills in the arts, in athletics, and in the humanities? Most students can cover many bases well, but it is critical for educators of adolescents to realize that every present investment in skill development comes with possibility costs and benefits. Broadening is likely to lead to generalized knowledge and to keep more doors open. Specializing is likely to lead to more highly developed specific skills, thereby opening particular doors more widely while closing, at least partially, others along the way.

Flow theory argues that the specializing approach is more likely to lead to experiences of optimal development—focused, localized experiences of optimal development. In turn, such experiences are likely to become core components of students' identities. Earlier schools of learning theory assumed that skill development in one area would transfer to skill development in other areas. That theory has been largely debunked based on extensive research, including studies derived from Fischer's skill theory, addressed above. Skill theory depicts a learning process in which experience in specific areas builds domain-specific skills supported by an integrated neural network. Skills become more complex through their application to progressively more challenging tasks. But they only become more complex in the areas in which they have been applied. Their complexity does not transfer well to other areas without practice in those areas. On the other hand, the experience of skill development in one area can provide the motivation and modeling needed to apply one's efforts in other areas. That is, the experience of building skills builds confidence and a sense of competence. The more confident and competent we feel, the more likely we are to venture into new learning activities.

This is precisely what Maggie had hoped would happen with Lorena. In fact, as Lorena's calluses grew thicker and her rowing strength and skill improved, she began to work harder at improving her writing. Running off to the boathouse immediately after school kept her out of fights, and the exposure to college students in the rowing program gave her new possibilities into which she could project herself. Watching the more experienced crews of college women slice by the boathouse in a perfectly synchronized blur and then seeing them laugh with each other, make playful jokes about one another, and even hearing about their doing homework together gave Lorena a positive association with what college might be like. Along with her relationship with Colby, this motivated her to step up her academic efforts to make the possibility of college a reality. But it was the experience of working with her boat's teammates that had perhaps the greatest impact. No longer did she have to hide her insecurities by lashing out or competing with threatening peers, and no longer could she rely on her quick verbal acuity to get her out of (or into) trouble. She was now part of a crew, learning to row in unison with her teammates as smoothly and quickly as she could, preparing for that task in sequential steps, becoming stronger and more proficient each step of the way. Sometimes, in the middle of a practice or a race, Lorena stopped thinking about what each leg and arm had to do and just did it, losing track of time, letting go of any worry, and losing herself in the process.

Internalizing possibility models

Although skill development may not be transferable across domains, models of skill building can be internalized and broadly used. Educators might call this phenomenon *learning how to learn* and might conceive of their work as *teaching how to learn*, as opposed to teaching only about a particular subject matter or the development of particular skills. Still, teaching how to learn does not bail us out either. There is still the reality that at some point in adolescence students will need to organize an inordinate amount of their energy around specific learning challenges if they are going to reach high levels of domain-specific competence, and making that investment is going to rule out similar levels of investment in other areas. Such decisions have enormous lifelong and even societal implications, including the clustering of certain groups of people in some professional arenas while others cluster elsewhere. This is why it is so critical that we co-construct *with* adolescents the choices they make and the meanings ascribed to them. By pointing out what might be gained and lost with their investment of time and energy, we help them to see more clearly the possibilities they are imagining and to recognize the ones they might be leaving behind.

This section would not be complete without a general reference to the role of sports in adolescent development. For many youth, sports are granted a uniquely privileged position among the options for skill building potentially available. The reasons behind this privileged status are fairly transparent and understandable. Sports provide a concrete means for having one's skills developed, tested, and displayed. They provide opportunities for social interaction and interpersonal skill building (despite the fact that some of these interpersonal skills might be viewed as less than healthy, depending on one's values). And by displaying one's athletic skills publicly, sports participation creates a context for bringing the sort of recognition and rewards that contribute to self-confidence and a related sense of competence.[6]

An overemphasis on skill building in the athletic arena, however, can leave too little energy available for investment in other forms of development, including academic development. Given the importance of so many of the benefits derived from athletic participation for adolescents (e.g., peer approval and admiration, physical strength or prowess, tangible experiences of challenge and success), it can be difficult for investments in activities that more fully pay off in the long term to compete for attention. The road to becoming a scientist or lawyer, for example, is not paved with the same immediate returns as athletic participation. There are no physics pep assemblies, no math cheerleaders. The student writers, like Janine and Julian in chapter 3, perhaps find their names in the school yearbook or newspaper but rarely in the town papers. Investment in nonathletic pursuits requires some blend of the capacity to delay gratification and the ability to appreciate private accomplishments.

Given this scenario, is highly accomplished athletic skill development a risk or a benefit? The answers, of course, are varied. Some athletes will be able to transfer the experience of challenging practices into the endurance and focus needed to succeed in challenging professional arenas. Some will organize their adolescent experiences so thoroughly around athletic pursuits and related social experiences that their academic and career possibilities will be compromised. Many others will fall somewhere in between: they will succeed in sports and academics, for example, but their energy will be spread broadly across a range of domains.[7]

The point here is that energy is finite and skill development requires energy. More specifically, higher levels of skill development require greater investments of energy. In general, the skills we develop orient us toward the possibilities that are likely to follow. Without the efforts of educators and other adults to encourage their sustained engagement in meaningful and challenging activities, adolescents may allow expediency, peer pressure, or the media to direct their energies, perhaps closing off the high-end skill development that requires sustained commitment and yields the greatest developmental payoff.

INVESTING IN POSSIBILITY: THE DEVELOPMENTAL ASSETS MOVEMENT

Whereas flow theory emphasizes optimal development in specific domains, other approaches point to basic necessities that children and adolescents need in order to thrive. The Search Institute, a nonprofit research organization focused on youth development, has fostered the increasingly popular notion of *developmental assets*. By intentionally choosing a name that implies investment, the Search Institute team has advanced the proposition that healthy youth development requires the investment of all people who care about youth. To concretize how this investment might be made, researchers from the institute created a developmental assets framework that depicts the key ingredients or assets that all children and youth need to grow up healthy.[8]

To simply matters further, the developmental assets framework was made symmetrical with an even number of twenty external assets and twenty internal assets. The external assets are organized into four broad clusters representing the essential environmental ingredients needed to nurture healthy youth development. The four external asset clusters include *Support, Empowerment, Boundaries and Expectations*, and *Constructive Use of Time. Support* includes positive relationships with family and nonfamilial adults, including teachers and other school personnel. *Empowerment* captures the importance of not just providing relational support but also of creating opportunities within the environment that encourage students to take leadership roles and make important contributions to their communities. *Boundaries and Expectations* emphasizes the importance of clear and consistent external parameters that help shape healthy behavior, including high academic expectations and the structures needed to support them. And *Constructive Use of Time* focuses on the importance of community resources and activities that allow students to invest their energy wisely and productively.

The internal assets represent the individual's internalized or developed strengths or attributes, and they too are organized into four central clusters: *Commitment to Learning, Positive Values, Social Competencies*, and *Positive Identity. Commitment to Learning* focuses on the internalization of achievement-related habits and emphasizes the relationship between achievement motivation and lifelong opportunity development. *Positive Values* summarizes the key moral and character development attributes—such as care, justice, honesty, and restraint—that have been associated with other healthy outcomes such as sustained friendships and physical health. *Social Competencies* focuses on the skills needed to grow interpersonally, in the world of work, and in other communal contexts. Finally, *Positive Identity* addresses the healthy sense of self that is derived from experiencing strong doses of the essential external supports and other internal assets.

The developmental assets model suggests that the external assets are necessary to building the internal assets. By creating a model built on language that lay people understand and with a structure that is easily memorable, the Search Institute's goal has been to help ignite a widespread movement to promote healthy youth development. They argue that the health of the country as well as our young people requires such a national commitment. Communities around the country and the world are in agreement. More than 600 communities across the United States and many more in countries throughout the world are adapting the developmental assets framework to meet their local needs. The institute's Healthy Communities–Healthy Youth initiative supports communities in their efforts to apply the developmental assets framework in a manner that fits with each community's needs and resources.[9] Rather than creating prescriptive approaches to building external assets in general, the Search Institute promotes and collects varying community models that show how the framework plays out in particular communities.

The developmental assets movement places the onus of responsibility for youth development at the societal level rather than at the individual or institutional levels (e.g., the public schools).[10] Within this framework, skill development would be scaffolded on a community infrastructure of care, support, and community resources. The more fully developed that infrastructure, the more likely it is that youth will be able to build the skills needed to live the life they choose. In fact, the internal assets could be renamed as skills—skills of empathy, skills of academic achievement, and skills of community building, for example. From this perspective, the schools and communities that are successful in providing the external assets youth need might be called skilled communities—communities skilled in the particular domain of youth development, communities whose citizens have invested the time and energy needed to promote the optimal development of their young people. Such communities provide an infrastructure parallel to Fischer's neural support networks: human networks of people and institutions coalescing to support possibility development for young people.

The developmental assets framework has endless implications for educators, in general, and for cultivating flow experiences and possibility development in particular. It implies, for example, that while intensive skill development might be promoted in particular domains at the cost of such development in others, the key to healthy development is assuring that our youth have access to a full range of supports, challenges, and opportunities. To provide caring relational support without opportunities for empowerment is inadequate. Similarly, to promote high academic achievement or athletic performance without a foundation in caring and supportive relationships also is inadequate. How, then, might schools play their roles within the larger community infrastructure of external assets? Where should educators and school personnel focus their time and energies?

Perhaps the most compelling example of education-based developmental assets work comes from the Traverse Bay area, a small town and surrounding rural community in northern Michigan. The larger Traverse Bay area won the support of 19 area school superintendents who all agreed to bring the developmental assets framework into their schools. Through their adoption of the model, the school systems found that they could organize their student education and support work around what they referred to as a common language. They also found that, although the external assets seem obvious—like activities and resources that relatively healthy communities such as theirs would provide in the natural course of things—many of these assets were actually lacking or inconsistently applied. Simple acts of kindness in the school hallways, for example, were not always carried out as one would expect, particularly under the stresses of daily teacher demands. The key for the Traverse Bay area educators was not found in the learning of anything new that the model provided but in the awareness that they inconsistently acted on what they knew was best for their students. Similar findings have been discussed in other communities as well.[11]

> When Lorena shared with her world lit teacher that she wanted to experience that selfless flowing feeling in other venues besides rowing, Ms. Petersen replied bluntly, "Lorena, you could convince a fish to buy water with your verbal skills, and if you put into your writing what you put into your rowing, you'd be a heckuva writer too. Bring that attitude you've got and that confidence you've built into your written work. Take the risk! Show the world what you got! I mean, if you make a mistake in here, unlike in a rowboat, you don't even get wet!" "I hear you. . . . I'm on it," Lorena responded with a self-satisfied smirk, "but it's called a 'scull!'"
>
> Maggie, Lorena's counselor, kept track of her progress and heard many anecdotes like this one. Although there were some speed bumps along the way (like when Lorena got sent to the office for telling another stu-

dent to "f——off" after he told her she was a "row ho"), by the time her parents were called in for a progress meeting with her teachers, things were definitely improving. Lorena was submitting homework on a more regular basis, keeping out of fights, beginning to raise her grades, and still remaining true to her reputation as a talkative but charismatic leader among her peers. She was considering the debate team coach's offer to join her club next year, and had recently placed a university sticker she received from Colby on her school binder. A few weeks before the end of the fall semester, in recognition of the quality of her work, Lorena's English teacher posted her A+ essay on self-improvement in the hallway display case. Its title, "Rowin' and Flowin'," brought some jeers, but Lorena took them in stride. "Yeah, it's a little corny," she admitted to herself, "but it's me."

CHAPTER FIVE

Relational Identity and Relationship Development

If they respect me, I respect them. It's simple as that. But if they gonna get up in my face, telling me this and that, like I'm stupid, then hey, I ain't gonna do their work. It's simple as that.

—Antwon Saladin, tenth grader, explaining why he
works "for" some teachers and not others

While flow theory emphasizes the role of challenging activities in promoting optimal development, relational identity and relationship development theory provide a different angle on optimal development. Drawing largely from the work of Carol Gilligan, Nancy Chodorow, Jean Baker Miller, and others who have followed in their relational psychology footsteps, this chapter presents identity development as it evolves within meaningful relationships and suggests that the development of an independent "self" might obfuscate our understanding and appreciation of our relational being. Specifically, relational psychologists have argued that classic identity theory—primarily, Erikson's work—places too much emphasis on individual uniqueness while grossly underrepresenting the relational interconnectedness so important in adolescence and across the life cycle.

Feminist relational psychologists have not been alone in emphasizing the fundamental role of relational connectedness in human development. In the 1940s and 1950s psychiatrist Harry Stack Sullivan began formulating what he called an *interpersonal theory of psychiatry*.[1] His theory not only called for an interpersonal approach to treating mental disorders but also articulated a developmental model that based mental health and mental illness on the evolving nature of one's interpersonal history. The main developmental implication of Sullivan's theory was that friendships, romantic relationships, and other interpersonal experiences outside the primary caretaking bond could have profound influences on lifelong development and mental health. While that presupposition might seem commonsensical now, it was quite radical at a time when the Freudian emphasis on the mother-infant relationship was believed to hold clear, lasting influences over the duration of the life span—influences that were deemed difficult to modify through subsequent interpersonal relationships.

The relational perspective has critical implications for educational practice. For example, are our classrooms and pedagogies overly oriented toward individual achievement and competition rather than collaboration? This question has a great deal of relevance for not only identity development but also career development. To what extent are we preparing our students to function within work relationships? Are our conceptions of student leadership too individually constructed? As our economy becomes more global, are notions of the relational self especially important? Questions such as these help organize this chapter around strategies for supporting relational development within school environments.

LEARNING AND RELATIONAL DEVELOPMENT

With Lorena's situation in chapter 4, it is important to remember how influential it was that she became part of a crew, how she learned to row in unison with her teammates and put differences aside in order to achieve something greater than she ever could have done by herself. In the rowing program, Lorena learned to relate and negotiate rather than "diss" and demand. She learned to trust her teammates and her coach because she could see that she was progressing in her skills and growing in her connection with others. Lorena even looked forward to being harangued on the water—to being yelled at to "Pull harder!"—because she knew that when everyone was back at the boathouse, she'd be treated like a valued teammate with skills and strengths the crew needed. She belonged in that boat just like she belonged in those relationships. This new capacity to be in relationship with peers and significant adults where a sense of trust and the ability to grow and take risks were foundational gave Lorena the developmental opportunities she needed.

She brought that development back into her school-based relationships, and her academic achievement began to rise.

In looking at disparities in urban student achievement, we consistently see relational factors at the center of the picture. Time and again students tell us they work hard "for" the teachers they like, teachers by whom they feel respected and valued or, as some students put it: teachers who treat us like *real people*. In schools where students experience a lack of agency due to restrictive policies and punitive disciplinary responses, or in classrooms where vulnerability to peer derision is seldom protected and assignments and class activities do more to expose ignorance than display knowledge, it is no wonder that adolescents often choose to construct adversarial relationships with adults in school. Like anyone else, youth want to be engaged as thinking, feeling, valued members of a community in which they are understood as stakeholders. If the adolescent's desire for autonomy is met with enforced powerlessness or if the need for connection yields only isolation, students rightfully resist. That resistance, if labeled as "defiance" or "disruption," often gets the student in trouble. This is why disciplinary interactions in classrooms can be so revealing—it is then that students' and adults' understandings of one another and the classroom situation are most exposed and most at risk, when the relationship is most tenuous. By paying attention to how our work with adolescents is relational rather than purely pedagogical or clinical, we open our eyes to the ways in which reciprocity, interdependence, and connection shape our decisionmaking and development.

Unfortunately, so much of education has become a numbers game. Standardized test scores are scrutinized at the national, state, and local levels, and while that scrutiny may seem objective and a bit abstract in the pages of our newspapers, it is experienced as very real and highly personal in low-performing schools and classrooms. More than ever, schools and school systems are judged on their numbers. Teachers feel that in very real ways, and that feeling is passed along to their students who are now performing not only for themselves but for their teachers, their schools, and even their racial/ethnic group as well, with the whole "team" being examined under a common microscope. No wonder students are crying out to be treated like real people. They risk being lost beneath, and perhaps confused with, the accumulating heap of progress indicators and percentile rankings that are espoused to represent them.

No wonder, too, that students view *their lessons* as the *teachers' work*. While it has always been the case that students would work harder in some classrooms than in others, play harder for some coaches than for others, now—more than ever before—students and teachers are "in it" together. They both get a report card. And the grade reports not only go home to be reviewed by parents; they get reviewed by the school principal, the district superintendent, the state department of education, and the national press. The stakes for the team are high. In prior eras low-performing students were "held back," carrying and marked by the full weight of the team's failure; now the larger team carries the burden. Success and failure have become public displays, celebrated and excoriated by a broadening fan base with vested interests.

We are not sharing anything newsworthy here, anything you, the reader, do not already know. But we reiterate the emphasis on high-stakes testing to underscore a point: student achievement has become a team endeavor to a new degree, and as a team, the players perform and are assessed on their performance collectively. As with other team endeavors, including those in athletics and music, there are, of course, individual stars and particular performers who struggle. But a musical production is judged largely on the basis of its overall presentation, not on the virtuosity of solo performances. Educational performance is now being judged similarly. But are educational performers really working together as a team? Do they possess and are they encouraged to possess team-oriented skills? Does the team share a common goal? Do the players share equally in success and defeat? And what do these questions mean for the emerging identities of the various team players?

VYGOTSKY, SULLIVAN, AND THE "SOCIOCULTURAL MIND"

Although the works of Vygotsky and Sullivan are rarely mentioned in the same conversation, their contributions should be examined side by side for their related influences on our understanding of human development. In chapter 1 we presented Vygotsky's emphasis on the interpsychological underpinnings of cognitive development, which argues that intellectual growth occurs through interpersonal connections that allow children and people of all ages to learn from and with one another.[2] Just as Vygotsky's contributions shifted the focus in cognitive development from an innately individual orientation to one that is more interpersonal and intimately interactive, Sullivan, as noted above, instigated a similar shift in the spheres of emotional and mental health development. Addressing the broad continuum from "normal" development to serious mental illness, Sullivan used clinical studies to show how mental health and mental illness were as much learned or socialized ways of being as they were individually inherited predispositions. Just as important, he developed a model of interpersonal psychotherapy for promoting mental health and treating mental illness.

Sullivan placed a strong emphasis on the school environment as a key contributor to healthy development, particularly for those students coming from difficult home lives. As he put it, schooling provides the best opportunity for healing the "warps" of early childhood. For Sullivan, development is anything but an either/or proposition. On one hand, we are all destined to be warped in various ways and to varying degrees by our upbringing; on the other hand, we all carry the possibility of transcending or substantially modifying our family histories through extrafamilial relationships, starting with those forged at school with teachers and peers. In many respects, Sullivan's clinical case studies foreshadowed the more contemporary resilience literature, which shows just how critical extrafamilial child-adult relationships are to overcoming early life difficulties—none of them more critical than teacher-student relationships.

Of Sullivan's many contributions to our understanding of human development, his depiction of *chumship* is especially poignant. Drawing on the now archaic meaning of *chum* as "close friend," Sullivan showed how this seemingly light relational experience was laden with developmental implications. According to Sullivan, chumship, if it occurs, typically appears in preadolescence, the period that bridges childhood with adolescence proper. By about this time—late elementary school, when children are approximately 11 or 12 years old—a fairly extensive store of relational experience has developed. Following the early years of connecting with and learning from parents and other family members, young children begin to experience a more extensive variety of relationships when they begin school. New adult authority figures enter the picture, and, for those children lucky enough to forge strong and supportive relationships with these new adults, models for mature behavior and healthy relating are substantially expanded. At the same time, classmates become candidates for a different and potentially exciting type of relational experience: genuinely reciprocal friendship.

In the early school years, friendship or peer relationships consist of sharing experience through parallel play, learning classroom skills side by side, and negotiating conflicts that arise through such difficulties as sharing toys, sharing other friends, or being overly competitive on the playground.

All these relational experiences are profoundly educational on multiple levels. Children not only learn academic lessons and build formal learning skills in school, they also learn about other people and the possibilities for alternative ways of being that they entail. This, Sullivan realized, was overlooked in the mainstream psychological theory of the time. He pointed out that emotional learning was believed to occur almost exclusively within the context of the family because of the intimacy required for such learning. If this belief was valid, what were the implications for children who grew up within particularly warped families, to use Sullivan's memorable terminology? Were they incapable of learning new ways of developing healthy emotional responses to the world, the world of their own inner lives as well as their relational connections with others?

It was in response to such questions that Sullivan formulated the notion of chumship out of his clinical observations as well as from his own self-reflections. Building on the progressively more complex understandings of relationships that evolve throughout childhood, preadolescents are poised to cultivate a new level of friendship. That level is marked by the capacity to genuinely recognize and empathize with another's experience, and as such, to deeply care about that person in a more profound way than was possible in earlier childhood. Sullivan argued that this new level of relating might be deemed the first experience of genuine love. That is, it is marked by a type of care that is rooted less in the give-and-take of what I can get from my friend (emotionally and otherwise) and more in a desire to connect with him or her out of care alone, and through that care to make his or her life more gratifying. Sullivan describes this as the first time in the life cycle when one has the capacity to care for another as much as for oneself.

Through the intense relational bond of chumship, the opportunity exists to radically reexperience and relearn the deep meaning of relationships, and through that learning process to come to see one's self and one's own relational possibilities in new ways. From a clinical perspective, Sullivan was one of the first to recognize that people hold the capacity to literally "treat each other" with the empathy and compassion inherent in healthy relationships. By seeing into and sharing one another's worlds, one's own world might be receptive to some restructuring. Common school-based interventions like group counseling are founded on such premises, as are adult approaches to addictions via 12-step programs. The primary rationale for cooperative grouping in classroom instruction also stems from this work.

These approaches are built upon the recognition that sharing insight into others' experiences is vital to understanding one's own experience and ultimately to changing those experiences where necessary or desired.

Before discussing more contemporary work that builds from Sullivan's original conceptions of relational or interpersonal interventions, it seems important to tighten the connection between his insights from the therapy world to those stemming from Vygotsky's developmental studies. Just as Sullivan showed how self-understanding and self-esteem were promoted interpersonally, Vygotsky articulated how all understanding, or cognitive development, is fundamentally an artifact of interpersonal or interpsychological relatedness. Ours is a "sociocultural mind" such that even the independent reader, seemingly reading in isolation from others, has been taught to read by having another share the workings of his or her mind within that arena. As discussed in chapter 1, the teacher—whether formal or informal—provides a human scaffold that helps the early learner learn to read. After children learn to read "on their own," the very act of reading serves to connect them with the ideas of the authors they encounter and the characters those authors introduce. In essence, from a Vygotskian perspective, even "independent reading" is highly interpersonal.

By linking Sullivan and Vygotsky, we are able to see how in the mid- to early twentieth century, clear models were emerging that allowed us to better understand how vital each person—each student—is to the broader development and education of others. Both of these theorists enjoyed fairly extensive followings in their respective fields, and each has had a good deal of influence on psychological and educational theory. Why, then, are so many educators deeply invested in individual learning practices, in models that often discourage student sharing and interactions? Why do we spend inordinate amounts of energy and time doing our best to manage the classroom by preventing students from interacting with one another? While no one would argue against the common refrain that our students must learn to be self-reliant, at least to a degree, we often underappreciate how important it is to get there through a supportive network of social, emotional, and intellectual relationships that optimize the opportunities for accessing the thinking and ways of being of others.

Such is the case with Steve Chang, a tenth-grade Korean American student in Mr. Harrison's fifth-period chemistry class. With both of his parents employed in a nearby biotech research facility, Steve has grown up in a household oriented toward academic and scientific achievement. While he sometimes experiences his parents' focus as pressure, he genuinely enjoys the process of discovery he has experienced in his science and math classes over the years, and his academic record (other than that one B+ in ninth-grade world lit) has been exemplary. On the social end, however, Steve sometimes struggles. With little free time available outside of orchestra (where he is first chair among the violins), his SAT prep class after school, and his advanced coursework in school, it is rare for Steve to simply hang out with friends unless it is over the Internet in chat rooms and through instant messaging. While his peers are often excited initially to have him as a teammate in cooperative grouping activities because of his well-known academic abilities, those relationships often become contentious and unproductive due to Steve's tendency to dictate what should be done and to react harshly and judgmentally when others express a desire to do otherwise.

Aware of this possibility, Mr. Harrison was a little worried when Steve ended up pairing with strong-willed Lorena on their science fair project. For 18 years, Mr. Harrison has fielded the most award-winning chemistry projects in the district's annual science fair, and he wanted this year to be no exception. Building on his reputation among students as a tough grader with a fun and friendly demeanor who makes his content interesting, Mr. Harrison pushes his students to use chemistry to investigate their worlds. Steve and Lorena, however, were having trouble. Lorena had come to the project excited about an idea that had come to her during one of her rowing practices, but when she presented the idea of studying the river's water quality by testing for pollutants in the river at numerous spots along its path through the city, Steve was less than enthused. "The parks and rec department already does that testing," he remarked, "which is why we should do something no one has ever done, something that will win." Annoyed at his dismissal and what she perceived to be Steve's obsession with his grades, Lorena remembered her rowing coach's mantra about how "crews that fail to work together sink together" and tried a new angle. "We could work with the parks and rec department to help them gather data because yo, I am in that water and I wanna know what's in it."

After a few more minutes of increasingly combative discussion, Steve formed the opinion that Lorena knew nothing about science and would bring his grade down if he allowed her ideas to prevail. Lorena, on the other hand, began to realize that if each of the project's elements weren't Steve's ideas, he wouldn't like it. Not wanting to get in trouble for fighting or saying something offensive, Lorena simply folded her arms, stopped talking, and stared out the window, at which point Steve raised his hand to ask for Mr. Harrison's mediation. Having watched the rising tension from afar, Mr. Harrison promptly approached the feuding duo. "What's up?" he asked. When they both responded simultaneously and angrily, Mr. Harrison put up his hands and said, "Whoa, whoa, whoa. Let's move this meeting to the hallway, shall we?" As the three of them shuffled out of the room, Mr. Harrison used those brief seconds to plan his approach.

SELMAN'S CLINICAL-DEVELOPMENTAL APPROACH TO EDUCATION

Robert Selman has built explicitly upon the work stemming from both the clinical and developmental psychology traditions outlined above.[3] Trained originally as a clinical psychologist, Selman subsequently was exposed to developmental psychology through the work of Lawrence Kohlberg.[4] As a postdoctoral fellow in Kohlberg's laboratory for the study of moral development, Selman focused specifically on the interpersonal aspects of morality and began questioning how children move from having little or no perspective on the interests and intentions of others to eventually recognizing what others want and need and how to coordinate those wants and needs with their own.

In Kohlberg's model of moral development, more mature levels are marked by the ability to act on progressively more complex notions of fairness and justice. Selman recognized that the development of these moral conceptions emerged largely within the interpersonal contexts of family and friendship. Having been exposed to Sullivan's interpersonal orientation to psychotherapy through his clinical training, Selman began to question how counselors and therapists might utilize peer relationships and friendships to study moral development within real-life relational contexts and to promote such development through those relationships. In early to middle childhood, Selman focused on the evolving capacity of children to share toys, take turns, and resolve conflicts without fighting. In preadolescence and onward, he drew on Sullivan's notion of chumship and studied higher levels of interpersonally based morality and friendship development more generally.

Drawing on the Piagetian underpinnings to Kohlberg's moral development theory, Selman first studied the evolving complexity of child and adolescent social and moral cognition. He termed this developmental phenomenon *interpersonal understanding*, and like Piaget, he examined the evolution from sensorimotor or physicalistic understanding in early childhood to more concrete but symbolic understanding in middle childhood to complex and abstract understanding in adolescence and beyond.[5] Within the interpersonal realm, sensorimotor understanding is marked by impulsive and unreflective actions with and toward others. Through those actions, the child learns to relate in a crude way—to reach for a parent, for example, to solicit a caring response, or to throw a block at a sibling to communicate frustration. These interactions are initially accidental or primitively intuitive and over time are shaped by responses from the interpersonal environment. To demonstrate the lack of reflection inherent to infantile interactions and, at times, the delayed or regressed interactions of children, adolescents, and some adults, Selman termed the lowest levels of interpersonal understanding *egocentric* and represented it as *Level 0* or showing no interpersonal perspective taking.

The first shift to more complex interpersonal understanding is marked by the capacity to adopt at least one perspective somewhat clearly, which Selman termed *unilateral* and designated *Level 1* (one perspective). Unilateral understanding is evidenced by "I" and "you" statements: "I like Lisa because I like bikes and she lets me ride her bike." "I don't like you because you always want to use my things." In both statements, one perspective is emphasized; there's little sign of the back-and-forth or give-and-take that marks *Level 2* understanding, which Selman labels *reciprocal*. Reciprocal interpersonal understanding is marked by the recognition that there are two people, each with his or her own wants and needs. There is a practical and equitable awareness of the value of helping meet someone else's needs through the relationship. Healthy reciprocal understanding is accompanied by proactive outreach to one's friend as a gesture of care and fairness, but that outreach typically carries with it an expectation that one's friend will return the favor. At this level, nothing is given for free. A return on relational investment is the expected course of action. After all, "that's only fair."

Most relatively healthy adolescents, and adults for that matter, act in accordance with a reciprocal level of social understanding most of the time, even though they have the capacity for *Level 3* understanding, which Selman terms *mutual*. Whereas reciprocal understanding implies a give-and-take, mutuality is defined by genuine care and concern for the other and includes an understanding of another's needs and interests that is not contingent upon one's own interpersonal agenda. According to Selman, Sullivan's notion of chumship is marked by mutual interpersonal understanding; indeed, having a chum increases the likelihood that mutual perspective taking will be enhanced.

Sullivan's and Selman's insights, while emerging from fields sometimes mistakenly considered by teachers to be too "touchy-feely" for their consideration, have clear implications for classroom practice. Adolescents' developing capacity to relativize their needs toward others ushers in expansive interpretations of history, biography, poetry, biology, and even disciplinary interactions. As unilateral understanding gives way to a more reciprocal orientation, relationships come to be built upon the assumption of fairness. This is why the "do as I say not as I do" approach can be particularly infuriating to an adolescent expecting simple reciprocity in her relationships. Disciplinary interactions in classrooms often expose the adolescent's overriding concern for fairness, which can challenge the teacher's need to differentiate approaches and relationships according to specific students' needs. Although adolescents can sometimes display a righteous indignation at perceived lapses in fairness, some of the best teachers capitalize on such expressions to explore whose needs are being privileged over others and why that might be the case. Questions about fairness can become growth-promoting discussions about relationships, needs, and negotiation. Teachers who engage youth reciprocity and probe their claims of unfairness will find a tremendous wellspring of intellectual and relational resources that can be channeled into academic achievement and the development of a critical citizenry. As evidence, countless activists, policymakers, politicians, social workers, clergy, and teachers trace their passion for justice to confrontations with unfairness they experienced in adolescence. This fact is as developmentally significant as it is politically and pedagogically useful.

If the adolescent's relational development proceeds optimally, the need for reciprocity may subside as mutuality takes its place. The pedagogical significance of mutuality, gained as it is from ongoing relational connection and experimentation, can be observed in classroom discussions when youth begin to unpack issues of causality, responsibility, and ethics with increasing sophistication. Empathy and compassion develop alongside the adolescent's ability to recognize and incorporate the needs of others. This is why some of the most talented middle- and high-school teachers tend to respond incredulously to questions about how they can tolerate working with teenagers. The fact is, it's fun for them. Indeed, participating in the co-construction of youths' relational development can be extremely gratifying, precisely because it provides opportunities to witness and affect adolescents as they develop in their capacity to be concerned for others.

It is no surprise, then, that Selman's model has been shaped over the last 30-plus years in ways that have particular implications for adolescent development and for those educators who work with adolescents.[6] Having studied how interpersonal understanding develops, he became particularly interested in the connections between interpersonal thought and action, with an emphasis on the disconnection between the two that is so often apparent. To study the action side of the equation, Selman explored what he called *interpersonal negotiation strategies,* which are the cognitively mediated actions people take to meet their needs within relationships, both close and distant relationships.[7] Working from the logic of the level system constructed for interpersonal understanding, Selman described Level 0 strategies as *impulsive* responses to the social environment. Although normative in its purest form for infants and very young children, impulsive strategies appear at all ages, for most people, under certain conditions. Level 1 strategies are characterized by *unilateral* demands, requests, or deferential behaviors that depict the capacity to hold onto only one person's perspective, either one's own or that of the person whose favor one is trying to win.

Adolescent interpersonal negotiation strategies build upon these earlier behavioral repertoires to become more sophisticated approaches to *cooperative* (Level 2) exchanges; that is, "you scratch my back and I'll scratch yours." In their most mature form, adolescent and adult strategies alike move from cooperative exchanges to mutually *collaborative* interactions. The strategic shift from cooperation to collaboration, in Selman's model, reflects a giving up of the singular, independent self to an interconnected, relational self. By defining this shift as a negotiation strategy, Selman implies that "higher-level strategies" are not always healthy or wise. Specifically, one should not assume a collaborative relational stance with a partner incapable or unwilling to participate at a similar level. As we shall see in later chapters, not all relationships promote growth, and some may even be counterproductive. There is a time to feel things out cooperatively, and a time to give one's self over to genuine, mutual collaboration. Determining when and how to make that shift is a complex act, one that many adolescents and adults may never master.

Knowing this to be the case, Mr. Harrison wanted to use the situation between Steve and Lorena as a way to enhance the capacities of both students to relate to each other productively. Because Lorena had been immersing herself (literally) in the river and in her academics as a result of her rowing experiences, Mr. Harrison wanted to be careful to preserve her enthusiasm and promote her continuing success in school. He realized that Lorena's gregarious nature and vast network of friends prepared her better for the process of discussion and negotiation than Steve, but few could match Steve's sophisticated content knowledge and the scientific resources he had at home. Mr. Harrison was hoping Steve might be able to model some of the academic skills Lorena needed to develop, but what Steve possessed in academic proficiency was matched by his tendency to isolate himself and withdraw from situations in which he would be expected to compromise.

As they turned to face each other in the hallway, Mr. Harrison was aware of all this, so he began by opening the discussion positively. "I think you two are ideally suited to work with each other. You each bring key knowledge and skills to this project, and I am excited to see what you'll create. Now, what seems to be the issue between you two?" In the conversation that followed, Mr. Harrison could see that Lorena was actively seeking collaboration as long as her input was incorporated into the design, while Steve seemed incapable of considering Lorena's positions and contributions unless they matched his. Eventually, Steve accepted that the water-quality study was a good idea, but after relenting on that point he refused to budge on any others. Picking up on some possible racial and gender tensions in their remarks and guessing that resolution would not be forthcoming by the end of the period, Mr. Harrison gave them each an assignment. "Okay. Sounds like some good work can be done here and that each of you needs to think through what you're prepared to do to make this project a success. To help you get to that point, I have an assignment for you. I want each of you to write down in neat and complete sentences answers to the following three questions." Taking a piece of blank notebook paper from his clipboard, Mr. Harrison wrote as he talked. "One, what do you think are the key elements that make this project important? Two, on which of those elements would you find it difficult to compromise? And three, which elements are negotiable for you?" He handed each of them a copy of the questions, congratulated them for their willingness to work it out, and watched as Steve and Lorena went back to their desks and prepared quietly for closing comments and dismissal.

The *thought-action gap*, as Selman describes it, is understood through his third component of interpersonal development, which he terms *personal meaning*.[8] Whereas interpersonal understanding captures social thinking or cognition, personal meaning reflects the multitude of ways in which individuals make sense of or come to value what they know. A person might know the benefits of cooperative strategies in general but choose to act unilaterally under certain conditions because he or she either does not know or trust the other actors in the relational play. If, for example, a student feels burned by prior cooperative efforts, a more self-protective unilateral stance may serve as an initial defense in early relationship formation. Just as thought and action grow developmentally in and through relationships, so does personal meaning. We come to make meaning of and value (or devalue) our interpersonal possibilities based on what we have experienced throughout our relational histories. In this way, interpersonal knowledge, action, and personal meaning are interconnected and constantly informing one another.

FROM "STRUCTURAL DEVELOPMENT" TO MORE PURELY RELATIONAL APPROACHES

Whereas Selman moved Kohlberg's moral-development model in an explicitly relational direction, he did so within the structural-developmental paradigm of neo-Piagetian theory—that is, theory that focuses on the developing structural complexity of the human mind. In this sense, there is an emphasis on developmental capacities and their corresponding competencies. The personal-meaning component of Selman's model, however, taps into the more purely experiential side of development: "What is it that I am experiencing within my relationships, and what do I care about most deeply?" Selman's focus on the negotiation of autonomy and intimacy in relationships incorporates Eriksonian insights as well. Thus conceived, relationships become developmental learning laboratories in which adolescents experiment with both egocentric and more accommodating orientations toward others. This helps us see how relationships always exert a push and pull on the self such that we need to connect and be known and also understand ourselves as autonomous agents, capable of self-efficacy and independent action. Adolescents in particular seem to feel this push and pull intensely as they co-construct their identities with one another and with us as educators. They want the intimacy of belonging but concurrently resist the potential to get lost in their relationships, to become too much what the other wants/thinks. The turbulent interpersonal dramas often seen in teen friendships can result in angst-ridden decisions about where to sit at lunch, what to wear to school, whom to dance with at the prom, whether to smoke that cigarette, what party to attend on Saturday night, and so forth, precisely because such events test the adolescent's relational development.

Like Selman, a developmental psychologist with prior clinical training, Carol Gilligan also worked in Kohlberg's moral development lab. In her groundbreaking book, *In a Different Voice*,[9] Gilligan presented an alternative interpretation to Kohlberg's moral development assessments, and in doing so spawned a generation of developmentalists who focused more on the experiential nature of interpersonal care and connectedness than on the cognitive capacities that underlie close relationships and moral decisionmaking. A key finding of Gilligan's reanalysis of Kohlberg's data and of her own future studies was the seeming gender difference in prioritizing care and justice as moral guideposts. Whereas Kohlberg's model showed men to value abstract fairness and justice principles more highly than women, and in this sense cast men as more principled than women, Gilligan's reanalysis showed that women's moral decisionmaking was rooted in meaningful interpersonal connections, which she termed an *ethic of care*.

Although contested on academic research grounds, Gilligan's original and subsequent findings have obvious implications for educators, and the relational phenomena she described can be seen on a daily basis in our schools.[10] We see students take strong moral or ethical stances to defend the honor of their friends and to stand up to authority figures in the face of what they believe is right and wrong. We see these same students engage in deplorable acts of ridicule, bullying, and worse with peers to whom they feel little or no personal connection. Are these students highly moral or highly immoral? Should they be educated in the principles of moral behavior that might allow them to treat the average person more considerately? Educators frequently lean toward the teaching of principles or rules in attempts to foster order within their classrooms and schools. How many of our classrooms have rules posted to dictate how students should interact? How rare is it that students get to construct and negotiate their own rules for social interactions? But as Gilligan and other relational psychologists warn, such rules will be fruitless outside of meaningful relationships. From this perspective, we become who we are—we come to see and understand ourselves and others—in and through relationships. To teach social development abstractly or to expect adherence to rules students had no role in making, then, is to leave out the relational scaffolding necessary to promote optimal interpersonal growth.

Relational continuity, a core theme that runs throughout Gilligan's work, has been used to underscore differences in how males and females are socialized, particularly as they transition from childhood into and through adolescence. Gilligan builds from the groundbreaking work of Nancy Chodorow, who fleshed out the gender implications of Freud's oedipal period of development.[11] During this period (approximately age three or four), according to Freudian theory, it is common for boys to disconnect from their mothers, at least to a degree, in order to identify more strongly with their fathers. This disconnection and strengthened male identification is followed by intense competition for the mother's affection. This early stage in male identity development, according to Chodorow, underlies the male emphasis on separation and competition. Girls, according to this perspective, undergo a very different identity step in early childhood. They remain connected to the original maternal caretaker and learn from her how to win their father's affection. Without a shift in the primary caretaking bond, girls maintain a more continuous identity throughout childhood. They remain identified with their mothers and learn from them how to stay in relationship with their fathers.

Although the extent to which gender differences play out in childhood identity formation varies across children—based, in part, on differences within family and community contexts—there is clear evidence from sociology and developmental psychology that boys in the United States are, in general, encouraged to be tough and independent while girls are encouraged to be caring and supportive. As contemporary options for gender roles have become more complex, traditional socialization practices have placed many older children and adolescents at risk for relational difficulties. In particular, Gilligan has underscored the struggles many girls face in standing up for what they believe in the face of relational scrutiny. That is, having been socialized throughout childhood to remain within the primary relational bond, it becomes difficult in early to mid-adolescence to challenge the opinions of family, teachers, and even friends. Certainly, this finding does not hold across the entire female population, and it applies to many boys as well, but the relational identity point here is that the separation boys experience in the oedipal period (early childhood) comes into play for many girls in adolescence.

Like Chodorow and Gilligan, Jean Baker Miller and her colleagues in the Stone Center at Wellesley College respond to psychodynamic and developmental theories that overemphasize the drive for gratification and the necessity of autonomy.[12] While never negating these as fundamental aspects of human becoming, Miller and her associates have long emphasized *authenticity* as a crucial element in healthy relational connection and growth. The goal of development, as Miller sees it, is not to individuate and separate from primary caregivers but to increase one's ability to participate in mutually growth-fostering connections, to be one's authentic self and to promote such authenticity in others. Relationships, then, are understood as both the means and the ends of our development. We relate so that we may learn to relate better. In Miller's conception of relational development, healthy relationships contain not only mutual empathy but mutual empowerment as well. Our need to belong and be understood compels us to enter into relationships with others, but, according to Miller, if that relationship is to be deemed healthy, each person must be able to respond empathically to the other. Growth-promoting relationships are thus characterized by connections in which each person's needs are considered and enhanced, where each person's identity is known and actualized as the self they understand internally. For teachers, counselors, and school psychologists to promote healthy relational development among the adolescents they serve, it is important to recognize that enhancing students' self-sufficiency and autonomy without also supporting their capacity to negotiate resources, power, and relational meaning with others can limit student growth. Just as each of us needs to be able to feel fully "myself," we also need to practice responding to and encouraging such expression in others. This is the hallmark not only of healthy relationships but of healthy communities and nations as well.

> The fact that relationship development, identity co-construction, and self-actualization go hand in hand is clear in Steve and Lorena's work on their science project. Although each was reluctant to write anything that

might be construed as negotiable in their assignment for Mr. Harrison, the fact that he expressed so much confidence in their project and their potential to work together gave both Steve and Lorena the push they needed to consider the other person's perspectives. Once Mr. Harrison got his fifth-period groups going on their science project tasks, he knelt down next to Steve and Lorena's table, greeted them with a "Good afternoon," and told them what he wanted to do with their assignment. "I want you to exchange the papers you wrote last night and, in pencil, put a check next to the things you like or agree with and then circle the parts that worry you. Does that make sense?"

"What if I don't agree with anything she wrote?" asked Steve.

"If you can't find something to agree on, you will fail the project, Steve, since it is a requirement that you work together, incorporating each other's contributions. But I'm confident you two won't let that happen." Pausing to check their body language for evidence that they're ready to give this a try, Mr. Harrison continues, "So, when you're done quietly reading, checking, and circling, put your pencil down and wait for the other person to finish. When you're both done, give the papers back and talk about the areas you both like first, then use that foundation to figure out how you'll deal with the differences. Okay?" When Steve and Lorena both sit up and lean toward their papers with pencils in hand, Mr. Harrison responds, "All right. You've got a great start here. Get to it." He then stands up but lingers for a moment to make sure they exchange papers and begin reading each other's work. When they do, Mr. Harrison walks away to let them sort it out on their own. Half an hour later, he looks over to see Steve and Lorena making a project timeline, drawing up a list of sampling locations and materials needed, consulting their textbook for the names of industrial pollutants and toxic bacteria, and entering each other's cellphone numbers into their phonebooks.

EDUCATIONAL MENTORING

In the scenario above, Mr. Harrison is as much a mentor as he is a teacher. The burgeoning field of youth mentoring focuses on the critical role of caring adult relationships in the healthy development of young people. Drawing on research from studies of resilience in child and youth development that highlight the importance of even one healthy nonfamilial relationship in the lives of young people, mentoring has become one of the country's fastest-growing developmental interventions. Although the majority of mentoring research targets formally organized one-to-one adult-youth relationships, such as those sponsored by Big Brothers Big Sisters of America, some scholars have emphasized the importance of "natural mentors," such as teachers or other caring adults in the community. These studies show that the availability of one natural mentor can yield long-term, substantial benefits for young people, such as increased self-esteem, stronger coping skills, and a more positive view of the future.[13]

Mentors accomplish their work through the power of close, trusted relationships, and they use those relationships to encourage the development of their protégés in any number of directions.[14] Mr. Harrison cares about Lorena and Steve as people as much as he values the quality of their education. Like his other students, they know that. Although Steve is fiercely protective of his stellar academic record, fully cognizant of its implications for competitive college admissions, he knows Mr. Harrison as more than a teacher who can support his academic success; he also knows him as someone he cares about, someone he trusts. Mr. Harrison is unique in that way for Steve, who tends to view his teachers more as practical stepping stones toward a promising future than as real people in the here and now.

For Lorena, too, Mr. Harrison holds a unique position. He broke through with her where his colleagues had experienced strident resistance. He broke through because he listened, even when she wasn't speaking. He heard a tone in her silence that alerted him to the inner struggles that Lorena never overtly shared with him. But she knew he heard nonetheless, that he listened, and for her the listening was what mattered. She didn't need to share the particulars of her life to experience his support; she simply needed to know he was there for her. Because he was there for her, she would do "his work" when she wouldn't work for other teachers. For Lorena, school work is relational work. It's a shared commitment made between student and teacher. Without that commitment, the work is just not worth it.

Relational teaching—teaching that builds on the student-teacher relationship to promote learning—might be deemed a particular form of natural mentoring.[15] Teachers who model ways of being in relationship for students teach more than content knowledge; they teach respect, care, collaboration, and a host of life skills necessary to ensure success and personal happiness. This is mentoring in the fullest sense of the word; and it is teaching that reflects a particular professional ethic, an ethic of learning through care and support. *Educational mentoring* captures the essence of this model for us: it is educating *to care*—for oneself, for others, and for the world around us; and it is educating *through care*—through caring for the student as the pedagogical priority.

CHAPTER SIX

Gender Identity Development

Relational psychology, as presented in chapter 5, holds critical implications for understanding the nature of gender identity development. In this chapter, we build upon the work of Carol Gilligan and other relational theorists to explicitly forge the connections with gender identity and its development. To what extent are gender identity theories helpful to educators? Why is it important to consider the similarities and differences in male and female identity development? To what extent are these differences overly determined by existing theory and research? The answers to each of these questions can open an array of strategies for promoting student development in our schools. In fact, students themselves continually espouse folk theories of gender-based development. By bringing their folk theories into mainstream educational discourse and debating them within the context of classroom discussions and written exercises, we may create an atmosphere that counters what Gilligan and her colleagues describe as the "need to go underground" in order to disguise who one is as a developing boy, girl, man, woman.[1] In short, using gender-based conceptions of development to promote learning and development itself requires opening up the dialogue on what it means to become a "healthy" man and woman. If that dialogue is not opened up in our school settings, it is likely to remain unspoken and underutilized throughout adolescence and beyond.

THE GENDER PLAY AND ITS ESSENTIAL "PARTS"
Just as adolescence itself is very much a matter of social construction, so too is gender identity development. The biological distinctions between girls and boys certainly influence the gender roles we all learn to play, but biology is

merely one prop, albeit a crucial one, supporting the larger performance. Other props, arguably more influential even than biology, stem from cultural expectations rooted in societal, community, religious, and family values. Through these cultural contributions we give meaning to our particular biological endowments and learn to use our gender differences in a wide variety of ways, the accumulation of which can come to characterize the chasms that often exist between the sexes. This is not to say that innate biological differences, including the role of hormones like testosterone and estrogen, have no impact on gender-role behavior. As contemporary research has made clear, biology and environment (or nature and nurture) continually interact to inform virtually every aspect of human social functioning.[2]

In their compelling depiction of how early adolescents learn to be the "opposite" sex, Sapon-Shevin and Goodman describe how social scripts come to serve as "gender-appropriate" learning guides.[3] Much of our gender scripting is implicit. We internalize *gendered* norms for masculinity and femininity that are picked up through family life, in the neighborhood, and throughout the media. Schooling, of course, becomes a major stage for acting out and refining initial gender roles. With an expanding cast of new performers in the early school years, gender scripts become more complex, including increased pressure to differentiate roles. Some girls become more "girlish" than others; some take on roles similar to those of boys. Many school-age boys compete for the role of leading man; others become independent loners, wanting little to do with social comparison or competition. By early adolescence, as Sapon-Shevin and Goodman put it, scripts have been so thoroughly presented and practiced that they have come to define what it means to be male and female within particular settings. In essence, the players are lost to the play itself. Their roles are so thoroughly scripted that modifying or breaking out of them takes extraordinary acts of insight and courage.

> Steve Chang is beginning to need some of that courage. Desiring connections with peers that last longer than a class period, an orchestra practice, or his SAT prep course after school, Steve begins to heed Mr. Harrison's advice and look for opportunities to "chill" with others for reasons beyond just the completion of schoolwork. He ventures into the school cafeteria instead of eating alone, attends after-school sporting events, and even goes to lift weights before school two or three days a week. Each of these forays has exposed him to the potential ridicule of his peers, but the threat

of having homework as his only companion is much worse. Plus, he's beginning to get a crush on Lisa Prescott, and Lisa Prescott doesn't date loners. Although Steve realizes he can't compete with the jocks' prowess and social command nor the skaters' alternative coolness (especially since Steve is self-conscious about being six feet tall, 140 pounds, and lacking in athletic skill), his new friends from weightlifting are giving him the sort of manly bonding experiences he though he'd never have. Lifting progressively heavier weights, seeing his muscles grow, and being able to spot (assist on heavy lifts) lacrosse and football players on the bench press gives him access to social networks not present in his academic pursuits.

As the weight lifting gave way to banter, which led to introductions and eventual invitations to trips to the mall, movies, and parties, Steve learned that if he was to relate to these other guys he had to become adept at making fun of others, exposing weakness, hiding insecurity, talking about girls, and scorning anything "gay." When he admitted he thought Lisa Prescott was "hot" one day in the weight room, a few friends laughed out loud until one said, "Dude. I heard she thought you were gay!" Steve laughed it off as quickly as he could in order to hide his deflation and rage, but he carried the comment with him all day. Still seething and hurt in his sixth-period world literature class, he noticed two boys pointing at him as he walked in from the passing period. While giggling, one of them turned to Steve and asked, "So, you wanna get with Lisa, huh?" Glancing to his left to see if Lisa, already seated in the room, heard the remark (she didn't), Steve's embarrassment choked a timely response. As he took his seat, he uttered the only thing he could think to say and simply shot back, "No! Shut up, fag!" As luck would have it, Mr. Harrison overheard only Steve's response, which is how Steve garnered his first detention and a mandatory discussion with him after school.

Lisa Prescott was unaware of what had just transpired because she was engrossed in conversation with two of her friends in the far corner of the classroom. Lisa's all-consuming focus on her relationships with her girlfriends was new behavior, however. In fact, had they chosen a valedictorian for her eighth-grade cohort at her upper-middle-class neighborhood middle school, Lisa would certainly have been it. As an articulate, well-prepared, charismatic, and no-nonsense 12-year-old, she was adored by her teachers and respected by her friends. During her freshman year at the much larger comprehensive high school, however, Lisa began to change. A "late bloomer," as her mother called her, Lisa noticed how boys started looking at her differently, for longer stints, often making comments about her body. She even caught seniors doing it. At first embarrassed by this, she later grew to crave the power those glances and comments conferred on her. She watched how older, less academically successful girls got most of the dates with the "hotties" at her school and consequently began to temper her contributions in class so as not to appear too "brainy."

Gradually shifting her focus from the academic to the social realm, Lisa spent hours on the phone or instant messaging with her friends about the countless mini-scandals erupting daily between various friends and groups at school. One of their favorite activities was to vote among themselves for the week's "school fool," the person that most exemplified what they thought they despised. In participating in this, Lisa sometimes worried about what others were saying about her behind her back, but the thrill of secrets and the promise of lifelong allegiances with her friends overpowered her feeling of vulnerability. To compete and con-form with her friends, she donned outfits with hemlines, shoulder straps, and bare midriffs that regularly pushed the limits of the dress code but drew increased attention from some of the most popular guys at school. She and her "fashion police" friends would line the walkway at the car-pool drop-off area each morning to scrutinize one anothers' style choic-es and sometimes denigrate those whose outfits failed to impress. But the stress of having to perform and criticize others like this each day depleted the energy Lisa had available for her studies, and her grades and academic confidence began to drop. Then, seemingly out of nowhere, the bottom fell out. Accused by one of her friends of trying to steal her boyfriend, her small and previously tight clique of girlfriends suddenly refused to speak with her. Lisa was cut off. Not able to face this ostracism in the lunchroom, where she would surely become the week's "school fool," Lisa ran crying to Ms. Petersen's room for refuge.

GOING UNDERGROUND

For more than two decades now, Carol Gilligan and her colleagues have pro-vided vivid imagery for staging the sort of gender plays seen in Steve's and Lisa's experiences above. Gilligan has explicitly described girls' development as, in many respects, learning how *to act* within overly prescribed roles. Through interviews that she and her colleagues conducted, Gilligan constructed an archetypal form of girls' and women's development. That form consists of a happy and confident childhood cultivated by an adequately nurturing early family life and initial school success. By early adolescence, according to the archetype, exuberant self-expression gives way to insecurity and self-silencing. This inward flight into hiding occurs in response to multiple layers of societal messages—messages that girls should be supportive and accommodating and that "appropriate" feminine behavior is neither loud nor aggressive. For girls accustomed to a full range of assertive expression, the transition from childhood to adolescence can be laden with social rejection. That transition can be marked as well by coaching from parents and teachers intended to help these rambunctious girls shed their childlike ways in favor of more refined ways of being and becoming—specifically, being in a manner that is "becoming" of a lady.

While this archetype clearly does not hold for all girls and women and may be more common to girls of White middle- and upper-middle-class backgrounds, the form has been embraced by a host of researchers and practitioners who find it common enough to warrant serious consideration by those invested in girls' and women's development. Working from a relational psychology perspective, Gilligan describes the process of going into psychological hiding as *going underground*.[4] In order to preserve important relational connections, many girls force parts of themselves into hiding, thereby making themselves more acceptable to the local status quo. But going underground to remain in relationship with others ultimately leads to disconnections from oneself. This, according to Gilligan and others, is a critical cause of adolescent female depression and a source of inauthenticity that carries lifelong repercussions. Sacrificing part of the self leaves one less resilient, less fully equipped to thrive and to defend oneself in the face of life's demands, including those demands to forego aspirations for a lead part in exchange for a "supporting role."

Gilligan situates adolescent development squarely within the sociopolitical reality of patriarchy, the male-dominated social order. Within our patriarchal system, she argues, girls and women become sexually objectified and socially limited due to their assumed capacity for care, relationship building, and intuition. Boys and men, on the other hand, are understood to possess less inherent capacity for these traits and instead are framed in terms of their strength, intelligence, emotional control, and leadership abilities. Although these assumptions hold little to no biological validity, the result is that adolescents learn to perform their gendered selves in response to these dictates. Each young person will respond differently, of course, based in part on the intersections of environmental support and temperamental predisposition. Some will opt for wholesale adoption of stereotypically sanctioned representations of their gender, while others will stop at nothing short of outright rejection of any such limits. What youth choose to wear, how they cut their hair, when or if they choose to wear makeup, how they speak, how they walk, the hobbies they invest in, the music they listen to, the relationships they build—all these things represent the ways in which adolescents respond to, shape, and express their gendered selves as they come to terms with patriarchal expectations.

The developmental import of Gilligan's work becomes clear when she analyzes the psychological costs of developing one's self and one's relationships within the prescriptions of patriarchy. As girls grow in their awareness of societal expectations, navigating the people and places that reward certain behaviors versus those that do not, they often confront the fact that they cannot bring their full selves into relationships with others, even close same-sex peers. As Gilligan describes the general dynamic, there is "the tendency in girls' lives at adolescence for a resistance that is essentially political—an insistence on knowing what one knows and a willingness to be outspoken—to turn into a psychological resistance: a reluctance to know what one knows and a fear that such knowledge, if spoken, will endanger relationships and threaten survival."[5] From this perspective, the difference between what girls know and want and the scripts they are expected to adopt produces psychological dissonance and the necessity for survival-based accommodation.

To seek out and maintain connection with others, Gilligan observes that adolescent girls often bring only the socially acceptable parts of themselves into relationships, withholding their full knowledge of themselves and the world and thereby sacrificing the authentic core of the relationship in order to save what they can. As girls take what they know about themselves—their needs and desires—and go underground with them, they shield the less valued parts of themselves from the judgment and ridicule of both peers and adults. Smart girls, tough girls, and athletic girls, for example, may be given countless messages that they are not adhering to the expected script and feel the press to step in line. They may be labeled as "uppity," "bitchy," or "butch," the message being that if they persist with the disfavored behavior they will lose friends and/or risk ostracism. Lisa Machoian's work has suggested that high intelligence can increase adolescent girls' risk for depression and suicidality because "brainy" girls are more likely to be rejected by their peers.[6] Likewise, educators may observe the former star sixth-grade student and intellectual leader of her class deciding to accentuate her social, sexual, and even deferential capacities as she transitions into high school and learns how to adapt to a society that values her body, her listening skills, and her willingness to defer to men more than her intellect, her capacity to lead, and her power.

In terms of how these patterns play out in schools, Sadker and Sadker identified a difference between "boys in action" and "girls' inaction" in classrooms, a distinction they traced to teacher practices that privileged boys' academic contributions while favoring girls' social skills.[7] Surveying numerous studies, Skiba et al. found that girls are highly underrepresented in advanced placement math and science classes, whereas "boys are over four times as likely as girls to be referred to the office, suspended, or subjugated to corporal punishment."[8] Ferguson and Connell have identified how teacher-student cross-gender interactions are shaped by expectations of masculinity and femininity.[9] Schools themselves are gendered spaces. When students establish relationships with teachers and negotiate power in disciplinary interactions, they do so in a society in which women outnumber men in the teaching profession by a three-to-one ratio,[10] even as schools continue to be "organized around the unacknowledged and devalued work of women."[11] "Ophelias," "queen bees and wannabes," "odd girls out," "lost boys," "bad boys," "real boys," and "super-predators" remain dominant monikers for the gendered way in which educators are taught to frame youth identities and behavior.[12]

Whether one agrees with the specifics of the developmental drama these theorists outline, the fundamental nature of the script seems hard to reject: for girls, the specter of adolescence commonly imposes a resocialization process organized around relational accommodation. In their studies of low-income girls of color, particularly African American girls, Michelle Fine and Nancie Zane found a variation on the accommodation theme.[13] In their study of girls in the Philadelphia public schools, they found that African American girls who dropped out of high school frequently appeared better adjusted than their peers who remained in school and than their male siblings. Many of them dropped out precisely because they possessed the character strengths and real-life competencies that allowed them to help support their families through employment, family childcare, or both. "Bein' wrapped too tight," as one of the girls in the study put it, forced them by default into predestined roles of caring for others, a destiny common to so many girls and women across time and cultural contexts.

> In Lorena's case (chapter 4), however, the specter of "bein' wrapped too tight" was offset by the strengths and skills she was building in both her rowing program and in school. She felt proud of her sculpted arms and taut legs and reveled in the positive attention she received from her teachers as a result of her efforts in school. Confronting the same messages Lisa Prescott faced regarding how to attract boys and secure friendships with powerful (i.e., popular) peers, Lorena felt compelled to tone down what one of her teachers called her "combative" nature, but she resisted doing so. She felt good about putting clueless people in their place, highlighting lapses in logic in classroom discussions, and discovering the most elegant way of solving an algebra problem. Resisting the gender scripts that would have her be deferential to boys and less invested in scientific ways of knowing, she located pockets of support where she was known and valued as strong and smart. Besides, she remembered, both Colby, her coach, and Maggie, her counselor, said that if the boys found her intimidating, "that was their problem." When the fashion police noticed her physique under the tank top she wore one day, saying, "Did you get that at Gold's Gym?" she merely rubbed her eye with a prominently raised middle finger and walked right by them, unfazed.

Although the scenarios depicted by Gilligan and those of Fine and Zane differ in detail, they are all organized around relational accommodation. Depending on the social setting and its needs, the adolescent girls in these depictions accommodate accordingly. In one scenario they defer leadership and responsibility *in order* to fit in appropriately; in another they are required to take exceptional responsibility *in order* to sustain their families. In each of these scenarios a demanding social order prescribes a particular form of accommodation to the needs and interests of others. In many cases, those needs and interests may match those of the girls themselves. In other instances, such accommodations are experienced as required necessities. They are neither chosen nor desired but, rather, are required self-sacrifices that enable friendship and family structures to function according to plan. To break out of the usual ways of doing things is to let others down. That is the message many adolescent girls hear, whether shouted and demanded explicitly or whispered and encouraged implicitly.

AN ALTERNATIVE MORATORIUM

In Erikson's model of identity development, described in chapter 2, a strong emphasis is placed on a very different type of enclosure than the underground to which Gilligan and her colleagues refer. Erikson emphasizes the role of an adolescent moratorium—a safe space—in which alternative ways of being can be explored before longstanding commitments to career and intimate relationships are made. Going underground is the inverse of this phenomenon. It is a removal of the self from desired expressions and explorations in order to remain accepted and desired. According to this model, the young woman who emerges from adolescence has not experienced a moratorium of the type Erikson describes. Rather, she has experienced a process of refinement—refinement of a socially acceptable way of being. She has learned to become what others want her to be, and in that sense has lost an opportunity to become the person she herself might have imagined.

A number of feminist scholars have observed that while the Eriksonian notion of a developmental moratorium does not always exist for girls because genuine exploration has been constrained, alternative processes can be cultivated to provide safe spaces in which to resist the patriarchal status quo and explore options for healthy development. In their edited volume *Urban Girls: Resisting Stereotypes, Creating Identities,* Bonnie Leadbeater and Niobe Way organize a range of compelling responses to the myriad ways in which development can be particularly challenging for low-income girls of color.[14] In combination, the contributions to this volume provide hopeful approaches to promoting healthy development. Although focused on urban girls' development, many of the insights presented can be applied to girls' development more broadly and, in fact, hold important implications for constructively altering boys' development as well.

Working with the metaphor of "home," with its implications of safety, warmth, and nurturing, Jennifer Pastor, Jennifer McCormick, and Michelle Fine describe the critical importance of constructing "homeplaces" where girls, and in this case, urban girls of color, congregate.[15] Such homeplaces provide for safe exchanges of ideas, intimate discussions of desire, and expressions of anger and frustration felt in response to the external world, the world that exists just beyond the boundaries of the homeplace. Home, as Pastor and her colleagues put it, should be a place to organize and gain support. It should be a place to organize around everyday activities of common interest, and, in the face of external opposition, home should be a place to gain political support for organizing to initiate change. There is a strong linking of family and politics in this depiction of the homeplace. Identity development, from this perspective, requires an *inner* sanctum of strong family support within which to gain validation for everyday being, and it includes the need for political backing that the family can provide in the face of *external* challenges.

Many educators have adopted the notion of a homeplace as a way of framing their teaching and counseling. Through activities that encourage critical analysis of social forces, approaches that invite emotional responses along with intellectual ones, relationships that expect open and honest sharing, and frequent attention to the political dimension of one's decisions, educators can create homeplaces within a host of school settings. To learn which school spaces adolescents consider homeplaces, one need only locate the teachers' and counselors' rooms where youth gather before school, at lunch, and after school. Youth tend to linger in these places precisely because they feel at home there—at home in a way that accepts them as fully as they're capable of showing up, and sends them out more fully capable of coping with the demands of the day.

> This is precisely why Lisa fled to Ms. Petersen's class when ostracized. Ms. Petersen had demonstrated her capacity to "get" the impositions and contradictions of high-school gender scripting from the first day of school when she had the class list all the colloquial or euphemistic terms for *male/man/boy* and *female/woman/girl*. After filling two blackboards with names and labels and eliciting lots of giggles, jeers, and cheers in the process, the students settled into "getting real" with one another in a conversation about what it means to be a man versus a woman in this society and in their school. Since that time, they have returned to that list and others like it to explore the operative symbols and tensions authors use to create characters and craft stories. In response to her always asking, "What's the author trying to get you to see?" Ms. Petersen's students began to ask that of each other, of the media, and even of their parents. Her classroom and her teaching became a place for

inquiry—any inquiry—where self-exploration was as valued as a well-written five-paragraph essay.

Teaching her students to resist easy answers and commonly held conclusions, Ms. Petersen helped many of them fall in love with metaphor and narrative as ways of revealing truths too complicated to communicate with mathematical, scientific, or historical language. Her tenth-grade world literature classes were currently engaged in lively analyses of the gendered implications of Chinua Achebe's Things Fall Apart. Their assignment at the end of the unit was to write a 1,200-word essay in response to this prompt: "Pick a character in Things Fall Apart and describe the gender barriers s/he confronts and how they affect her/him. Then, compare these to the gender barriers you confront and how they affect you." Recognizing that the emotional impact of Lisa's ostracism was profound, that the other girls involved would need to be addressed, and that it was 17 minutes until the bell would ring to signal the end of lunch, Ms. Petersen called in Mitch Guillermo, the school psychologist, to help with the situation.

Conferring in the hallway outside Ms. Petersen's class while Lisa sobbed by herself inside, they decided that the best thing for Lisa was to be removed from classes for the rest of the day and given an opportunity to unpack what had happened in a safe space. Before going in to accompany Lisa to the counseling office, Mitch got the names of the other girls and asked Ms. Petersen to have the office send them to Maggie Lang, one of the school counselors. As Ms. Petersen left to do that, Mitch entered and sat next to Lisa. "Had a hard day, huh?" Lisa nodded, still crying. "Well, we're gonna cut you some slack for the rest of the day so we can help you figure out what's going on." "I know what's going on," Lisa muttered between muffled sobs." "Okay," Mitch replied, "I imagine you do. So let's go and figure out what to do about it. Let's get a glass of water and go over to my office." Before they left the room, Lisa reached in her backpack, pulled out her essay for Ms. Petersen and placed it on her desk, saying, "That oughta explain some of this mess."

HOMESPACES FOR HEALTHY RESISTANCE

Janie Ward's contribution to *Urban Girls* provides a variant on the homeplace metaphor, not unlike the alternative spaces of Ms. Petersen's classroom and

Mitch's office. The *homespace* Ward describes is not so much a physical place within a particular system, whether family, school, or community setting, but rather a collective psychological space designed to promote healthy resistance to oppression. For the Black youth in Ward's study, that space is the critical consciousness of racism passed on from African American parents to their children. Without such consciousness, according to Ward and other authors, healthy resistance cannot be developed. In fact, without the proper attunement to racial discrimination faced by African Americans and other groups of color, resistance can be distorted and turned destructively against the self and others.[16]

Ward and her colleague Traci Robinson differentiated two forms of resistance among African American girls that have important implications for educators.[17] The first form, *resistance for survival*, is focused on "quick fixes" in response to racial discrimination and can be marked by such short-term strategies as avoidance or critical attack. Such defenses can serve an immediate self-protective function but tend not to have longer-term strength-building implications. A student who refuses to do homework for a teacher who frustrates her, or a student who gets in hallway fights with classmates who disrespect her, may be exhibiting the sort of resistance that helps her survive that day; at the same time, however, she may be enhancing her risk for longer-term difficulties if the behavior persists repetitively.

Resistance for liberation, according to Robinson and Ward, moves beyond survival behavior through collective, thoughtful responses to racism and other forms of oppression. These responses are constructive by definition, in that they are designed to build up the strength and self-esteem of the young women using them. They are organized around long-term liberating goals, including success in school and career as well as relational and community life. Resistance for liberation requires the support of others who are critically conscious of oppression, whether that be family support, support from school, or from others in the larger community. Students who exhibit collective and calculated responses to perceived injustices or who courageously stand up against their peers' self-destructive behaviors are often demonstrating a resistance for liberation. As educators working in systems sometimes ill-prepared to deal with "resistant elements," we not only need to facilitate such growth and action in our students; sometimes we may simply need to get out of the way.

Whereas experimentation is a key factor in Erikson's conception of adolescent development, resistance holds that place in developmental conceptions such as those described here. In this vein, resistance provides protection against accommodation to an oppressive status quo. It is a protective factor against the risks of racism as well as sexism, classism, and homophobia. As noted above, lessons gleaned from the girls' development literature hold implications for all adolescents. How, for example, does resistance factor into boys' development? What role does it play in becoming a man?

RELATIONAL THEORY AND BOYS' DEVELOPMENT

Unfortunately, many homeplaces for boys are spaces that breed homophobia. They are spaces that socialize boys into masculine stereotypes of toughness and independence, thereby discouraging sensitivity and intimate caring. To care is to be feminine, and to be feminine is to be gay. There is perhaps no more common slur in our school hallways than "faggot"! In many middle and high schools, it can be heard during virtually every transition from one class period to another. To be tainted with this slur, in many cases, results not only in having one's psychic self attacked but in having one's physical safety placed in jeopardy as well.

Jean Baker Miller has argued convincingly that the excessive valuing of autonomy and independence inherent in traditional identity theory has reinforced a sense of isolationism among many boys and men, thereby reducing their opportunities for mutually beneficial growth. To break from the perception of autonomy by embracing same-sex friendship in particular ways is to break away from manhood itself. Yet the distancing that is normative to male development, in many respects, shortchanges male adolescents in their opportunities to learn from and grow with one another. Because male relationships often lack the intimate mutuality more common among girls and women, according to Miller and her colleagues,[18] there is little mystery behind the differences in relationship maturity and emotional understanding that emerge between the sexes.

The sociologist Michael Kimmel has shown how pervasive masculine scripting is across all levels of U.S. society.[19] Breaking from the hypermasculine script, as Kimmel describes it, requires its own form of resistance. If boys are to benefit from caring connection with others, particularly other boys and men, they will need their own education in resistance. They must learn to resist the very images of manhood that are held up for them on television ads, in the music they listen to, and, perhaps, within their families and communities. Accommodating to the dominant male script brings with it the preservation of distance. At the same time, resisting the script can bring intense scrutiny and even violent reprisals. Examining the effects of patriarchy and its correlate, homophobia, Kimmel offers insights into boys' gender identity development. He notes that the "hegemonic definition of manhood is a man in power, with power, and a man of power" and that much of what we see in adolescent male behaviors can be traced to this definition. Although layered with racism and classism, Kimmel asserts, "Whatever the variations by race, class, age, ethnicity, or sexual orientation, being a man means 'not being like a woman' . . . so that masculinity is defined more by what one is not rather than who one is." The persistent need to prove that one is a man produces a "chronic sense of personal inadequacy" in boys and men and a fear that others will see that "[they] are not who [they] are pretending to be."[20]

Kimmel argues that adolescent boys see their peers as "a kind of gender police." Walking into any gathering place for boys and asking who is a "sissy"—or any popular pejorative variant on the term—is likely, according to Kimmel, to provoke a fight that depicts the social order. Let there be no question who is the top man and, more importantly, who is not on the bottom. Kimmel cites a survey in which women and men were asked what they were most afraid of: "Women responded that they were most afraid of being raped and murdered. Men responded that they were most afraid of being laughed at." It is inevitable that with this pervasive sense of fear and constant awareness of being policed that violence becomes the "single most evident marker of manhood," especially as boys enter adolescence and begin to form identities as men.[21] The resulting masculine identity and the aggressive posturing to ward off potential ridicule demonstrate to others an adherence to the ideal male archetype.

Kimmel's work shows how boys and men learn to cope with this fear, doubt, and shame by adopting behaviors of "exclusion and escape . . . to keep their fears of humiliation at bay" through what he identifies as the "manhood of racism, of sexism, of homophobia."[22] Homophobia, for boys and men, becomes the fear that other boys or men will unmask or emasculate them, revealing to the world that they do not measure up, that they are not real men. Boys and men then become afraid to let other boys and men see that fear. Since real men are supposed to be fearless, the experience of being afraid is often accompanied by shame. If the adolescent boy, for example, recognizes his fear and has no one with whom to discuss it nor opportunities to resist it in productive ways, the fear serves as a sort of internal proof that he is not as manly as he pretends to be. It is this shame at not measuring up, Kimmel points out, that leads to boys' violence or silence, which in turn keeps other people believing they actually approve of the things that are done to women, to minorities, and to gays and lesbians in our culture.

Without safe-enough spaces in our schools to take on these issues, both the violence and silence in boys' masculinity posturing endures unimpeded, wreaking havoc not only in the social realm but also creating distance in the educational process. Learning—fully engaged learning—requires vulnerability. It requires the capacity to leave oneself open to criticism and to willingly seek and provide support. These are not "masculine traits," which is why for so many boys, particularly from late elementary school onward, "school learning" is seen as the educational terrain of girls. Boys' learning happens in the "real world."

In her portrayal of the urgency Black mothers experience in teaching their daughters to resist racism, Ward draws on the "tongues of fire" imagery provided by bell hooks in her captivating essay on Audre Lorde.[23] To "tell it like it is" with no holds barred, according to Ward, is deemed essential to survival among many in the Black community. While shattering the precious illusion of safety, bald *truth-telling*—and the scarring it inflicts—provides painful protection against the inevitable deeper wounds of racism. That desire for protection notwithstanding, Black mothers with their tongues of fire have obvious and critically essential battles to fight, battles staked upon the very survival of their families and their children. But who stands up for the adolescent boy, particularly the White boy, who is expected to resist the privileges of patriarchy? Who finds it urgent to tell the truths necessary for that resistance? In most cases, no one.

The dominant male script, with its emphasis on toughness and auton-omy, is perceived to come with age-old benefits. Toughness is associated with power, power with control, control with authority, authority with priv-ilege. Privilege allows for the exercise of autonomy, or the right to act freely according to one's wishes. Why would anyone willingly give up his "right-ful" role in this script? The answers are not obvious, which is precisely why education is critical to this issue.

Because of its complexity, understanding gender requires careful study. Ironically, although gender identity development is central to adolescence, it is only studied toward the end of that period, if at all, and only by the select few who attend college and are exposed to feminist theory in one form or another. Yet middle- and high-school language arts classes—not to mention math, science, and history—are replete with gender dramas that would allow for critical discussion on this topic. But who would hold that discussion? And how far would they take it?

COMING OUT AND UP FROM UNDER

Going underground in search of self-protection, at the risk of losing one's authentic self, has obvious parallels in the developmental realities of gay and lesbian youth. Although we discuss sexual orientation extensively in chapter 9, we introduce it here for its relationship to gender identity development. The vast majority of gay boys, for example, clearly identify with being a boy and yearn to be recognized for who they are—boys who are every bit as male as their heterosexual peers. But the gender scripts for gay boys are complicated in ways that make it difficult for such recognition to occur. The conflation of sexual orientation and gender identity creates unique challenges for gay boys as they attempt to claim and express their own experiences of masculinity. In a society where masculinity is so commonly associated with violence, including violence toward any "other" who threatens the comfort of male privilege, expressing alternative forms of maleness can be dangerous, even life threatening.

It is little wonder, then, that gay boys, or those who imagine they might be gay, hide out in the closet. In the closet, at least, there is some space to be "me," even if I must be alone with myself. At least there is self-preservation, or so the theory goes. But a closeted life is a life without validation, at least authentic validation. The partial self let out for public recognition is a fractured self. Holding it together requires a delicate balancing act, particularly as the weight of the hidden pieces grows. And the energy used in simply "holding it together" leaves far too few reserves for the everydayness of adolescent life. Ordinary things like going to a dance, to a football game, or to a friend's house can become extraordinary concerns due to the self-monitoring required for proper presentation. But what are the alternatives? To be seen "for real" is too risky. Knowing one's sexual orientation, it is feared, would lead to a castigation of one's entire being. Better, then, to let a partial self go public; if part of me is destroyed, I still have the rest.

Obviously, this is not a scenario conducive to optimal development. The energy needed to hide is lost energy. It is energy that cannot be used in the pursuit of flow experiences, as described in chapter 4, through which people are free to lose themselves is deep experiences of creative endeavor.

Although the pain associated with the struggle to survive can be transformed into creative expression—humanity, of course, is replete with such examples—this is a route to creativity that most of us would choose to bypass. It is also the case that for every transformation of suffering into creativity, there are more examples of suffering turned to human destruction.

As educators, our job is to promote learning and creativity through safe and enriching experiences. Optimal learning requires the presence of intact, fully present students. If parts of our students are closeted and hidden underground, we all lose out. Our classrooms and our schools in general become partial learning environments, with our students' collective energy short-circuited by multiple barriers to full expression. In this vein, gender identity work in our schools is the work of freedom fighting. It is a fight for the freeing of authentic expression, for the full presentation of all our students. It is the fight to help our students be fully present as learners, as classmates, as the people they see themselves to be.

All this is hollow rhetoric, however, without the leadership of educators in our schools. The truth telling that Ward speaks of with respect to racism holds in the arenas of gender identity and sexual orientation as well. Our schools must become the all-encompassing homespaces in which these truths can be told and heard. They must become spaces in which girls in hiding can emerge to refind lost aspects of themselves and in which gay and lesbian youth can find safe exodus from their closeted hideouts. But these examples touch only the tip of the iceberg. The heavy scripting of adolescent gender identity forces most youth to hide critical parts of themselves and in so doing robs them of vital opportunities for optimal development.

Jerry Callahan is an 18-year-old senior in a White, working-class public school. He will graduate in about three months and is very much looking forward to "wrapping up my school career for good," as he puts it. He's a big guy, but, he says, not the "macho type." "I mean I'm tough, mostly because I'm so big . . . and because I have a bad temper at times. But mostly I'm the funny type, the life of the party." Not only is Jerry the life of the party, but he attends and initiates a lot of them. He drinks hard, like most of his friends, but a little more than most, perhaps, again, because he's "so big." He says that when he drinks, "I don't get mad and go out looking for fights like some of the guys, I just get funnier. But, still, it never fails . . . at some point, once everyone's drunk, someone pushes me into a fight, trying to prove that they can handle the big guy . . . and that's when I just have to f——'em up . . . " Jerry adds this last piece without obvious pride, more with a sense of resignation. It is part of the script for a man like him, the kind of young man who, despite his good-natured sense of humor, gets used by others who are trying to define their own masculinity.

By most accounts, Jerry seems firmly in touch with himself, mostly comfortable in his identity. He claims to have relatively little regret over his self-proclaimed underperformance academically. "I'm basically a C, D student, and I know I could be getting at least Bs and Cs. But that's really not me. It might hurt me in the long run. But school just ain't my thing." He does, however, acknowledge two school-related regrets: "So most people think I'm really funny. I think I'm pretty funny. And I'm an actor. When I look back now, I wish I'd tried out for the school plays. I see those kids in the plays and I know I could have done so much better. But we all [Jerry and his male friends] looked at it like a gay thing, like all the guys in the theater club are fags. But they're not even . . . and who cares if they are. That's up to them. I don't have a problem with that. But it's just that we looked at it like that, so I never got into it. That's my biggest regret, that I let that gay thing get in my way of being in the school plays, which I know I would have really liked."

The other thing is music. "I wish I would have joined the school band. But that kind of had a gay or sissy thing connected to it too. You know, it was the guys that didn't play sports. My friends don't really play sports either, but none of 'em would even think of joining the school band. And that's kinda funny because we all love music and we play music in people's garages. We kinda have our own band . . . but, still, I wish I had joined because I could have gotten lessons for free, and probably would have learned to play an instrument, like the saxophone, that I could never afford on my own."

Jerry is neither gay nor female, nor is he a student of color coping with racism. Although he is of working-class background, he articulates no explicit form of class-based prejudice, although one could argue that social class barriers factor prominently behind the scenes of his story. But Jerry was not closeted nor seeking protection underground for the reasons described above. Rather, he hid part of himself in order to fit the male gender script he co-constructed with his male peers through their embeddedness in the larger community and society, in which they have been deeply socialized. If Jerry could have brought a fuller self to school, perhaps he would have succeeded in theater and band activities, as he suspects, and perhaps these successes would have profoundly altered his feeling of connectedness to education more broadly. Given this alternative scenario, perhaps Jerry would not be looking so excitedly toward "wrapping up his school career for good."

CHAPTER SEVEN

Racial Identity Development

Despite our best efforts to the contrary, the ways in which others see us profoundly influence how we see ourselves. Therefore, race and ethnicity as "external" identity markers hold particular salience in American society, given our extensive history of immigration and racial diversity. Along with this reality come the influences of racism and ethnic discrimination, which indelibly shape the experience of growing up for so many youth of color in the United States. Drawing on the Eriksonian tradition of *identity crises* presented in chapter 2, in these next two chapters we examine the impact of racial hierarchies, the legacy of racial and ethnic oppression, and the ongoing challenge of constructing a cohesive yet multifaceted identity in contexts that privilege some as they oppress others. In the process, we review the work of key researchers and theorists in order to establish the importance of attending to race and ethnicity as they affect both the adolescent and the school-based professional.

It is in these chapters that the framing of teaching and counseling as a political undertaking is most underscored (although it is sustained throughout the chapters on gender, class, and sexual orientation as well). Going beyond stage theories to recognize the developmental significance of reading the world sociopolitically and looking at how youth are situated within it, these chapters variously frame identity as identit*ies*, as performances, and as masks we don in order to move across different contexts. Examining the developmental significance of racial pride and multicultural literacy, we present the ethical imperative of specifically attending to racial and ethnic identity issues with a focus on how school-based professionals can best address injustice in their daily practice.

In matters of race and ethnicity, it is necessary to work reflexively (with critical self-reflection) and reciprocally with youth who come both from dominant and marginalized groups in order not just to facilitate healthy development but also to move toward dismantling the discourses and assumptions that perpetuate racism and ethnic discrimination in our schools and communities. In addition to the effects of stereotypes based on people of color, the developmental effects of *Whiteness* are examined as well, leading to methods that hold the school-based professional accountable for doing the necessary work to effectively accompany adolescents as they construct their identities in response to what can be injurious racial categories.

WHY THINK OF RACE DEVELOPMENTALLY?

When a student enters your school, classroom, or office, she brings with her the layers of historical and cultural experiences that have shaped the identity she inhabits. What she presents to you as "me" is the most recent iteration of her internalized life experiences, a representation contingent on her context at the moment. Because of context-based roles and assumptions, the identity she presents to you may look very different from the one she offers to her peers, family, or other adults at school. How often does it happen that a student has significant problems in one or two classes but has none whatsoever in others? In all likelihood, the contexts in which the problems are surfacing are quite different from those in which they are not (e.g., a different teacher, different subject matter, different peers). When a student's behavior shifts from setting to setting, it may indicate the extent to which particular contexts represent identity threats, whereas others represent opportunities for optimal development.

The same holds for adults. A school principal, counselor, and teacher all take into account the demands of their context and present to those within it the identity/identities they believe are most appropriate to the situation at hand. As with students, our identities shift as we move from setting to setting, and our behavior and decisions shift with them. When in the role of spouse or life-partner, we assume a different identity than when we are in the role of teacher or vice principal; this is as it should be, since each setting has its own peculiar set of demands. Problems in one context experienced concurrently with successes in another suggest different threats and opportunities in these contexts as much as they point to how our identities shift according to setting.

Conceived in this way, identities can be understood as *performances*, strategically constructed to provide the best chances for personal safety and ever attentive to feedback from our various audiences. Identity as performance is not solely the achievement of a singular cohesive self, durable and immutable across differing contexts; rather, it is also, at least in part, a context-derived and context-driven representation of who we are at that moment for that particular setting. Understanding identity in this way allows us to make visible the factors that shape how we see and represent ourselves, and it illuminates how adults and adolescents co-construct and position one another in every interaction in which identities are performed.

If we are to meet adolescents "where they're at," we need to attend to the primary influences that shape their identities. Race is precisely one such influence for many youth. Howard Winant represents the larger issue of racial influence as follows:

> In U.S. society, race is a fundamental organizing principle, a way of knowing and interpreting the social world. . . . As we watch the video-tape of Rodney King being beaten up by Los Angeles police officers; compare real estate prices in different metropolitan area neighborhoods; select a radio channel to enjoy while we drive to work; size up a potential client, customer, neighbor, or teacher; or carry out a thousand other normal tasks, we are compelled to think racially, to use the racial categories and meaning systems into which we have been socialized.[1]

Regardless of our own racial identifications or those of the kids we serve, our work with adolescents occurs within a social context laden with racial meaning. Students and teachers alike are routinely asked to select a specific racial identity when filling out forms and taking standardized tests, which, if you've ever been present for such tasks, inevitably produces numerous quandaries that seldom get the attention they deserve: "My mom is Puerto Rican and my dad is Black—which box do I check?" "I'm German and Lithuanian—why am I only allowed to select White?" "What does 'other' mean?" Teachers in classrooms across a diversity of settings consistently face racialized language (the "n" word, "Brown Pride," "Kiss Me, I'm Irish"), encounter dangerous stereotypes propelled by the media and reproduced by teens, observe sharp divisions among students (and faculty) along racial lines, and confront racist comments in hallways and classrooms, not to mention the teachers' lounge. Administrators, too, must balance the interests of various community groups often divided by racial distinctions, which creates enormous challenges for school reform efforts. Yet these anecdotes only scratch the surface of how racial identities get produced, reproduced, challenged, and resisted in our schools. Given this, it is surprisingly rare to find school spaces in which both adults and youth are encouraged to question racial meanings and their effect on learning and development. Framing such discussions as *developmentally necessary* opens up the possibility for them to occur in ways that enhance opportunity, perspective, and freedom.

Thinking and working developmentally means looking for as many interpretations of what might be happening to/in that person as possible; in the United States, this can rarely be done without considering the impact of race. In countless research reports, district and state studies, and mainstream media articles, racial identity is identified as a primary concern in adult and youth experiences in our schools and a key factor in understanding school reform, teacher performance, and student success. Accordingly, there is an ethical imperative to investigating race as it functions developmentally. Consider, for example, such high-profile and highly racialized school issues as the "achievement gap," the myriad perils and possibilities associated with "urban education," and the demographic profiles of the U.S. teaching force (largely White, middle class, and female) versus the students served by it (largely students of color). The race-based implications here can hardly be overemphasized.

Because the legacy of race can be painful and oppressive, working with racial identity development theory and translating it into practice can produce some of the most confusing and anxiety-ridden situations we face in our work with adolescents. "Did she say that because I'm White?" "Did he do that because I'm Black?" "How am I being understood as a *raced* person?" "How am I understanding others as *racialized* people?" Actively attending to such questions can help us understand one another in our struggles to confront the everyday realities of social hierarchies. We contend that racial identity development as it comes to bear on our work with adolescents should not be considered an accessory to the classical developmental approaches (i.e., relegated to a small addendum chapter or lecture subsumed within the canon of cognitive and relational interpretations), nor should race-based developmental inquiries be dismissed as "identity politics." To the contrary, racial identity development is, in many cases, as much at the core of adolescent co-constructions of the self as other critical organizing experiences. Given the influence of racial dynamics in our schools and communities, to ignore race or claim to do applied development work in a "color-blind" manner approximates malpractice. Put bluntly, racial identity development is not just for people of color. All of us—White, Black, Latino/a, Japanese American, Hmong, Chinese American, Native American, Haitian American, Laotian, and so on—are "raced" (identified and assessed in relation to our perceived racial background) in our society, and the process of identity formation is forever tied to that experience. If we work with adolescents and wish to meet them where they are, we must "go there," to where they live racially, even when—and perhaps particularly when—going there takes us beyond our educator comfort zones.

A WORD ON THE SOCIAL CONSTRUCTION OF "RACE"

Scientifically, there is no such thing as "race." As many biologists and geneticists have pointed out, including the late Stephen Jay Gould,[2] there exists as much genetic diversity within any racial group as there is within the human population as a whole. There is no biologically sustainable reason for establishing "races" as distinct subgroups within the human species, which is why Omi and Winant call racial categories "patently absurd reductions of human variation."[3] That there are unique bodily features (skin color, hair texture, shape of eyes, etc.) distributed according to regional ancestral origin supports nothing "racial" except an appreciation for the ways in which our species adapted to specific environments over hundreds of thousands of years.

So where does the concept of race come from? In short, race is a concept created in the modern era as a way of drawing distinctions between peoples such that some might benefit at the expense of others. Slavery in the seventeenth, eighteenth, and nineteenth centuries is inextricable from the invention of race, which was used to legitimize the exploitation and murder of millions by designating certain "races" as subhuman in order to treat them as chattel without violating the Enlightenment notion of freedom. Scientists enamored of the social-engineering possibilities of eugenics later expanded the use of the term in the twentieth century, giving rise to the arbitrarily racialized subcategories of "Negroid," "Mongoloid," and "Caucasoid," and ultimately providing the Nazi regime with its rationale for a master Aryan race. In the contemporary U.S. context, racial taxonomies have long been and continue to be employed to ascribe value to White European American cultural patterns by differentiating the White norm from "other" people of color. The current use of the term "people of color" is itself an artifact of that differentiation, suggesting as it does that one is either White or nonWhite.

The scientific and historical analyses debunking the biological validity of race and the enduring social consequences of the concept have been widely detailed. The purpose of surveying such work so briefly here is not to diminish its importance but to point out one simple fact: *race is a social construction*. It was created largely to divide people, giving power to some while taking it from others. Like all social phenomena, it morphs and moves depending on the power dynamics of the context. For example, throughout U.S. history, federal, state, and local governments have employed various strategies to classify and sort people based on race. Originally, government officials used only the categories of "White," "Negro," and "Indian." For a time, the Irish were considered "Black" and therefore exploited and oppressed. Later, "Latino/a" and "Asian" were added as classifications, which gave rise to "Chicano/a," "Hispanic," "Chinese Americans," "Orientals," "Pan-Asians," and "Asian Pacific Americans" among others. As Kincheloe and Steinberg point out, "Analysis of such categorization indicates both the slipperiness of racial grouping and the American attempt to force heterogeneous racial configurations into a single category around similarities in skin tone, hair texture, and eye shape."[4] Regardless of its lack of basis in scientific fact, "race" functions as a segregating marker of power in nearly all societies on earth.

In working with youth, it is important for us to recognize that although race does not exist scientifically, it certainly does exist socially. By holding onto this recognition, we can enter into race-based analyses with youth as developmental allies, joining our students in constructing positive racial identity experiences and making transparent for critique and civic action the multiple ways in which racism and its implications affect all of us, educationally and otherwise.

DEVELOPMENTAL ALLIANCES

If we are to accompany youth as they attempt to construct healthy identities and resist oppressive contexts that limit their potential, we must learn to recognize and confront the ways in which injurious racial categorizations play out in their lives. Since none of us emerges from raceless upbringings or race-blind professional contexts, and none of us works in schools bereft of racial issues, we cannot expect to perceive youth experiences from a neutral place. Simply put, we are subject to the same racist social forces as our students. Denying the salience of race in our work with youth may in fact contribute to the legacy of racist, exclusionary, and debilitating practices in schools. In fact, research has indicated that endorsement of "color-blind" racial attitudes is significantly associated with greater levels of racial prejudice and a mistaken belief that society is just and fair.[5] Taking this into account, providing optimal developmental experiences for adolescents requires us to examine the ways in which race has affected our own growth. We use the term *developmental alliance* to describe work with youth around such politically charged developmental issues as racial oppression. The term implies a personally and politically collaborative approach to addressing complex developmental barriers. It also implies that while youth are the primary authorities of their own experience, adult alliances are critical in helping cultivate authoritative responses to oppression.[6]

We draw upon developmental theory, not to assess the relative "stage" of adolescent growth experiences, but to find guidance for accompanying youth as they make meaning of those experiences with us, to participate in their transformations as they participate in ours. Being in developmental alliance means expecting this transformation to be reciprocal—we expect to grow in our relationships with students just as we hope to promote growth. At times such working relationships can engender feelings of discomfort, fear, sadness, and anger. Indeed, dialogues about race, especially with adolescents for whom such issues are quite raw, can produce dramatically different reactions in different people. Michelle Fine and her colleagues describe this realization when working through race issues with a class of diverse students, asking:

> Is it possible that Whites work "optimally," that is, uninterrupted, when [they] *don't* have to discuss race and ethnicity and that students of color can only be engaged and most unburdened when race and ethnicity are squarely on the table? . . . It seems likely that students of color are "stuck" until "race" is discussed, while White students are "stuck" once race is discussed.[7]

Confronting the negative consequences of racism in our school environments, even when it entails seeing ourselves "in the unflattering light of another's angry gaze,"[8] serves to enhance our own growth just as it does our students'. It is important for us to recognize that racism is not just the aberrant behavior of morally repugnant individuals but is also part and parcel of institutionally sanctioned social policies and ways of knowing and relating to one another. Using the developmental alliance framework gives us a foothold for acting on this recognition. We simultaneously confront racism and contribute to positive racial identity development for ourselves and our students when we join them in collaborative and critical working relationships, including relationships that cut across racial lines.

REEXAMINING STEREOTYPE AND PREJUDICE

Ameliorating the effects of racism in adolescence requires attending to the ways youth understand themselves and others racially and how that develops over time. Lisa Delpit has pointed out that "We do not see through our eyes or hear through our ears, but through our beliefs."[9] We understand (and misunderstand) one another, in part, through stereotypes culled from our individual and collective belief systems. We are bombarded by sensory data every day: sights, sounds, tastes, smells, touches, feelings. Our brains manage all this information by grouping input into simplified conceptions or containers—schema, as Piaget referred to them (see chapter 3). From this perspective, stereotypes are a natural form of cognitive development, a way of making sense of sensory data. They are particularly dangerous if too durable but, as cognitive schema, serve as starting points for more complex understanding if they are flexible enough to be altered by new experiences. This places a good part of the onus for changing stereotypes on those contexts that provide meaningful learning experiences: schools, family, and community, for starters. Like stereotypes, prejudice generally is understood as a pejorative assessment of a person or group. There are important differences, however, between attending to our prejudices, trying to rid ourselves of them, and acting as if we do not possess them. All of us are prejudiced by virtue of ingrained habits derived from living in the world; we make prejudgments of familiar people, places, and things based on past experience. We cannot overcome our prejudices fully, but we can recognize them with practice and learn both to modify and respond to them constructively. When we risk putting our assumptions on the table, we open the possibility that others may do the same. A stance that "this is the way it is!" leaves little opportunity to negotiate perspectives; any ensuing dialogue becomes a battle for the ascendancy of one perspective over another. On the other hand, statements like "I see it this way because of where I stand" create openings. The ensuing dialogue then revolves around experience and perspective. Multiple truths can coexist and be held accountable for the actions they inspire. Speaking in terms of agendas, assumptions, and perspectives frees us to see what's at stake for one another rather than falsely determining who is pure and innocent and who is clouded by their prejudices.

Because we live as if the way we think of the world is the way the world truly is, it is important to uncover and examine those critical prejudgments that affect our everyday lives. Racial prejudice is one of these critical areas: we are deeply socialized to make prejudgments in this area and typically untrained in understanding the multiple ways in which race and racial identity influence those around us. Racial identity development theory can provide assistance in resocializing us, and our students, into being more racially conscious. It provides clues into how the uncovering might occur and direction for examining what we find.

RACIAL IDENTITY DEVELOPMENT THEORIES

As educators working in alliance with adolescents struggling to become themselves within and against racial stereotypes, we might ask ourselves the following questions:

- How do the youth we're working with make sense of racial categories? How do we make sense of these same categories?

- How do adolescents orient their identities toward one race (or several) as they come to understand that certain contexts marginalize some and privilege others based on racial categories?

- How might our students' identities (and our own) be affected by racial hierarchies? What do we notice and what decisions do we make based on that information?

- What is "optimal racial identity development"? What is the end goal?

- How do youth (and adults) reproduce harmful racial ideas? How do youth (and adults) resist or transcend them?

- What interventions might inspire a deeper, more integrated, and flexible racial identity?

- If one has more fully explored one's racial identity, might that contribute to higher levels of academic achievement? Is a student who has a complex understanding of their "Blackness" or "Whiteness" or "Puerto Rican-ness" more likely to have elevated academic potential?

As a first step in taking on such complex questions, it is essential to find colleagues with whom we can discuss ideas, confusions, and potential strategies. Such race-based discussion can be enhanced by drawing upon resources from racial identity development theory, a literature with which most educators have had little exposure throughout their training and professional development.

That literature generally frames racial identity as a mental orientation toward racial group membership, "a psychological template which operates as a 'world view' and serves as a filter for race-based information."[10] Race, then, has everything to do with personality and developmental processes since we come to know ourselves and others in part through racial categories. For the most part, as depicted in figure 7.1, racial identity development theories demonstrate how the individual comes to terms with those categories and moves toward positive self-evaluation and group membership.

The role of differentiation

Freud's theory of personality differentiation is a good starting point for understanding the trends summarized in figure 7.1. Freudian theory begins with the simple observation that children are born without the awareness that they are psychologically differentiated from their mother and/or father, and then gradually learn that they are separate and unique from their parent(s) as they grow older and their sense of self develops. At some point during this process, children learn that they are not only distinct from their parent(s) and people more generally but that they also are members of specific racial groups. They learn to affiliate with their "own group" and distinguish themselves from "other groups," just as they learn to affiliate with and differentiate from such other social groupings as gender and social class. Each differentiation of the self from particular people, groupings, and roles brings with it specific developmental dynamics. With respect to racial differentiations, patterns of exclusion, inclusion, oppression, and privilege in the young person's environment affect how her ego transforms race-based information into an identity that can effectively manage the demands of the Freudian id (innate drives and impulses) and superego (internalized societal expectations). Responding to these dynamics in their environment, children and adolescents forge identities that both align with and differentiate from the racial categories they confront in their daily lives. This process can exert powerful demands on an adolescent's psyche as he negotiates when to resist race-based characterizations and when to comply with them.

As children grow into adolescents and adolescents into adults, they interact with different racial groups, stereotypes, and expectations, and in the process, if the conditions support it, their identity grows more complex and flexible in its ability to manage race-based information. Because of their new cognitive abilities, adolescents in particular often seek out ways in which they can experiment with identities in order to differentiate themselves from family, friends, and the racial categories that may limit them. However, as discussed through Selman's work in chapter 5,[11] social-cognitive development

FIGURE 7.1:   Typical Trends in Racial Identity Development Theories

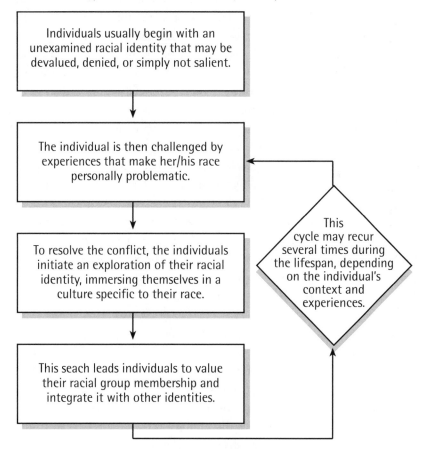

Adapted from D. E. S. Frable, "Gender, Racial, Ethnic, Sexual, and Class Identities, *Annual Review of Psychology* 48 (1997): 147

in adolescence is marked by the emerging ability to understand what others might be thinking and to coordinate one's own perspectives with those of others in increasingly proficient and complex ways. This means that differentiation is more the unfolding of an interpersonal self-authorship (i.e., a "me-in-relationship-with-you") than it is the solidification of an isolated identity apart from others (i.e., a "me-not-you"). Spencer and Dornbusch stress that the adolescent "'looking-glass self,' in which one imagines how others react to one's behavior and personality, affects the adolescent's identity development" in profound ways. They contend that "for minority youth, the stigmas of racial stereotypes, often reinforced by poverty, have the potential to distort the image in the mirror."[12] Such nuances to the theory of differentiation allow us to recognize the empathic possibilities intrinsic to identity development as much as they highlight the potential for adolescents to align their perspectives with racialized assessments of themselves and others.

The intensity with which teenagers form tight allegiances to social groups—even as they seek out ways to express their individuality and push back against the constrictions those groups represent—can be seen as evidence of this process of differentiation in relationships. For example, a Latino boy may have strong, positive, and affirming familial associations with what it means to be "Brown," learned through relatives and friends in a tightly knit community. The psychological need to differentiate from that racial identity may be low in early childhood since his acceptance and value may be affirmed by those with whom he identifies. However, when presented with racist language and attitudes at his large, diverse high school, that identity may be challenged and even assaulted, forcing a differentiation from home and/or friends or a willful negation of the harmful identities being presented to him. Either way, this young person is thrust into a complex set of competing racialized demands on his identity.

Reading racialized performances developmentally

If a student begins devaluing or ignoring his familial connections or chooses to decorate his notebook and backpack with declarations such as "Brown Pride" in order to make clear from whom he is differentiating himself, it behooves those in developmental alliance with him to find out how he is making sense of it all. What does the phrase "Brown Pride" mean to him? How does he understand it in terms of his relationships with family, friends, teachers, etc.? What does he feel like when he sees it or says it? How does he understand it as a label for him and not others? Spencer and Dornbusch suggest that the developing adolescent mind often makes for complex answers to such questions:

> Adolescents have the ability to interpret cultural knowledge, to reflect on the past, and to speculate about the future. With cognitive maturity, minority adolescents are keenly aware of the evaluations of their group made by the majority culture. Thus, the young African-American may learn as a child that Black is beautiful but conclude as an adolescent that White is powerful.[13]

Adolescent performances of racial identities evident in such symbols as "Brown Pride" or "Black Power" are sometimes read by adults in schools as threatening, as gang-related monikers, or even as evidence of "reverse racism." In classifying them this way, a developmental opportunity is lost. To think developmentally and to act in developmental alliance requires us to read expressions of racial identity in adolescents as exploratory performances— "This is who I think *I* am—what do *you* think?"—and therefore engage them as invitations to dialogue. Left to develop these symbols and identities in isolation without the social interaction they call out for, the adolescent may construct an overly rigid definition of the self, unable to accommodate new or conflicting representations of herself or others outside that framework. This rigidity can develop in victims of racism as much as it can in perpetrators: White youth, for example, exposed primarily to racist ideologies and representations who refuse to assimilate racial information that conflicts with a supremacist worldview.

Throughout these processes, educators can assume a vital role in opening dialogue about racial identities and the diversity of possibilities available within any single racial group. Seen developmentally, conversations with youth about how they understand themselves and others racially become occasions for connection and expansive thinking, whereas the avoidance of such engagement can exacerbate school-based segregation and prejudice.

THE BLACK-WHITE BINARY: A HISTORICAL STARTING POINT

As discussed above, the concept of race is inherently a gross reduction of the complexity of any person or people. To employ racial distinctions to help explain how adolescents and adults organize their identities is, arguably, to participate in the reification of those very categories. At the same time, ignoring the "reality" of race in the lives of young people is to miss a critical component of their lived experience. Therefore, throughout the remainder of this chapter we attempt to show how racial categories function developmentally so that school-based practitioners can engage youth at the level of their identity challenges. We begin by exploring the two most dominant racial categories in U.S. history: Black and White. By entering racial identity development theory first through an examination of these two categories, we do not mean to suggest that other "races" possess experiences any less salient or unique. In fact, all such groups have complex histories, cultures, and ethnicities that have been compared to and distinguished from the Black and White developmental theories outlined below. In table 7.1, we attempt to depict this diversity by surveying multiple theories in order to show how they both build upon and differ from those pertaining to Blacks and Whites. In chapter 9, we explore how ethnicity complicates race as a developmental reality, a fact that rightfully challenges the notion that racial identity development can be reduced to a Black-White binary.

African American racial identity development theory

Recognizing the contributions and limitations of Erikson's and Marcia's models in accounting for the impact of race on identity development, several theorists have expanded their work to include crises and commitments that revolve specifically around the ways in which individuals respond to racialized experiences in their lives. Returning to Antwon's case from chapters 1 and 2, recall how his relationship with Ms. Petersen devolved due to missed opportunities for communication and mistaken perceptions layered with racialized meaning.

> As Antwon moves through his school days increasingly afraid of failing, confronting the holes in his academic preparation, trying to find the "right" friends, and sometimes being disappointed in his teachers' capacity or willingness to help him, he encounters several different expectations about how he should understand his "Blackness." One lesson, in his social studies class during Black History Month, emphasizes the uniqueness of African American heritage, instilling in Antwon a sense of pride in Black achievements. Later that day, in a discussion of *Things Fall Apart* in his world literature class, Antwon confronts the oppression endured by Africans and the connections between the colonial legacy in Africa and

TABLE 7.1: Models of Racial/Ethnic Identity Development

Model and Population	Stages or Statuses of Models					
General Identity Model						
Marcia (1980)	Identity Diffusion	Foreclosed Identity	Moratorium	Achieved Identity		
Generalized "Minority" Identity Models						
Atkinson, Morten, & Sue (1989)	Conformity	Dissonance	Resistance & Denial	Introspection	Synergetic Articulation	
Phinney, Lochner, & Murphy (1990)	Diffusion/Foreclosure	Search/Moratorium	Achievement			
Ponterotto & Pedersen (1993)	Identification w/the White Majority	Awareness, Encounter, & Search	Identification & Immersion	Integration & Internalization		
Carter (2000)	Conformity	Dissonance	Immersion/Emersion	Integrative Awareness		
Ethnic- or Race-Specific Models						
Arce (1981)—Chicano Identity	Forced Identification	Internal Quest	Acceptance	Internalized		
Ruiz (1990)—Chicano Identity	Causal	Cognitive	Consequence	Working Through	Successful Resolution	
Kim (1981)—Asian American Identity	Ethnic Awareness	White Identification	Awakening	Redirection	Incorporation	
Helms (1990)—White Identity	Contact	Disintegration	Reintegration	Pseudo-Independence	Immersion/Emersion	Autonomy
Cross (1991)—Black Identity	Pre-Encounter	Encounter	Immersion/Emersion	Internalization	Internalization/Commitment	
Wilson (1996)—Indigenous American Identity	"The emphasis of the Indigenous American worldview on the interconnectedness of all aspects of an individual's life challenges the compartmentalized structure of developmental stage models" (p. 310).					

Adapted from J. G. Ponterotto and P. Pedersen, *Preventing Prejudice: A Guide for Counselors and Educators* (Newbury Park, CA: Sage, 1993).[71]

current intergroup relations in North America. Unlike the previous characterization, this depiction inspires in Antwon feelings of rage and a desire to resist relationships with those who represent the oppressor. On his walk home, Antwon listens to music from a politically conscious rap group, which heightens his awareness of hypocrisy, discrimination, and the calculated efforts by some either to keep people of color down or to push them to rise up. The cumulative intensity of these experiences results in a complex blending of anger, pride, despair, and hope. Stopping by a park on the way home, a White friend of Antwon's makes an argument for a humanist stance, emphasizing the interconnections among all humans regardless of race. This discussion and the connection he feels with this White friend causes Antwon to temporarily reject racial categories as a way of explaining differences among people, to claim "We're all the same inside." Upon arriving at home and switching on the television, he watches a situation comedy and then a reality show, both of which portray the connections between African Americans and mainstream/dominant American society in a way that tacitly advocates an assimilationist stance yet builds humor around interracial misunderstanding. This first makes Antwon think about how to fit in and how to reject those who seek to resist, but in talking about it with his mother later, the same subject matter reinforces his belief that racial differences are to be extolled and defended.

Each of these encounters presents quite different messages about who Antwon is supposed to be and how he is supposed to understand himself racially. The identity statuses formed in response to these messages are as mixed, contradictory, and rife with power dynamics as the messages are. As if these issues were not confusing enough, research suggests that adolescents must also manage the tension between public perceptions about one's race (i.e., others' judgments about one's racial group) and more private assessments (i.e., the feelings about others and oneself as members of a racial group).[14] It is not hard to imagine Latino/a, Asian American, Native American, and multiracial adolescents tackling similar issues and being compelled to ask difficult questions of oneself in response: Given these demands, what identity will I adopt/construct? Who do I think will accept it and who will reject it? Which relationships will be strengthened by the identity I adopt/construct, and which ones will be threatened? What identity will guarantee me the most safety and gratification? What are the social benefits and liabilities of constructing this identity versus others? How is this possible identity depicted in the media? What does my family want of me, and how might that conflict with what my friends seem to want? These are some of the many questions that arise as adolescents begin to see how their relationships and identities are affected by racial categories; these are also the questions that arise, explicitly or implicitly, when school-based professionals work with youth and colleagues of different racial backgrounds.

To begin to envision a common developmental pathway through these questions, racial identity development theory can be an enormous help. William Cross's model of Black racial identity development helps describe how African American adolescents confront identity issues in markedly different ways than Whites, and it suggests how those differences affect teacher-student and student-student relationships. Cross's model ascribes a five-stage process to Black racial identity development, in which an African American's self-definition and connection with others proceeds through eras marked by the ways in which the individual makes sense of and responds to racial categories and interactions.[15] Summarized by Fischer and Moradi, the five stages as a whole trace "a progressive movement away from a pro-White, anti-Black stance to greater flexibility in attitudes toward Black and White people and cultures."[16] Like other status-based models,[17] however, Cross's schema allows for the possibility that individuals may return to earlier stages when confronted with new encounters. Table 7.2 illustrates the major transitions and characteristics of each of the stages.

According to Cross's model, African Americans proceed through an ebb and flow of phases marking the individual's capacity to form trusting relationships with Whites and feel secure in their own identity as Blacks. Designing instruction and interventions to meet the needs of African American youth without considering these dynamics not only misses the possibility for rich conversations about self-in-society but may also create conflict. For example, expecting Black adolescents who may be in the Immersion/Emersion stage to work collaboratively with Whites—both teachers and other students—may be experienced by the Black adolescent as a willful negation of his need not to be associating with the perceived oppressors. This is not to say that such groupings should be avoided or that White teacher–Black student pairings are necessarily problematic; rather, they should be undertaken with the full developmental realization that conflict

TABLE 7.2: African American Racial Identity Development

Status	Beliefs and Values	Actions and Affiliations
Pre-Encounter	adopts many of the beliefs and values of the dominant White culture; considers Blackness a "physical fact" that plays an insignificant role in one's everyday life; has not given much thought to race issues; race is a hassle, an imposition, something better left undiscussed; Eurocentric cultural perspective; pervasive belief in U.S. meritocracy	seeks assimilation into dominant White culture and may distance him/herself from other Blacks; somewhat dumbfounded and naïve during racial discussions; argues that personal progress is a matter of free will, initiative, rugged individualism and personal motivation to achieve; advocates for an abstract humanist stance when confronted with a race-based analysis; if sensitive toward racial issues, can become anxious over things or people being "too Black" and thus failing to project the best race image
Encounter	one is "caught off guard" in a confrontation that exposes the relevance of race to one's identity and worldview; the encounter can be positive or negative but generally forces one to question the validity of an assimilationist stance; begins to recognize own membership in a group targeted by racism	encounter can occasion confusion, alarm, or depression and often results in anger expressed toward those perceived as having "caused" their predicament (i.e., Whites); "inner-directed guilt, rage at White people, and an anxiety about becoming the right kind of Black person combine to form a psychic energy that flings the person into a frantic, determined, obsessive, extremely motivated search"
Immersion/ Emersion	transitional period in which the individual demolishes the old perspective and simultaneously attempts to construct what will become his or her new frame of reference; has made the decision to commit herself or himself to change; more familiar with the identity to be destroyed than the one to be embraced; immerses self in world of Blackness, which is often framed as a liberation from Whiteness; some anxiety when one worries about being or becoming Black enough; eventually emerges from the dichotomous and oversimplified ideologies of the immersion experience and discovers that "one's first impressions of Blackness were romantic and symbolic, not substantive, textured, and complex"	surrounds oneself with symbols of one's racial identity and actively avoids symbols of Whiteness; may adopt African names, become intensely interested in African or African American history and engage in a fervent search for inspiration in Black culture; proves one's Blackness by attaining some sort of group membership, "an audience before which to perform and a set of group-sanctioned standards toward which to conform"; articulated or enacted need to confront oppression; expresses "overwhelming love & attachment to all that is Black" that brings about "selflessness, dedication, and commitment to the Black group"

Internalization	anxiety over "Am I Black enough?" turns to confidence in one's own personal standards of Blackness; reconstitutes a durable and steady understanding of one's identity; may reference a bicultural or multicultural orientation in which one's concern for Blackness is concurrent with an acknowledged validity of cultural traits gained through nonBlack associations	rage at White people turns to anger at oppressive systems and racist institutions; urgent need to define oneself against White society evolves into a sense of liberatory destiny that can sustain long-term commitment; dissatisfaction with simplistic thinking and simple solutions; less defensiveness; willingness to establish meaningful relationships with Whites who demonstrate race-critical consciousness and actions; readiness to build coalitions with other oppressed groups
Internalization-Commitment	finds "ways to translate [her/his] personal sense of Blackness into a plan of action or a general sense of commitment" that can be sustained over time	able to perceive as well as transcend race as an organizing principle in one's life and worldview; Blackness is understood as an expression "shaped, voiced, and codified by a particular sociohistorical experience"

Adapted from W. E. Cross, *Shades of Black: Diversity in African-American Identity* (Philadelphia: Temple University Press, 1991), 189–223.

may arise as a result of active identity work, and that such conflicts are not necessarily a result of actions taken by one party or another. We can and should seek to have racially diverse students and teachers work with one another, but we also need to be aware of the ways in which those relationships are influenced by racial identity development and be prepared to respond in an informed manner when we recognize the need.

Since Antwon was suspended for the graffiti incident (chapter 2), his relationship with Ms. Petersen has grown increasingly adversarial. Although he likes the novel *Things Fall Apart* and especially enjoys the ways in which race has been infused into their class discussions and activities, he feels as if Ms. Petersen doesn't "get" how racist her own actions can be. Expressing this frustration to one of his "crew" after school one day, Antwon says, "It's like she expects me to fail, so she looks for every mistake I make and bosses me around in class until I wanna just bust out. I mean, she doesn't get on, like, Lisa Prescott for that sh——. She picks on me 'cuz I'm Black." Antwon's frustration with Ms. Petersen and his naming of the situation as racist comes on the heels of months of progressively more conspicuous displays of his race sensitivity. Wearing Tupac Shakur and Malcolm X T-shirts, growing his hair out and styling it into various cornrow designs or a large "fro" when many of his peers have shaven heads, restricting his close relationships to friends of color, and listening (often in class with his CD-player and headphones on) to Public Enemy, KRS-ONE, and the X-Clan, Antwon broadcasts his desire to engage Blackness and sometimes reject Whiteness. Strutting with a newly affected hitch in his walk, Antwon adopts a slower cadence in the hallway and often "fronts" other students by squaring off his shoulders and tilting his head back in a threatening manner as he makes his way to class. Taking this streetwise "cool pose" from the hallway into the classroom, Antwon prepares himself to combat any and all instances in which racism might be present.[18]

After numerous attempts to influence Antwon to shift his behavior into more "productive and cooperative" modes, Ms. Petersen has enacted a "zero tolerance" policy when it comes to his off-task talking and distractions in class, as insightful and race-critical as they sometimes are. She tells him that she values his class participation and his work on recent assignments but that she cannot allow him to distract other students, nor can she permit him to derail class discussions into tangential topics. Knowing that Antwon may read this as a dismissal of his contributions (indeed, Antwon does experience it this way, especially since they are discussing a novel replete with multiple racial implications), Ms. Petersen urges him to "consider the needs of the class as a whole" and work on resisting his "impulsive desire to insert race into every class discussion." Claiming to a colleague that Antwon "sees everything I do as racist when I am simply pushing him to do his best," Ms. Petersen is aware of the racialized meaning Antwon is making of her actions, and she possesses a genuine desire to learn how he sees things that way. However, as a fellow teacher reminded her, "We must teach all of our kids—not just one—and if one is a pain in the neck, we gotta get 'em outta there."

This advice collides with her concerns about Antwon's claims of racism in her mind as she opens the door to her fourth-period class and waits for him to slowly make his way into the room just as the tardy bell rings. With the instructions on the board indicating what the students are to do for the first half of the period, Antwon takes his seat with his groupmates, one of whom is Lisa Prescott. After ten minutes of circulating and prodding various groups to begin their work, Ms. Petersen notices that Antwon's group seems to be socializing more than working productively. When she asks the group for a progress update, Lisa claims she has been trying to get everyone to work while Antwon claims Lisa has been taking control and telling him what to do.

Ms. Petersen responds by asking Antwon, "Well, what have you done so far?"

Incensed that Ms. Petersen apparently sided with Lisa, Antwon exclaims "Man, you're only asking me 'cuz I'm Black!" Pushing back his chair and rising to go to the pencil sharpener, Antwon points his pencil at his groupmates and asks Ms. Petersen, "Why don't you ask them what they've done?" Realizing that she and the situation are now being read racially and that Antwon is walking away from her while she is talking, Ms. Petersen asks Antwon, "Will you please come back and sit down?" to which Antwon snaps back "I'm sharpening my pencil!" Not wanting to escalate the situation, Ms. Petersen busies herself by reading Lisa's paper while she waits for Antwon's return. When he sits back down again, Ms. Petersen defends herself, saying, "I am trying to help your group do the best it can and that means checking on your progress. I am asking you what's up just as I will ask the others in a moment, Antwon."

As she says this, Antwon scans the classroom for nonBlack students currently off task, remarking, "Those White dudes over there aren't doin' nuthin', but you aren't yellin' at them."

Realizing that she wasn't going to prove an absence of racism (and silently wondering to herself if she was indeed picking on Antwon unnecessarily), Ms. Petersen tells him, "We'll talk about this after class, Antwon. Please see me then, but right now all I am asking is that you and your group use your class time to work on the project, not socialize."

In their discussion after class, Ms. Petersen asks Antwon if he really thinks of her as "a racist."

"Sometimes," he says as he looks into the hallway for friends.

Ms. Petersen asks, "What can I do to convince you otherwise?"

"Stop picking on me," he replies quickly.

"Well, if you mean holding you accountable for your behavior, trying to get you to do your best, and removing you from the room when you're disturbing others, I can't stop doing those things, Antwon." As he stood there waiting to be excused, Ms. Petersen remembered that Antwon and Julian were friends, so she remarked, "Julian hasn't claimed I am a racist or that I pick on him because he is Black. How do you explain that?"

Quietly, with a measured pace, Antwon replies, "Ms. Petersen, Julian isn't Black. He's Haitian. You're pickin' on me 'cuz I'm Black, and you don't pick on him 'cuz he isn't, and that's racist. Can I go to my next class now?" Not knowing what to say or how to make sense of Antwon's explanation, Ms. Petersen simply writes Antwon a pass to Mr. Campbell's world history class upstairs.

Given situations like these and the markedly different developmental issues in each of Cross's stages, it is easy to see how classroom, cafeteria, bus stop, assembly, and hallway interracial conflicts might arise from the ways in which adolescents organize their identities around racial categories. Although it may be youth of color who often resist, reject, or rebel against a racialized experience or utterance, it is developmentally counterproductive to blame them for illuminating it; rather, it is critical in such moments to remember that the dominant culture fuels these crises of identity and creates the possibility for conflicts to emerge between differently empowered or devalued youth within those hierarchies. All adolescents and youth need to be shown the effects of their language and actions and be held accountable for them. As school-based professionals, the trick is to see how adolescents' language may suggest the ways in which they are orienting themselves racially. The ideal intervention is to engage what they say and do, and to find out how they understand and experience their words and actions.

What Cross's developmental model suggests is a movement through phases where emotions and attitudes shift depending on one's awareness of and confrontation with racial differences and that there are some phases in which it makes perfect sense to expect conflict. To suppose that Black youth will move through these phases of identity development without experiencing conflict in their relationships with White peers, White teachers, or other White school personnel is to ignore the developmental insights this model supplies. Too often, adults unfamiliar with the particulars of racial identity development theory are unaware of how certain behaviors associated with each stage may actually be psychologically healthy and developmentally necessary, even if experienced by Whites as scornful or threatening. This lack of awareness contributes to such labels as "rude," "disrespectful," "volatile," "reverse-racists," or simply "dangerous" being applied to Black youth who may be struggling with identity concerns in the Immersion/Emersion stage. Consequently, those youth who perceive the injustices and inequities from a marginalized position and resist them in words and actions often get stereotyped into the "angry Black male" or the "angry Black female" archetype. This label may be experienced by adolescents as a reduction or a dismissal, especially when their critiques are heard only as artifacts of a "phase they'll get through."

For the adolescent, one's racial identity is not experienced as a phase—it is experienced as "me." It is important to keep in mind that experiences of marginalization and discrimination strike at the deepest levels of identity and radically shape how individuals relate to others and to the world. Being conversant with racial identity development theory gives us the tools to interrupt such labeling and help prevent our students from being misunderstood because of it.

Taking these insights into account, it is no surprise to Mr. Campbell that Antwon is getting in trouble for his race-sensitive orientation, his tendency to react with anger at fairly straightforward requests, and his resistance to classwork. Mr. Campbell remembers doing the same things himself back when he was in high school. But now, Mr. Campbell has three years of experience as a classroom teacher and a lifetime of experience as an African American male. Although his middle-class upbringing sometimes complicates his ability to understand Antwon's behavior, Mr. Campbell can and does relate to Antwon better than most of his other teachers. Seldom *requesting* that Antwon do anything and more often *telling* him what he *will* do, Mr. Campbell pushes Antwon to resist the racism he observes around him but to think hard about the effects of that resistance on his long-term prospects for success.

"Look," he says to Antwon as they eat pizza in his classroom during a Friday lunch, "fighting racism by getting angry and speaking out is one thing—and it is a good thing—but letting that anger get the best of you so they have reason to throw you out of school is letting them win. You wanna resist racism? Get A's, go to college, and get the power you need to protect yourself from its effects. Just do it with integrity and a commitment to help others like you."

Realizing his comment could be understood as tacit acceptance of Ms. Petersen's alleged racism, Mr. Campbell reiterates his support for her. "Ms. Petersen is an excellent teacher. Who else does such a good job teaching Achebe and Antigone and actually talking about race issues and working with you all to pass your state exam? She cares, she wants you to succeed, and she may pick on you until you get there."

Sensing that Mr. Campbell was protecting his colleague at the expense of seeing how race impacts his relationship with her, Antwon remarks, "Then she oughta do a better job at picking on all students, not just the Black ones. All she wants to do is prove to me that she isn't racist when I know she is."

"I hear you, Antwon," replies Mr. Campbell, "and you know more than anyone what it's like to be you, and it's important for you two to be able to talk these things through. But keep in mind that she doesn't see it the way you do, and she has more power in this situation. You must find a way to be true to what you know without making things a hassle for yourself. What can I do to help?"

Antwon thinks for a moment, then asks, "Can you talk to her about it?"

"Sure thing. But you must promise to tone things down for a few days until I do. If you go off in class or tell everyone I am on Ms. Petersen's case, you'll set me up and put me in a tough spot with her. You know what I mean?"

Rising to leave for his next class, Antwon mutters, "Yeah, Mr. Campbell, I get it."

White racial identity development theory

Racial identity development theory has primarily been applied to people of color, as if to suggest that European Americans have no "race." This fact has been remedied in recent years with significant work on White racial identity development.[19] Researchers in this field point out, however, that even when White racial identity development is discussed, "it is done in terms of [Whites'] political views or in terms of how they view people in *other* racial groups"[20] rather than how Whites come to know of themselves as White. This is not surprising, due to the fact that "Whiteness" has long been the racial-cultural norm in the United States. Consequently, people of color are often forced to construct identities in response to a dominant culture most closely associated with Whites, and in which Whites are often not aware of themselves as "raced" unless forced to respond to "others" who are "nonWhite."

This difference in orientation to the dominant culture explains why anxiety and conflict often arise when Black and White identities interact with one another, especially in classrooms of adolescents where so much identity work is occurring. This fact is underscored when we realize through racial identity development theory that both Black and White adolescents (and adults) often seek to define themselves in contradistinction to the other (a not-White identity versus a not-Black one) on a social playing field that is anything but even. Despite the meritocratic rhetoric of public education, schools have been and continue to be instrumental in reproducing the racial hierarchies of the larger society in which White is privileged and Black is marginalized.[21] Black-White identity encounters therefore cannot be understood without interrogating these power differentials. Seen in this way, any developmental practice that proceeds as if these encounters occur in a raceless or somehow color-blind ecology is not only counterintuitive but developmentally negligent.

Thinking developmentally about how White adolescents acquire and construct a racial identity requires us to consider the processes through which they make meaning around their identities as White people, particularly in terms of how they think about and respond to people of color. According to Janet Helms, White racial identity development necessarily involves both the rejection of racism and the adoption of an antiracist White identity. In order to achieve the latter, Helms contends that a White person "must accept his or her own Whiteness, the cultural implication of being White, and define a view of the Self as a racial being that does not depend on the perceived superiority of one racial group over another."[22] Helms's model has six statuses, the first three of which proceed toward the abandonment of a racist identity while the last three reflect a movement toward a nonracist White identity (see table 7.3).

The insights in Helms's model suggest how important it is to think developmentally when analyzing and addressing adolescent behavior in schools. Being able to read an adolescent's comments and actions with an eye toward the ways in which they are organizing their identity around racial constructs can help us assist them. For example, Lisa Prescott's difficulty in working with Antwon and her tendency to boss him around in group work may stem from her distrust of his abilities and her lack of relationships with any students of color. Having moved into the large, comprehensive Central High from her suburban, mostly White middle school, Lisa may possess unexamined assumptions about what students like Antwon are like and are capable of academically. As a result, she may need to be pushed on those assumptions and given multiple opportunities to consider the impact of her thinking. When a White adolescent like Lisa presents a Contact, Reintegration, or even a Pseudo-Independent status, it is quite possible that he or she may experience difficulty in working with peers or teachers of color, particularly if the peers or teachers are in Cross's Immersion/Emersion stage. Developmental mismatches like these have the potential to produce rapidly escalating conflicts that emerge both from misunderstandings and actual discriminatory acts. Robert Carter has analyzed these mismatches and characterized them into four different types.[23] His typology, seen in table 7.4, helps us see how contrasting social locations and developmental levels shape how people enter into and understand relationships across racial differences.

When we incorporate such theory into our work with youth, it is important to realize that developmental analyses such as Helms's and Carter's are
not meant to excuse racist behavior, eliminate accountability, or defend ways
of communicating that harm others. Instead, such theory allows us to consider what might be going on for White adolescents as they construct their identity, and how we might help them move toward anti-racist modes of self- and
other-understanding. To do so is to open the possibility that White adolescents may see themselves and others more expansively and to participate in
the interruption of the racism that places the development of all of us at risk.

Mr. Campbell peeks his head into Ms. Petersen's room during her prep
period the next Monday and asks, "Got a minute?"

"Sure," she says. "What can I do for you, Lionel?"

He takes his seat and, after asking Ms. Petersen how she's doing, begins
by describing his discussion with Antwon. "Antwon came to talk to me
the other day, and he's feeling pretty angry about a lot of things."

"Yeah, I've noticed. He called me a racist last week in class and it made
for some pretty tense moments. I'm not sure what steps to take to
address his concerns. What do you think is going on?"

"Well, I talked with him about what he notices in school and in society,
and it seems he's become sensitized to injustice, specifically around race
issues, and he is beginning to see how some of his school experiences are
racialized."

"Did he tell you about our interaction?" Ms. Petersen asked.

"He did. I was clear with him that I had the utmost confidence in you as
a talented and devoted teacher and that you cared deeply about his academic and personal development. I also reiterated how you are charged
with teaching a whole classroom, not just him, and he got that. But he
really feels as though he is undervalued and dismissed by you sometimes,
that you pick on him because he's Black. So he asked me to talk with you
about it and I said I would, as long as he agreed to take some responsibility to work things out. What do you think is going on?"

Thinking for a second, Ms. Petersen answered, "Well, I think two things
are going on. One, Antwon's got a fire in him that just recently got lit,

TABLE 7.3: White Racial Identity Development

Phase	Status	Beliefs and Values	Actions and Affiliations
Phase 1: Abandonment of Racism	Contact	possesses naïve curiosity or timidity and trepidation about people of color learned from friends, family, or the media; seeks limited interracial or occupational interaction wth people of color unless that interaction is initiated by people of color who "seem White"	oblivious to own racial identity; benefits from institutional and cultural racism without necessarily being aware of it; may enjoy being racist since a confrontation with moral dilemmas in being so has not occurred; may say things such as "You don't act like a Black person," or "I don't notice race"
	Disintegration	conscious though conflicted acknowledgment of one's Whiteness; guilt, depression, helplessness, and anxiety may occur when the individual confronts the emotional discomfort of not being able to rectify an appreciation of morality, freedom, democracy, compassion, dignity, and respect with the oppression and injustice occasioned through racism	first acknowledgment of White identity; to reduce dissonance, individual may avoid further contact with people of color, attempt to convince significant others that people of color are not so inferior, seek information from Whites and/or people of color that either racism is not the White person's fault or does not really exist; individual may interact only with those who can be counted on to support the new belief
	Reintegration	out of a desire to be accepted by one's own racial group, the individual accepts the belief in White racial superiority and the inferiority of people of color; privileges and preferences are believed to be earned and race-related negative social conditions are assumed to result from people's of color inferior social, moral, and intellectual capacities	idealizes Whites; denigrates people of color; selectively attends to and/or reinterprets information to conform to societal stereotypes of people of color; cross-racial similarities are minimized or denied; any residual feelings of guilt or anxiety are transformed into fear and anger toward people of color

Phase 2: Defining a Non-Racist White Identity		
Pseudo-Independent	begins to question his or her previous definition of Whiteness and the justifiability of racism in any of its forms; begins to acknowledge the responsibility of Whites for racism, but cultural or racial differences are likely to be interpreted by using White life experiences as the standard; no longer comfortable with a racist identity; begins searching for a better definition of Whiteness	intellectualized acceptance of own and others' race; submersion of the tumultuous feelings about Whiteness that were aroused in previous stages; may feel commiseration with people of color and disquietude concerning racial issues/jokes/slurs in White peer groups; often as uncomfortable with Whites as with people of color
Immersion/ Emersion	honest appraisal of racism and significance of Whiteness; attempts to redefine White identity positively; successful resolution of this stage apparently requires emotional catharsis in which the person reexamines previous emotions that were denied or distorted; the individual may feel a euphoria akin to a religious rebirth	replacement of racial myths and stereotypes with accurate information about what it means and has meant to be "raced" in United States history; may ask of self, "Who am I racially?" or "Who do I want to be?"; frequent immersion in stories of Whites who have made similar identity journeys; may participate in White consciousness-raising groups; changing people of color is no longer the focus and is displaced by efforts to change Whites
Autonomy	the individual attains racial self-actualization; no desire or need to oppress, idealize, or denigrate people on the basis or racial group membership exists; it becomes possible to abandon personal racism and resist cultural and institutional forms; increasing awareness of how other forms of oppression (sexism, classism, homophobia, etc.) are related to racism	internalizes a multicultural identity with non-racist Whiteness as its core; he/she internalizes, nurtures, and applies the new definition of Whiteness in situations aimed at ending oppression and establishing justice; actively seeks opportunities to learn from other groups; openness to new information and new ways of thinking about racialized interactions

Adapted from Janet E. Helms, *Black and White Racial Identity: Theory, Research, and Practice* (Westport, CT: Greenwood Press, 1990), 49–66.

and he needs to find a place or some relationships that can help him deal with it. Sounds like he found you, which I think is perfect. And two, I think Antwon sometimes uses his ' 'cuz I'm Black' claim to get me to back off and lower my expectations for him. And it's tricky, because it does make me back off. It does make me think twice. And I have lowered my expectations on occasion out of fear of being perceived as a racist. But the truth is, he needs to work harder, and it's possible he may not pass the state test if he doesn't, so I'm torn. I want to hear his concerns and look into whether I do have some racial blind spots, but I also don't want him to ever get away with using that claim manipulatively, as a crutch. You know?"

Leaning back in his chair as he considers her remarks, Mr. Campbell says, "Wow. I'm glad he has you as his language arts teacher. Sounds like you're on it. I think that's great. I have a suggestion for how you might talk to him about it sometime if you'd like to hear it."

"I'm all ears, Lionel."

"Okay. So it's like this: Antwon needs to know that you understand and are willing to consider his perspective on your interactions as valid. He wants to talk about the impact. Now, if you're like me, when someone claims I did something I don't think I did, I want to talk with that person about what I meant. I wanna talk about my intentions. The way I think it might work well for you both is to focus on the difference between Antwon's view of what's going on and how it impacts him, and your view of what's going on and what your intentions are."

"That makes sense, Lionel. I'll give it a try."

"And here's the trick. You gotta let him start and let him get all the way through explaining what he sees and how it impacts him. Let him talk about interactions and his understanding of them, but make sure he tells you how that made him feel. Don't interrupt him unless it's to ask for further clarification. Just listen. Then, you tell him what you heard him say, repeating back to him what he observed, and validate it as real. Ask him if he feels like he's been understood, and if he says yes, then and only then do you describe what your intentions are. You might consider high-lighting your concerns about lowered expectations, the state exam, and

TABLE 7.4: Racial Identity Development Applied to Social Interactions

Type of Relationship	Developmental Level of the Person with *More Power/Privilege*	Developmental Level of the Person with *Less Power/Privilege*	Characteristics of the Relationship
Parallel	both at the same level		Both persons express the same type of attitudes about their own race and the race of others. The relationship is self-validating and socially confirming, placid but stagnant. The person with less power acquires no new information about how to deal with racial stimuli. Neither party is presented with opportunities to challenge their racial identity status.
Regressive	less advanced	more advanced	From the perspective of the person with *more* power/privilege, the relationship produces anxiety, resistance, and anger. Little growth is facilitated in either party even though the possibility exists here for the more powerful/privileged person to learn from the less powerful/privileged. Often the person with more power/privilege claims to be misunderstood and seeks to clarify her/his intentions at the expense of the impact their expressions may have caused.
Crossed	less advanced	more advanced	The person with *less* power/privilege feels disregarded, devalued, and dismissed in the interaction. There is likely conflict and suppression, and the core dynamic often centers around expressions of oppositional positions in which the less powerful/privileged person's experiences and feelings are often denied. Here the less powerful/privileged person may seek to have the impact of the more powerful/privileged person's comments or actions understood, and she may be less concerned with the apparent intentions underlying that expression.
Progressive	more advanced	less advanced	The more powerful/privileged person is in a position to help the less powerful participant deepen his understanding of issues surrounding race and racial identity. Depending on the communicative qualities of the relationship, the less powerful/privileged person may be open to hearing and incorporating some of this knowledge as he complexifies his racial identity status.

Adapted from R. T. Carter, "Reimagining Race in Education: A New Paradigm from Psychology," *Teachers College Record* 102, no. 5 (2000): 864–97.

your perception that he sometimes does the ''cuz I'm Black' thing to keep from having to do work. Make sure he can hear that you're working to safeguard his success. Does that makes sense?"

"Yeah, that helps a lot, Lionel. Where'd you come up with that?"

"A buddy of mine is one of those 'diversity trainers' for corporations, and he uses that approach all the time. Seems to work when folks are coming to a racial situation from different perspectives."

Mr. Campbell and Ms. Petersen continue to compare notes on Antwon for a while before parting so they can get back to grading papers. Whereas she was worried about her declining relationship with Antwon before her meeting with Mr. Campbell, she now looks forward to hearing what Antwon has to say. She's curious as to whether he will openly share how he is making sense of their interactions in class. She wonders too how she will respond if Antwon maintains his resistance. Her friend Lionel made this all seem so clear, and seemed to have a great deal of faith in her capacity to reach Antwon. How rare it is to have a colleague who is so insightful and honest, she thought. "I hope I can deliver on his faith in me," she says just loud enough to hear as she stares at her stack of papers, realizing she better get focused if she's going to get home before dark.

CHAPTER EIGHT

Ethnic Identity Development

IT'S MORE COMPLICATED THAN A BLACK–WHITE BINARY

Racial and ethnic identity development are complexly interrelated processes that extend far beyond the Black-White starting point presented in chapter 7. What sense do we make of a 15-year-old Haitian immigrant who does not think of himself as Black even though he has been attending U.S. schools since early childhood? And how do we understand this boy's cousin who was born in the U.S. to Haitian immigrant parents but presents a very different identity, displaying a "hardcore" attitude more aligned with his Black friends than his cousin? What might be going on developmentally for a Latina who is thrilled about her upcoming quinceañera when in the presence of her family and Chicano/a friends but largely silent on the issue at school? What do we make of the Hmong student who resents having to fill in the "Asian" bubble on his college applications? If, as educators, we hope to grapple with these questions at a level commensurate with their complexity, we must look carefully at the many intersections of race and ethnicity, and the multiple identity options these intersections provide.

We began our presentation of race and ethnicity by underscoring the tensions we have seen in Black student–White teacher dynamics, and to begin where the country's race-based struggles have been centered historically. But the Black-White analysis presented in chapter 7 is intended to serve as a starting point for exploring the more fine-grained race and ethnicity interactions that emerge in our work. To help fill in the gaps in the academic literature on racially and ethnically marginalized youth, ethnic identity has emerged as a distinct developmental concept from the void left by race-based analyses that focused solely on White-Black dynamics.[1] Although disparate in their histories, sociopolitical contexts, and geographic locations, many ethnic groups in the United States share with people of African descent the marginalizing experience of being outside and below the dominant White "majority."[2] A number of identity development theories of nonBlack people of color trace paths similar to the ones outlined by Cross. Tatum, for example, points out that although the identity development of Asian, Latino/a, and Native American people is not included in Cross's theoretical formulation, "there is evidence to suggest that the process for these oppressed groups is similar to that described for African Americans. In each case, it is assumed that a positive sense of one's self as a member of one's group (which is not based on any assumed superiority) is important for psychological health."[3]

Because there are striking similarities between aspects of racial and ethnic identity development, it is common to conflate the two concepts. Race is indeed part of ethnicity and vice versa, but they are not the same thing. Researchers such as Janet Helms have compellingly argued for separating the

TABLE 8.1: Summary of Characteristics That Distinguish Race from Ethnicity

Race	Ethnicity
Defines group member's position in a societal hierarchy	Does not define a definite place in a societal hierarchy
For most people, is not mutable	Is mutable for all people
Does not define a single culture	Defines a single culture
Implies knowledge of racism and own-group racial stereotypes	Implies knowledge of own-group culture
Determined by law and custom	Determined by in-group desires
For most people, lasts across generations	For most people, virtually disappears after three generations
Can generally be recognized by out-group members	Can rarely be recognized by out-group members
Does not require the person to do anything to belong	Requires some familiarity with group's culture to belong
Does not require infusion of immigrants or visits to homeland to persist	Requires an ongoing infusion of immigrants or sojourns to a homeland to persist

Adapted from Janet E. Helms, "Toward a Methodology for Measuring and Assessing Racial as Distinguished from Ethnic Identity," in *Multicultural Assessment in Counseling and Clinical Psychology*, ed. G. R. Sodowsky and J. C. Impara (Lincoln, NE: Buros Institute of Mental Measurements, 1996), 143–92.

two categories in research and practice. Drawing upon her arguments, table 8.1 compares ethnic and racial characteristics in order to show how the categories may be considered distinct. Leistyna, however, argues for collapsing them into a single term, *racenicity*, to underscore how any analysis of either race or ethnicity must account for the necessary interaction of the two terms.[4] Addressing one part of the equation without the other is inherently inaccurate, according to this view. Regardless of whether you come down on the side of Helms or Leistyna, the key insight here is to realize that the two categories, race and ethnicity, are layered and integrated. Although researchers and theorists still disagree on the precise definition of *ethnicity* and how it might be distinct from *race* as well as *culture*, the very debate attests to the richness of the topic and its relevance for the youth we serve.

Before delving into the terms we employ to make sense of this contentious topic, we must situate our presentation within the power dynamics that shape it. It has been well established in countless studies that racist and ethnocentric curricula, disciplinary practices, behavioral expectations, policies, assessments, and pedagogies persist in U.S. schools.[5] Well-intentioned educators expend a great deal of energy extolling the virtues of public education as a great equalizer despite much evidence to the contrary. Such rhetoric obscures the social stratifications that are reproduced and reinforced in our schools and can inhibit the development of the constructive alliances necessary to confront these stratifications.

Beyond its political significance, ethnic identity development has enormous implications for psychological well-being. In numerous studies, ethnic identity has been positively associated with self-esteem, self-confidence, and purpose in life. Based on their research, Martinez and Dukes state that "a stronger ethnic identity lessens the impact of negative stereotypes and social denigration in the individual by providing a broader frame of reference for the self that includes additional sources of identity."[6] Because the accumulating research on ethnic identity holds clear implications for developmental understanding and educational practice, our intent for the rest of this chapter is to present emerging issues in ethnic identity development from contemporary theory and research, and to use that knowledge to create scaffolding for educators to support their students and to counter the rhetoric and practices that can deceive us into thinking the playing field is even. Specifically, a better understanding of the processes of ethnic identity development should provide educators with insights required for creating a healthier school climate, designing more culturally relevant lessons and pedagogies, and providing more diversely competent support services.

SHIFTING DEFINITIONS, FIXED SIGNIFICANCE

The literature on ethnic identity development in adolescence builds upon, departs from, and at times rejects such psychological identity theories as Erikson's. Virtually every term employed to define ethnicity is highly contested, as ethnicity itself is a contentious category arising from inquiries that often are politically charged. Our goal is to survey ways of understanding ethnicity that can help educators think broadly about what might be at stake for their students when they confront who they are ethnically. Consistent with the literature, we largely retain Erikson's notion of an identity crisis in order to probe the ways in which specific ethnic groups often handle the differences between the pride they feel in their identity and the ways in which it may be devalued by the mainstream. In doing so, we draw upon more flexible descriptions, such as identi*ties*, *identifications*, *performances*, or even *masks*. Since a primary task of adolescence is "learning to express the multiplicity of one's identity in personally meaningful and socially acceptable ways,"[7] part of thinking developmentally about the ethnic issues adolescents face means preparing ourselves to perceive the complexity of their identities as they change from one day and setting to the next.

In an effort not to restrict our presentation to the *intra*psychic at the expense of the *inter*psychic, we recognize that ethnicity is as much a social phenomenon as it is a psychological one. Humans are "internalized culture," as Vygotsky put it. The legacies of stereotypes, ethnic clashes, intergroup misunderstandings, and institutional decisions exert profound effects on the internalized cultures we become. Just as we come to understand who we are psychologically through our experiences with primary caregivers and other close relationships, we come to understand ourselves ethnically through the cultural affiliations with which we feel most closely connected over the course of our lives. In this sense, culture mediates psychology; our psychological selves are culturally mediated; the outcome of this mediation is our ethnic identity. In the spirit of Erikson's identity statements across the life cycles: "I am who I experience myself to be within my own cultural affiliations, and, perhaps, in opposition to the cultural affiliations of others."

The notion of ethnicity is difficult to pin down partly because, as Hernandez Sheets notes, it operates at two levels—individual and group—

and in two domains—self-given and other-ascribed.[8] To study how those levels and domains interact, one must decide which topics and influences will be ignored as much as which ones to emphasize. Fischer and Moradi and also Phinney identify three traditions of theory and research on ethnic identity that shape what gets revealed and concealed.[9] One tradition emerges from social identity theory, which typically addresses the individual's sense of belonging or "groupness," which, in turn, is believed to help maintain an individual's positive self-concept. Other researchers and theorists come from the identity-formation tradition, which, according to Fischer and Moradi, generally assumes "a process similar to ego identity formation that takes place over time as people explore and make decisions about the role of ethnicity in their lives." A third tradition includes those working within "an acculturation framework whose focus centers on ethnic involvement, or on individuals' acquisition, retention, and maintenance of cultural characteristics."[10]

For educators, it is important to consider insights from each of these traditions, to reflect on the role of belonging, self-esteem, identity formation, and the level of cultural investment students exhibit toward their core ethnic group or groups. The temptation to narrow one's focus may be necessary for researchers as they gather data and disaggregate it in order to make claims about what they have discovered, but for those working with adolescents in schools, the approach needs to be broad and comprehensive. That also makes it complicated. But selectively picking and choosing emphases here holds little practical justification.

To understand ethnic identity development adequately enough to apply it in our work, we must synthesize what have been found to be common components of ethnicity and characteristics of ethnic identity. Ethnicity generally refers to distinctions based on national origin, language, religion, diet, styles of dress, modes of communication, and other cultural markers. This makes it seem nearly synonymous with culture, but as Hernandez Sheets points out, "The concept of *ethnicity* is narrower than the concept of *culture*, and although they are related, it is not a one-to-one relationship. Ethnic identity formation and development is influenced by membership in an ethnic group identified as a distinctive social group living under the shaping influence of a common culture."[11] Given this observation, it makes sense to augment our developmental analysis with insights from sociology and anthropology.

SOCIAL AND ANTHROPOLOGICAL INSIGHTS

Ethnic identity development in the United States evolves through the individual's experiences of dominant cultural norms relative to messages received from one's family and friends. Two theories of acculturation account for this process: the *linear model* and the *bidimensional model*. The linear model ascribes an inverse relationship between ethnicity and acculturation (i.e., the more people acculturate, the less they retain their ethnicity, and the less they acculturate, the more they retain their ethnicity) and therefore "assumes that individuals either maintain strong connections to their native cultures or develop strong ties to the dominant culture." The bidimensional model "assumes that an individual's relationship to that person's own culture is distinct from that person's relationship to the dominant culture."[12] Because this theory assumes that people can be bicultural, accentuating or minimizing their ethnicity or even expressing multiple authentic identities depending on the requirements of the context, it lends itself to a more flexible understanding of how adolescents may develop their ethnic identity. While the linear model may have merit when it comes to recognizing the extent to which people are sometimes compelled to assimilate in an either/or fashion (i.e., "either you're American or you're not"), restricting our understanding to such a binary ignores the range of resolutions adolescents construct to manage the tensions between self and society.

As with the theories of acculturation, sociologists and anthropologists divide into two camps as they explain the notion of ethnicity. There are primordialists who "maintain that ethnic groups are essentially cultural groups . . . [who] share a common tradition and history . . . bound together by birth . . . [where] the loss of culture signals the loss of ethnicity." Ethnicity then, from the primordialist perspective, is "an emotional attachment to one's cultural heritage."[13] Instrumentalists, however, argue that ethnicity is less an issue of emotional attachment and instead argue that ethnic groups are interest groups, relied on when political or social interests make it advantageous to do so. While instrumentalists do not equate culture with ethnicity, they often point out that culture is used strategically to mark ethnic group boundaries. Instrumentalists emphasize the ways in which the cultural practices of specific ethnic groups change according to the group's needs over time and in different contexts and stress the agency many individuals possess when they choose whether or not to identify as a member of an ethnic group.

For example, many Whites in the United States choose to accentuate a symbolic ethnicity during holidays, festivals, or in association with sports teams, specific cuisine, or neighborhood affiliations, in that they highlight their Irish, Italian, Scotch, Finnish, Lithuanian, Dutch, French, or French Canadian roots. For people whose appearances, language, and cultural characteristics mark them as mainstream, "ethnic identity is an option that can be appealed to whenever it is desired."[14] While this is true for some Whites, others uncritically assimilate the cultural criteria of dominant racist values and practices and as a result are unable to situate themselves historically. As Martinez and Dukes put it, "Their ethnic identity is so secure and taken for granted that they are unaware of it."[15] As such, taking on a symbolic ethnic identity is a matter of choice for most Whites: those who claim a nonmainstream ethnic identity are typically able to pass in society as a "nonethnic" member of the dominant majority and benefit from the privileges that that apparent lack of ethnicity confers. For others, however, such a choice may not be an option. Hernandez Sheets points out that "the assumption regarding choice denies the fact that ethnicity is often imposed on people,"[16] that people are often categorized by others in a manner outside their control. This categorization is inseparable from power relations that are often mediated by racial, linguistic, and cultural characteristics devalued by the dominant majority.

As an example, Lorena Chávez, a Chicana with darker skin and a discernible accent whom we last met in chapter 6, does not have a choice as to whether she will be "ethnic" when she enters mainstream U.S. society—that choice is already made for her. Sometimes the categories themselves impose a certain choicelessness, as is the case with pan-ethnic labels that lump together various ethnic groups into one. Differences between Brazilian, Colombian, Salvadoran, Nicaraguan, Costa Rican, Honduran, Guatemalan, and Mexican cultures render the term "Latino/a" essentially meaningless for many. The term "Asian American" glosses over crucial historical, cultural, religious, and linguistic differences among Filipino, Vietnamese, Hmong, Cambodian, Japanese, Chinese, Mongolian, Burmese, Nepalese, Tibetan, Taiwanese, Bengali, and Balinese immigrants (to name only a few). Steve Chang (whom we met in chapters 5 and 6), is often referred to as "Asian" by his teachers even though he understands himself to be Korean or Korean American, depending on the context. The differences between Haitian, Dominican, Puerto Rican, Cuban, Trinidadian, Bajan, and Jamaican students make the term "Caribbean American" somewhat baseless as well. However, sometimes pan-ethnic terms work for certain students. Such is the case with Julian Thomas (chapters 2 and 3) in that he prefers to be understood as "Caribbean

American" or "Haitian" rather than "Black" due to the societal implications of being associated with what he has been taught to recognize as the "Black underclass." Such designations are layered with racialized meaning, and this is evident in the ways Whites, too, have had pan-ethnic categories imposed on them. As Cornel West observes, "European immigrants arrived on American shores perceiving themselves as 'Irish,' 'Sicilian,' 'Lithuanian,' and so forth. They had to learn that they were 'White' principally by adopting American discourse of positively valued Whiteness and negatively charged Blackness."[17]

In the end, what is important for the educator to remember here is that the acceptance or rejection of the categories used to label ethnic groups has everything to do with who is doing the naming and what its purpose is. Categories are often imposed merely as a matter of convenience and, like the primordialist and instrumentalist positions above, are seldom able to capture the diversity of ethnic expressions and experiences found in our society and schools. Efforts at explanation through reduction may offer hope for understanding broad trends, but they come at the expense of the diversity that gave them life in the first place. So we need to be careful with categories and typologies, even though they serve definitional purposes. To meet the needs of our students, it is essential to find out from *them* what terms they use to describe themselves and then look to theory to help us contextualize and use that understanding in our work.

> Lorena Chávez has been confronting ethnic labels and trying to figure out which ones make the most sense since she was a young child. She remembers being asked by her third-grade teacher, "Where are you from?" and being laughed at by the class when, in response, she gave her street address a few blocks from the school. Now, when she's asked that question, she simply responds "Here," and if asked for her "nationality," she puts her hands on her hips, scowls, and says, "I'm a U.S. citizen." But these questions and her answers to them belie a deeper ongoing struggle within Lorena as to which parts of her are Chicana and which are more aligned with the majority culture. Perhaps the proudest day of her life thus far was during her freshman-year quinceañera when her father placed high-heeled shoes on her feet, her mother a tiara on her head, and she paraded through the ballroom filled with family and friends, recognized for the first time as a young woman. Since that day, however, she's become more and more aware of the demands placed on her iden-

tity as she negotiates ethnically and racially charged situations. In some settings, she is a Chávez; in others, she is a Chicana, a "loud Latina," a "feminista," a rower, or just a Central High student, each venue requiring different aspects of her to rise to the surface and others to be hidden. Living in an ethnic enclave community between Fifth and Washington where most of the Chicano-Latino community resides (and becoming aware of the fact that outsiders pejoratively refer to it as "little Tijuana"), Lorena has grown up among a tightly knit extended family. Speaking mainly Spanish and observing all the cultural traits she associates with being *Mexicana*, Lorena's ethnic identity as a child leaned much closer to the Mexican than the American part of her hyphenated identity.

As she moved into middle school and high school, however, her outspoken tendencies and her refusal to allow any perceived disrespect to go unchallenged got her into fights, particularly when that disrespect pertained to her ethnicity. The opportunity to become a rower helped divert some of that intensity into athletics, and the development she experienced on the river motivated her to apply herself academically and to invest in relationships with non-Chicana friends. She learned to love being on the river, being an athlete, and feeling smart in school. But such experiences often exposed a bifurcation in Lorena's identity, as if the Chicana parts of her could only compete with the "gringa" aspects. Admitting to one of her Black friends in the rowing program that she mostly prefers to speak Spanish, Lorena explains, "Like I'd rather speak Spanish because I guess I feel it in my body more, you know? Like I feel at home in it, like I can relax into it. English feels like somebody else's words, you know? And my P.E. teacher? He like always talks Spanish with me and it's so fun 'cuz none of my teachers speak Spanish, yo, except for him, even though he sounds funny 'cuz like he learned it in Spain in college and stuff. But I know like I have an accent and that some people in jobs or businesses or whatever don't like that."

With increasing regularity, Lorena peppers her conversations like this with allusions to college and the job world beyond high school, hedged as they are by an awareness of discrimination. The rowing experience introduced her to those possibilities, and they have provided her with thrilling visions of possible futures even as they scare her with the prospect of growing apart from her family and ethnic origins. Projecting herself into adulthood as a coach, an athletic trainer, or a doctor of sports medicine, Lorena's college and career ambitions force her to examine her ethnic identity and confront the fact that, as a Chicana, she never feels as valued outside her community as she does inside. While her parents are thrilled with the idea that she may be the first to attend college, some members of Lorena's family are less enthusiastic. Referring to the stereotypes some outsiders have of her, Lorena admits to her coach, "People just expect me to have babies and make tamales. And like, my grandmother I think would love that, but I don't wanna do that, you know? I don't want to live my whole life between Fifth and Washington, okay? I'm just afraid that if I leave I can't ever come back."

GENERAL DEVELOPMENTAL INSIGHTS INTO ETHNIC IDENTITY

As Lorena's example demonstrates, questions of ethnic identity cut to the core of who adolescents understand themselves to be. Who am I in connection with others who are ethnically similar to me? Who am I in response to the mainstream culture? How must I change the way I represent myself depending on who is with me and where I am? How do my school experiences shape the growing understanding I have of my ethnic self? Adolescent questions like these demonstrate how a developmental approach is essential if we are to understand the processes by which youth organize their self-concepts and form attitudes toward their own ethnicity and the dominant culture. Research indicates that the processes by which adolescents ethnically self-identify and gain a sense of belonging and pride in their ethnic group seem to be present regardless of the group to which one claims membership.

Like the identity development models explored in previous chapters, crisis and commitment are essential markers of a person's ethnic self-concept. Crises occur as the adolescent (or child or adult) confronts the different messages received about her ethnic identity, namely those emerging from ethnic peers and mentors as well as those coming from the dominant culture. Commitments are formed based upon perceived levels of safety and opportunities for full expression of the self. Isajiw defines this process "as a manner in which persons account for their ethnic origin, locate themselves psychologically in relation to one or more social systems, and in which they perceive others as locating them."[18] Individuals need a firm sense of group identification in order to maintain a sense of well-being; simply being a member of a group provides individuals with a sense of belonging that contributes to a positive self-concept.

A person's positive self-concept, however, also depends on the extent to which she can bring that identity into society beyond her ethnic group and experience it being valued. If the dominant group in a society holds the characteristics of an ethnic group in low esteem, then ethnic group members are potentially faced with a negative social identity. This is the crisis: how to reconcile the external experience of being marginalized with the internal need to feel safe and secure in one's identity. If an ethnic identity gets neglected or forced underground, significant stress and emotional turmoil can result. The developmental as well as the academic implications of this are clear.

Figure 8.1 depicts the ways in which the resolution of ethnic identity varies according to the ways in which one identifies with both the majority group and the ethnic group. Each of the four resolutions can be psychologically and socially healthy for the individual, just as each may be unhealthy. All resolutions depend on the context(s) in which the individual lives. This chart indicates that a particular adolescent's perceived ethnic characteristics signal nothing about how committed they may be to their ethnic identity.

FIGURE 8.1:   Effect of Varying Identifications with Majority and Ethnic Group

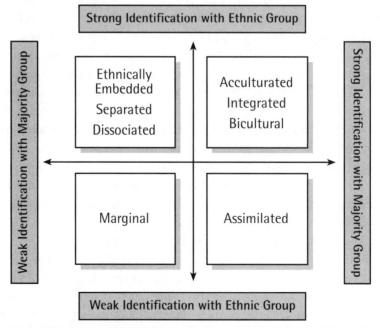

Adapted from J. Phinney, "Stages of Ethnic Identity Development in Minority Group Adolescents," *Journal of Early Adolescence* 9, no. 1-2 (1989): 34–49.

Each individual must resolve the crisis of ethnic versus dominant identifications, and there is no singular "healthy" or "correct" way to do this.

Similar to figure 8.1, figure 8.2 depicts people's orientation toward their ethnic identity, with the two axes being their psychic investment in assimilation versus ethnicity. It shows that the resolution of a person's ethnic identity naturally follows the decisions they make (or are forced to make) and the energies they devote to it. Stressing the distinctiveness of one's own group leads either to a traditionalist adherence to one's home culture or to a more pluralist orientation toward others, depending on the level of investment in assimilation. Conversely, being less invested in one's own ethnicity leads to either an isolationist or integrationist orientation, depending on the individual's level of commitment to assimilation. Again, what is important for the educator to realize is that all these orientations have the potential to be healthy or unhealthy. Being isolationist may make good sense for an adolescent unmotivated to become "American" and also unconcerned with his ethnic distinctiveness. Such an individual may be surveying the landscape for a while in a sort of identity moratorium (see chapter 2) and may decide to remain somewhat isolated in order to explore identities in context without having to endure too many risks. Likewise, a different adolescent with a more pluralist orientation may have the capacity to express her identity in ways that mesh with both her ethnic culture and that of the mainstream. Still, as she seeks to remain in relationship with peers and family, she may face others who have different orientations and will have to confront their demands that she choose one or the other. That her orientation may be healthy does not mean it will be experienced as easy, nor does it mean she will necessarily be well received by all others. Accordingly, it is important for educators to realize that these and other explanatory models suggest general trends and should not be used as diagnostic tools to label people. Though it may be helpful to see in a student such as Lorena how she may be moving from an ethnically embedded, traditionalist orientation to one that is more bicultural and pluralist, unless the adults in her life are in conversation with her about how she experiences her ambitions and how they compete with connections to her ethnic heritage, those designations are only guesses. What adolescents are responding to—their contexts—needs to be ascertained in order to understand how their identity is situated and how they may best be served by their school.

In terms of ascribing stages to an adolescent's ethnic identity development, Phinney's model is perhaps the most useful. After analyzing numerous studies, she developed a three-stage progression that roughly encapsulates

FIGURE 8.2: Orientations toward Ethnic Identity

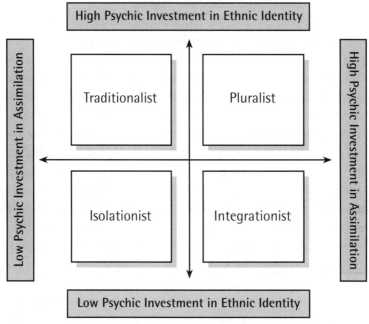

Adapted from A. L. Goodwin, "Growing Up Asian in America: A Search for Self," in *Asian American Identities, Families, and Schooling,* ed. C. C. Park, A. L. Goodwin, and S. J. Lee (Greenwich, CT: Information Age, 2003), 19–20.

the many models, which differ according to specific ethnic group experiences (see table 8.2 for examples). In the first stage, the individual possesses an *unexamined ethnic identity*. This is characterized by a preference for the dominant culture, a general disinterest in ethnic considerations, or an unexamined positive ethnic attitude absorbed from parents or other significant adults. Drawing a distinction between an unexamined ethnic identity that is diffuse and one that is foreclosed, Phinney observes that "young people may simply not be interested in ethnicity and may have given it little thought (their ethnic identity is diffuse). Alternatively, they may have absorbed positive ethnic attitudes from parents or other adults and therefore may not show a preference for the majority group, although they have not thought through the issues for themselves—that is, are foreclosed."[19] For adolescents with foreclosed unexamined ethnic identities, ethnicity is basically an unconsidered yet fundamental part of who they are. There is neither a commitment to the identity nor a crisis that would cause them to question it. Their ethnic identity *just is*, central to who they are in an unexamined way. For adolescents with diffuse ethnic identities, views of ethnicity are derived from others and received in an unquestioned manner.

In Phinney's second stage, the adolescent begins to search for an authentic ethnic identity that can resolve the conflicts experienced when confronting both the ethnic and mainstream groups' expectations. Similar to the moratorium status described by Marcia and the encounter stage illustrated by Cross, the *ethnic identity search* may occur in response to an interaction or event that compels the individual to recognize his ethnicity. An adolescent in this stage often immerses himself in his own culture by reading texts, speaking more often in his native language, attending cultural events, or visiting ethnic museums. Many adolescents in this stage may reject the values and impositions of the dominant culture as a way of maintaining cultural boundaries and preserving an unsteady but growing recognition of the salience of ethnicity in their lives. This may sensitize such youth to issues of tolerance or the rhetoric of diversity often expressed in schools, which can cause the searching adolescent to be critical of the normative assumptions that often lie beneath such messages. Teachers, counselors, and administrators unaware of the developmental aspects of ethnic identity may mislabel such behavior as combative or destructively rebellious and miss the opportunity to engage their students at the very heart of their current development.

When the ethnic identity search process settles, at least temporarily, into a state of critically reflective equilibrium, according to Phinney, a deeper understanding and appreciation of one's ethnicity is achieved. When adolescents (or adults) enter Phinney's third stage, they are said to possess an *achieved ethnic identity* status. Here, the individual "[comes] to terms with two fundamental problems for ethnic minorities: (a) cultural differences between their own group and the dominant group, and (b) the lower or disparaged status of their group in society."[20] Adolescents with achieved ethnic identities may not always demonstrate a high degree of ethnic involvement, since it is quite possible that they could be confident in their ethnicity without wanting to maintain their cultural characteristics such as language, dress, diet, religion, etc. As with previous stage models, many theorists have suggested that the ethnic identity development process does not end with an achieved ethnic identity, since individuals may further explore their identities as they grow older, immerse themselves in new contexts, or rethink previous resolutions and modify them based on new relationships. Thus, these three stages may imply a cyclical process as much as they do a linear one. What is becoming increasingly clear in the research, however, is that adolescents who examine and value their ethnic identity as a crucial feature of their lives are more likely to demonstrate prosocial behaviors and academic success than those who possess diffuse or foreclosed ethnic identities.

TABLE 8.2: Representative Quotations from Each Stage of Ethnic Identity Development

UNEXAMINED

Diffusion

"My past is back there; I have no reason to worry about it. I'm American now." (Mexican American male)

"Why do I need to learn about who was the first Black woman to do this or that? I'm just not too interested." (Black female)

"My parents tell me . . . about where they lived, but what do I care? I've never lived there." (Mexican American male)

Foreclosure

"I don't go looking for my culture. I just go by what my parents say and do, and what they tell me to do, the way they are." (Mexican American male)

"If I could have chosen, I would choose to be American White, because it's America and I would then be in my country." (Asian American male)

"I would choose to be White. They have more job opportunities and are more accepted." (Mexican American male)

MORATORIUM

"I want to know what we do and how our culture is different from others. Going to festivals and cultural events helps me to learn more about my own culture and about myself." (Mexican American female)

"I think people should know what Black people had to go through to get where we are now." (Black female)

"There are a lot of non-Japanese people around me, and it gets pretty confusing to try and decide who I am." (Asian American male)

ACHIEVED

"People put me down because I'm Mexican, but I don't care anymore. I can accept myself more." (Mexican American female)

"I have been born Filipino and am born to be Filipino. . . . I'm here in America, and people of many different cultures are here too. So I don't consider myself only Filipino, but also American." (Asian American male)

"I used to want to be White, because I wanted long flowing hair. And I wanted to be real light. I used to think being light was prettier, but now I think there are pretty dark-skinned girls and pretty light-skinned girls. I don't want to be White now. I'm happy being Black." (Black female)

Adapted from J. Phinney, "Stages of Ethnic Identity Development in Minority Group Adolescents," *Journal of Early Adolescence* 9, no. 1-2 (1989): 44.

Steve Chang, however, is feeling few of the benefits of an achieved ethnic identity these days. Having more or less possessed an unexamined ethnic identity throughout his childhood, Steve mostly associated with the White friends in his middle-class neighborhood. Whereas some of his "Asian" peers at Central High (who are really Cambodian, Hmong, and Vietnamese) had a much less privileged upbringing, Steve's upper-middle-class household allowed for extracurricular activities and parents with enough social capital to safeguard Steve's education and be available to him to help with homework in the evenings. Benefiting from the "model minority" myth in school, his teachers largely expected him to do well academically and praised him when he did. Lurking underneath these calm waters, however, was a growing sense that the ways in which he was being perceived did not match what he understood of himself internally. This was made obvious to him in sixth grade, when he invited a neighborhood friend who was White to stay over at his house on a Saturday night. Everything was going well until it came time to sit down to dinner. His friend refused to eat the spicy red pepper, garlic, ginger, and mustard-enhanced meal and asked to go home. Distraught that his friend abandoned him, Steve suddenly understood himself as different. From his diet to the language he often spoke at home to the ethnically homogeneous evangelical church he attended with his family on Sunday, Steve had to confront the fact that he was not mainstream, not White. This painful realization in middle school led to a partial retreat into his studies and his violin, activities through which his efforts and accomplishments would be lauded by everyone—everyone, that is, but the peers whose praise he craved the most.

Sort of hanging back and watching, listening to the social cues and surveying the ethnic and racial landscape of his high school, Steve slowly began to formulate theories about how he might fit in. Opportunities to explore his gender identity development through weight lifting and homophobia afforded access to White friends at school that were previously unavailable to him when he had focused solely on academics and orchestra. But those relationships were troublesome, both because those boys often used Steve as the butt of their jokes (as was the case with his revealed crush on Lisa Prescott) and also because they routinely marked him as "other," despite his best efforts to assimilate. They would ask him for help on their math or science homework, assuming that because he was "Chinese" he'd be good at such subject matter, as if that were all he did or could do. Although he didn't mind helping them with their work since he felt it might secure friendships, their erroneous ethnic labeling more than annoyed him. If he bothered to correct their careless ignorance and identify himself as Korean, invariably someone would ask, "You're from Korea?" to which he'd have to correct them again and say, "No, my parents are." And if the inquiry proceeded farther than that (it usually didn't), they'd often ask, "North or South Korea?" Not wanting to launch into a basic history or geography lesson, Steve would simply reply, "Uh, South," but he'd walk away from such interactions a little hurt that he was again made to feel so different when he was working so hard to fit in.

Although Steve's parents and teachers have largely supported his efforts to integrate since he has expressed such tendencies mostly in the form of academic and musical success, given the recent messages of exclusion he's been receiving from his peers, his attempts to assimilate into what he understands to be the dominant culture of Central High are beginning to manifest in risky behaviors. The homophobic remarks and heightened masculinity he performed to resist the feminizing taunts he received from the "jocks" have gotten him into a couple of near-violent altercations. Although he enjoyed the "props" he received from some of the lacrosse players when he "fronted" a ninth-grader who had made fun of his violin playing, he was petrified of actually having to fight one day to prove he was tough. Hanging out after school with some friends who share his love of video games, Steve gets introduced, first, to cigarettes, and to marijuana soon after. At school, his grades are beginning to drop and he begins to adopt a sort of laissez-faire attitude about school in general, propelled by an increasing devotion to violent video games and the use of marijuana. Keeping his parents in the dark with regard to these new activities, and hiding from his friends the fact that he can read and speak Korean and is playing a key role in the planning of the upcoming Korean Festival in a nearby park, Steve is forced to live in two drastically different—and for the moment, irreconcilable—worlds.

Steve's case and the studies noted above make it clear how important ethnicity can be to adolescents constructing their identities and how critical it is that we find ways to promote such development. As educators, we are ideally positioned to hear the myriad ways in which students are making sense of who they are ethnically. These statements are windows into how adolescents may be understanding their ethnic identity, and as such they can help us to know how they are orienting themselves toward their ethnic group as well as the dominant culture. Table 8.2 presents a sampling of typical statements made by adolescent research participants in Phinney's study across three ethnic groups (the Asian American group in her study being pan-ethnic). This table and Phinney's model suggest that significant overlap exists between the ethnic identity development experiences of youth from different ethnic groups. However, many researchers have found variations ranging from subtle to profound in the developmental progressions of different ethnically identified youth. Table 7.1 in chapter 7 is an attempt to present graphically some of those differences.

NARROWING THE SCOPE

While we have presented the more general theories of ethnic identity development and refrained from going group by group to discuss the ways in which each differs from the others, we have done so at the risk of glossing over the countless and momentous distinctions that make ethnic groups and ethnic identity development so unique. As Phinney contends, "The task of understanding ethnic identity is complicated by the fact that the uniqueness that distinguishes each group and setting makes it difficult to draw general conclusions across groups."[21] Indeed, specific ethnic group research will always be fluid, since it depends on culture, which is ever shifting and dynamic, for its definition. The point in surveying recent generalized theory in ethnic identity development here is not to impose a model on all ethnic groups, because to do so would be to ignore the contexts that give each group its richness. Rather, the purpose here is to think developmentally about the social and psychological forces that compel an adolescent to understand herself ethnically and to conceive of ways to participate in that process in order to provide optimal developmental experiences, both in and outside of the classroom. We have chosen not to present a survey of the research and theory describing ethnic identity development as it differs across specific ethnic groups, because to do so would either require more space than we can devote to it or would so drastically reduce the complexity of each group's experience that it would render our treatment dangerously simplistic. Table 7.1, incomplete as it is, suggests that there is much more out there to learn. Difficult as it is to find time amid the realities of our work, it would behoove the educator particularly concerned about such matters to take the general theories detailed here and then consult the research most relevant to the immigrant and ethnic group populations present in one's school.

With these caveats in mind, however, it is useful to examine how researchers and developmentalists understand at least one group, if for no other reason than to demonstrate how much can be learned as the focus is narrowed. When investigating the evolution of specific groups' self-described ethnicity, sociologists used to turn to the *straight-line assimilation theory* to explain the progression of ethnic identities in families across time. This theory understood ethnicity to proceed linearly as the generations progressed, from an immigrant identity struggling to succeed to one that is wholly "American" and economically successful. Adherents to the theory claim that each generation becomes more "American" and raises its social status higher than the previous one. The critique of this "melting pot" theory is that it "pays little attention to the economy in which the immigrants and their descendants work,"[22] leaves little room for agency, and ignores the possibility of a multiplicity of identities within the single person. Newer theories note distinct differences in the ways in which subsequent generations of immigrants, especially immigrants of color, experience U.S. culture and both choose to and are forced to live within it.

For example, jobs that appealed to first-generation immigrants are often turned down by second-generation children reared on U.S. soil. Reasons for this are varied: they learn to evaluate the labor market according to U.S. versus home-country standards, and they do not "have the long-range goals that persuaded their parents to work long hours at low wages; they know they cannot be deported and are here to stay in [the United States]." From the second-generation immigrant's perspective, immigrant jobs may seem demeaning. If schooling fails to offer the means to attain employment beyond such jobs, if the family lacks the social and cultural capital to secure higher-status jobs, and if the young second-generation immigrant is forced to endure the tribulations of concentrated poverty and crime, the potential for a decline in physical health and social well-being rises. That this "second-generational decline" seems to be most pronounced in "poor young men with dark skin if only because all other things being equal, they seem to be the first to be excluded from the labor market when there are more workers than jobs"[23] suggests how highly raced, classed, and gendered this pattern can be. That similar patterns existed a century ago for southern and eastern White European immigrants when they were characterized as "races" points to the arbitrary and shifting construction of "race" and its use as an instrument of control in ethnic populations. An analysis of the differences in the experiences, decisions, and identities between first- and second-generation immigrants of color can therefore illuminate the extent to which ethnicity, race, class, and gender constructs affect adolescent development in this culture and in this historical moment.

Mary Waters's work explores the extent to which contemporary Caribbean American immigrants of color and their children face very different choices and constraints than earlier White immigrants because of the way in which they are defined racially by other Americans. Taking into account the developmental impact of racial and ethnic hierarchies in American culture, Waters rejects the straight-line assimilation model that "assumes an undifferentiated monolithic American culture," choosing instead to stress the fact that immigrants enter a "consciously pluralistic society in which a variety of subcultures and racial and ethnic identities coexist."[24] As an alternative to the straight-line model, Waters draws upon the work of Portes and Zhou, who advocate *segmented assimilation* as a more appropriate descriptor.[25] The focus in this theory is not on the extent to which one assimilates into American society but into what sector of society that assimilation occurs:

> The mode of incorporation of the first generation creates differential opportunities and cultural and social capital in the form of ethnic jobs, networks, and values that create differential pulls on the allegiances [and developing identities] of the second generation. For those immigrant groups who face extreme discrimination in the United States and who reside in close proximity to American minorities who have faced a great deal of discrimination, reactive ethnicity emerges in the first generation. The second-generation youth whose ties to American minorities are stronger and whose parental generation lacks the degree of social capital to provide opportunities and protection for the second generation are likely to develop the "adversarial stance" that American minorities such as poor Blacks and Hispanics hold toward the dominant White society.[26]

Because Waters found in her research that Caribbean immigrants generally believe "it is higher social status to be an immigrant Black than to be an American [B]lack," she concludes that "part of becoming American for the second generation involves developing a knowledge and perception of racism and its effects and subtle nuances."[27] These patterns are not restricted to Caribbean American populations. In fact, Portes and Zhou found parallel examples of segmented assimilation in Mexican immigrants to the United States, suggesting that the dynamic extends beyond "Black" populations.

Stressing the impact of racial discrimination in the development of ethnic identities in the United States, Waters departs from Portes and Zhou, however, when she asserts that the "social capital among the first generation and the type of segmented assimilation among the second generation *varies within ethnic groups as well as between them*," adding that the "key factor for the youth [she] studied is race."[28]

> The daily discrimination that the youngsters experience, the type of racial socialization they receive in the home, the understandings of race they develop in their peer groups and at school affect how strongly they react to American society. The ways in which these youngsters experience and react to racial discrimination influences the type of racial/ethnic identity they develop.[29]

To explain the various identities chosen, performed by, or forced upon these second-generation immigrant youth, Waters describes three classifications: immigrants who identify (1) as Americans, (2) as ethnic Americans with some distancing from Black Americans, and (3) as immigrants who maintain an identity that "does not reckon with American racial and ethnic categories."[30] The differences between these three classifications are the result of varying degrees of distancing from what is stereotypically constructed to be the "American Black."

Waters's second classification, the ethnic-identified second-generation immigrant youth, best highlights the differences between the first and third. Recognizing society's and their parents' frequently negative portrayal of poor Blacks and searching for opportunities to differentiate themselves from those images, second-generation immigrant adolescents accentuate their ethnicity over their race (identifying as Haitian, Jamaican, Trinidadian, etc.), note distinct differences between themselves and Black Americans, and stress that being Black is not synonymous with being Black American (recall Antwon's comment about Julian in chapter 7). In making distinctions between themselves and what they considered the stereotypical Black

American to be, Waters's research subjects described "the culture and values of lower-class Black Americans as including a lack of discipline, lack of a work ethic, laziness, bad child-rearing practices and lack of respect for education." In addition, the ethnic-identified second-generation youth in Waters study claimed that "American Blacks are too quick to use race as an explanation or excuse for not doing well" and perceive that "Whites treat them better when they realize they are not 'just' Black Americans."[31] Notions of White supremacy are evident here, and it is clear they exert a strong influence on developing adolescents' understandings of their identities, relationships, and the social strata within which both are manifest. In fact, several studies have indicated that first- and second-generation immigrant students tend to decline academically the longer they are exposed to U.S. norms.[32]

Because these same ethnic-identified second-generation adolescents often receive messages (overt and covert) from Whites that they are the exceptions to the rule (with the rule being that most Blacks are not to be emulated), these adolescents face the realization that unless they declare their ethnicity, Whites will assume by default that they are Black American. As a result, many teens cope with this dilemma by inventing ways to broadcast their ethnicity often through accents, clothing, music, and even styles of walking. These "broadcasts" have profound implications in their relationships with parents, siblings, and peers, since the ethnic-identified second-generation adolescent may form an identity in opposition to their peers and aligned with their family. This process of identification may also lead to distancing from and friction with Black Americans, an acceptance of negative stereotypes of that group, and a perpetuation of White supremacy.

Those who can be categorized within Waters's first classification, the American-identified second-generation immigrant youth, follow a path that is closest to the one suggested by straight-line theory. These youths adopt the Black American culture as their peer culture primarily because they were born here and it represents the most powerful and pervasive means of building social and cultural capital in the spheres closest to home and school. These adolescents learn to view "being a Black American as being more stylish and 'with it' than being from the islands." "In the peer culture of the neighborhood and the school, these teenagers describe a situation in which being American is higher social status than being ethnic." For instance, several girls in Waters's study described "passing" as Black American in order not to be ridiculed or picked on in school. As a result of this pressure, they take on the identity of Black Americans and become disdainful of their first-generation immigrant parents' lack of understanding of the American (racist) social system, which can lead to obvious conflicts with parents.[33]

Despite the insights these classifications supply, real-life adolescent ethnic identity development can be much more complicated. As a case in point, consider Julian Thomas's situation. Born to Haitian refugee parents who consider their circumstances in the United States to be far superior to what they faced in Haiti, Julian has learned to hold assimilation in high regard. While his parents are careful to distinguish the sectors of society into which Julian is expected to assimilate (i.e., alignment with White mainstream cultural traits is deemed better than "Black" ones), Julian struggles to rectify the messages he receives from home with those he receives at school. Being childhood best friends with Antwon presented no challenges to his foreclosed identity because they liked the same things, got along famously, and neither found any reason to examine their differences. But when Antwon started getting in trouble in middle school, Julian's parents became uneasy about their friendship. Worried that Julian would get seduced by what they understood to be Antwon's slide into ganglike misbehavior and academic underachievement, they restricted Julian's after-school availability and stressed the need to be a strong student, a respectful representative of his Haitian upbringing, and a grateful example of the sort of success an immigrant to the United States ought to champion. This ethic sunk in and propelled Julian's academic success for a few years. His friendship with Antwon became tense and more distant during that same time, however. His retreat into isolation and comic books as depicted in chapter 2 was due in part to confusion about his ethnic/racial identity and the friends with whom he was supposed to associate.

School-based professionals could play a significant role in helping students like Julian navigate the tricky terrain of ethnic identity development. Attending to the differences between what mainstream culture often values and what the student's home culture may deem important—and then looking for ways in which race is infused in those evaluations—is an important part of applied development work with adolescents. In a culture steeped in the "American Dream," it is easy for educators to privilege the decisions and developments of the ethnic-identified adolescent over those representing a stereotype of "American Black" or the American-identified second-generation immigrant. Without critical analysis of these social forces and their developmental implications, educators can inadvertently perpetuate the ethnocentric and racist constructions that influence their students. Adolescents who confront these issues and look for faces and spaces where they can be discussed may become suspicious of educators who claim to care but demonstrate little awareness of the challenges they face. These adolescents often experience being followed in stores, discriminated against at job sites, and profiled by police, and if the significant adults in their lives are unable or unwilling to discuss these experiences, their development may move "underground" and manifest itself in unhealthy behaviors.

For both ethnic-identified and American-identified youth, school context can be as crucial as the family. A school with a high African American population may pressure second-generation immigrant students like Julian to identify racially. Similarly, a neighborhood school in or near an ethnic enclave community may make it possible to avoid thinking much about American categories. The differences between the first and second generations can produce conflict both in school and at home, since the children are identifying as Black American and the parents (and many educators) often possess negative opinions of that group. One consequence of this may be that teens either internalize the negative assessment of their identity or dissociate from their parents' worldview, both of which may lead to profound identity conflicts impossible to resolve without focused attention on both ethnicity and race.

> One day, when asked by Ms. Petersen to compare his experiences as an African American with one of Achebe's characters' experiences as an African, Julian corrected her, saying, "I'm Haitian." At lunch that same day, Antwon confronted Julian about his response to Ms. Petersen, saying, "Fool, you think you're not Black? I got news for you, dude—White folks only see your Black ass, not that Haitian flag you're always waving around, and you best get some knowledge about that, yo. I mean, you're darker than me, dude!" Having worked with Mitch on his Chameleon/superhero alter ego, Julian learned that flexibility and adaptability were desirable traits and that being different in different spaces and relationships was absolutely okay. But the familiar pressure to identify more as Haitian than Black was always present. As Julian began to experiment with various aspects of his identity and tried to resolve the differing societal, peer, and parental expectations that attach to various

aspects of his ethnic and racial identity, the esteem of his peer group became increasingly important, at times eclipsing his desire to please his parents. Knowing that he was learning from Antwon valuable race lessons he was not receiving at home, and aware of the fact that he was enjoying elevated popularity as a result of being associated with Antwon, Julian had every intention of maintaining that friendship. To maintain a strong connection with his parents, however, Julian had to keep his friendship with Antwon "on the DL." And so, as Julian's ethnic identity unfolds, he faces a significant dilemma: how to pass as Black with his friends (because not to do so is to be labeled uncool and be relegated to an "international" or "immigrant" status rather than a "student of color") while also retaining his Haitian-ness (which keeps him close to family and the support structures he has depended on to achieve academically). Add to this the fact that he recently began dating Janine, a White girl, and it is clear Julian's ethnic identity development is front and center, organizing much of how he understands himself and those significant others with whom he is in closest relationship.

Waters's studies illuminate situations like Julian's, in which competing pressures to identify either ethnically or racially make it difficult for adolescent immigrants of color to feel authentic as they move between school-based and familial relationships. This can lead to sharp divisions within communities of color, the dynamics of which are rarely investigated nor understood by a largely White teaching force. Educators who inform themselves of the sociocultural dynamics in their students' lives and their impact on developmental crises such as Julian's enhance their capacity to reach and teach youth for whom such dynamics are so crucial. When we are in conversation with youth about the racial and ethnic hierarchies to which adolescents are subject and within which they participate, we are able to co-construct the meanings they make of their experiences and note where optimal and unhealthy development may occur. Opening that conversation to include students' original developmentalists—parents—may prove enormously beneficial as well, since the pressures ethnically identified youth experience often arise through transitions from school to home. Creating school spaces where students do not have to abandon parts of their identity in order to belong, where regular dialogue about ethnocentric and racist dynamics in the school community is commonplace, where the development of cultural competency is stressed in the faculty and staff as much as it is in the students, where inclusive rhetoric is supported by inclusive pedagogies and relationships, where strong content mastery among the faculty is as valued as knowledge of the social and emotional needs of students, where counselors and school psychologists are well trained to discern the impact of ethnic and racial categories on student development—these are school spaces and practices most conducive to healthy adolescent ethnic development. Welcoming adolescents into the co-construction of these spaces can provide growth-inducing experiences for all involved.

CHAPTER NINE

Developing a Sexual Identity Orientation

Identity has a way of circling back on itself and finding the loose ends. In fact, much of the integrative work of identity development is a matter of figuring out just what to do with the dangling strands of our lived experience. It would seem best in some cases to simply cut the ends, to not have to deal with them any longer. It would even seem preferable at times to extract entire strands by the root. But that tends not to be the way identity operates. In the good cases, the strands become braided into varying degrees of integrity. They are wrapped up and around related experiences to create stronger, intricately woven strands bound together by purpose and need. In other cases, they are roughly knotted or merely clumped together, connected in ways that provide vague definition at best, in ways that call out for further attention, for a working out of the knot in our stomach that leaves us feeling a bit uneasy.

Sexuality provokes this sort of circling back. It creates loose ends from our experiences that at times become integrated into our self-understanding through wonderfully interwoven themes of pleasure and human connection. In other cases it leaves us stranded in confusion and pain, feeling knotted up inside in ways that seem inescapable and, despite intense efforts to the contrary, irreversible. Either way we are compelled to return in our repeated efforts to bring further meaning to these experiences and to bring these experiences into alignment with a deeper meaning of ourselves.

By late elementary school—fourth and fifth grades—the mysteries of human sexuality begin to assert a different kind of developmental pressure than what has typically been felt beforehand. Preadolescence, the period connecting late childhood and adolescence proper, can be a bridging of multiple challenges. It is a time for creating new experiences that can be innocently exhilarating and precociously confusing. It is a time when the mere brushing of arms in the hall can elevate a young person's heart rate, and a time to vaguely anticipate a first kiss after playing tag in the park just before sunset. But for some youth it can also be much more, much more than they are ready for, and much more than they could ever have anticipated.

Jerry, whom we first met in chapter 6 through his reflections on his high-school experience, remembers the fifth grade all too well. Having not yet cultivated the sense of humor that would win him popularity as "the funny big guy," he was a relatively shy fifth grader. He had a couple of close friends who were also on the quiet side, but when the three of them were together, there was no limit to the fun they had and trouble they could find. Jerry's friend Ben was the youngest of three brothers and was particularly good at figuring out what the older boys were up to. And Pat, who, like Jerry, was an only child, wanted to find out anything about the older boys that Ben could report. For the most part, Ben's reporting was pretty routine. His 17-year-old brother got a car, and that was cool to learn about. Ben even got his brother to give him and his two pals a ride through the city a couple times.

But Pat was eager to know more. "Who's your brother's new girlfriend, Ben?"

"I don't know her name yet," replied Ben. "He just started going out with her last week after dumping that girl Lucy. She was a slut anyway. That's what my brother said to his friend on the phone."

"What's a slut?" asked Pat. "You mean she's having her period?"

Feigning disgust at his friend's ignorance, Ben shouted back, "No, you idiot. A slut's the same thing as a 'ho'! Damn, you're stupid."

At this point Jerry was rolling on the ground with laughter, imagining he knew what Ben was talking about, and sharing in the hilarity of Pat's ignorance. Before long all three boys were laughing uncontrollably and playfully punching one another.

"Hey," Ben said, breaking up the hysteria, "wanna see something awesome? Come check this out. My brother has these DVDs hidden in his room. I found 'em when I was looking around the other day. You wanna see some sluts, Pat? You'll learn what they are for real!"

The boys found Ben's brother's stash of pornographic material, and, since Jerry's parents weren't home, they slipped away to his basement to watch one of the DVDs. Having sneaked a view already when he first came upon his find, and having seen bits and pieces of his brothers' hidden magazines over the past two years, Ben knew what to expect. But Jerry and Pat were shocked into a sudden and confusing awareness of a whole new world. Jerry had once seen his mother's breasts when she was coming out of the shower, but that had been his only awareness of seeing a naked female body. And Pat had little more visual experience than that. They'd seen provocative music videos and risqué magazine covers, but this DVD experience was of a completely new universe.

After half an hour of viewing in nearly stunned silence, Ben began to get edgy. "All right guys. I told you you were gonna see some sluts! You see what I mean now, Pat?!"

Barely able to speak, Pat mumbled, "You mean that's what your brother's girlfriend was like?"

"Yeah, man!" replied Ben, in an emphatically confident tone. "That's what I'm talking about. That's why he dumped her!"

Jerry remained fixated on the DVD, hardly hearing his friends, still shell-shocked by a "reality" that effectively brought an end to his childhood innocence.

All too frequently we hear stories of sexual trauma that shatter the innocence of childhood. We hear of boys and girls molested by respected authority figures who violate their most sacred trust: the security and well-being of their own children, their neighbor's children, and the young people in their schools and religious institutions. While these traumas rightfully grab headlines when they come to light, scenarios like the one in Jerry's basement are passed off as "boys being boys." In fact, most of the time they remain hidden experiences, never coming to the attention of adults. They rarely come into full consciousness for the preadolescents (typically late elementary school) or even early adolescents (typically middle or junior high school) who experience these events, either; rather, they remain etched in vivid imagery somewhat akin to intensely colorful abstract art. Without adequate contexts from which to interpret such "artistic" expression, the young viewers are left to make of it what they will. While Pat was clearly affected by what Ben showed his friends that afternoon, Jerry's system was fairly traumatized. He could not leave the images, perhaps because he had no place to store them away. They remained vividly haunting, pulling at his senses for further definition, compelling him to make sense of what those people were actually doing and, at some level of his consciousness, what that meant about him.

This beginning of his sexual history, if you will, is one of those loose ends that Jerry would struggle to come to terms with throughout his adolescence and into his young adulthood. Time and again he would circle back to this early experience, finding himself back in the basement, either literally, with another DVD he would steal from Ben's brother or a new secret source he had discovered, or figuratively, obsessively thinking about the scenes he had witnessed when he could not focus on algebra. Like many boys coming into adolescence in the late twentieth and early twenty-first century, Jerry's sexual training was supplied primarily by the visual media. In many cases boys pore over magazines they find; in progressively more cases today, they view pornography on the Internet. For good reason, caring adults worry about children being victimized by sexual predators who now have extensive access to tens of thousands of children and adolescents through chat rooms and other venues.

The impact of pornography and less graphic sexually stimulating media, such as sex-themed television dramas and provocative music videos, extends far beyond the devastating effects of overt victimization, however. It provides an enormous number of youth with their most extensive exposure to sexuality education. Given that chat-room predators and pornography marketers have aggressively joined the ranks of sexuality educators in contemporary American culture, what is it that they teach? Although the media-based curriculum may be diverse in sexually explicit content, a common theme runs through each presentation: Get more! Get more than you currently have, more than you're currently getting, more, even, than you have ever imagined. The for-profit media is designed to seduce. The same holds for a chat-room predator. The goal is to persuade the viewer or participant to want what is being advertised, and to want it enough to come back time and again. Consumer sex, sex as ubiquitous consumption; this is what the media curriculum features in order to survive. Profit margins are the high-stakes tests of the consumer sex industry. The industry fails if consumers do not buy in, over and over again.

A key question for this chapter is how to counter the media-based sex-ed curriculum in our schools. What should we be teaching about sexuality in the face of the massively funded marketing campaign that bombards our children daily? These are extremely challenging and important questions. Educators spend an inordinate amount of time encouraging students to "buy in" to the general process of schooling—to focus, to pay attention, to turn in home-work on a regular basis. But buying into school has become exceptionally difficult for students sold on the alternative curriculum: the nonstop, media-based sex-ed curriculum marketed to students all hours of the day and night. It is difficult to concentrate on the mundane everydayness of school when one's senses have been oversaturated and overstimulated by an overdose of graphic sexual imagery.

SEXUAL SCRIPTS

The lessons learned from marketed sex education have a range of lingering effects, not the least of which is the intensive sexual scripting modeled by the actors and other "performers." Like the gender scripting discussed in chapter 6, sexuality scripting creates the staging within which males and females are expected to play particular roles. But a central problem, according to Sapon-Shevin and Goodman,[1] is that the scripts are expected to be learned through something akin to osmosis rather than being taught or made explicit. Boys and girls are expected to naturally learn their roles as a matter of becoming men and women. Implied in all this is that sexuality is a naturally inherited trait rather than a learned behavior, or some combination of the two. When the organism matures, the relevant parts (the physical parts as well as the parts we play) will follow suit. Also implied in this script is that if the development of sexuality is a natural function of human biology, existing prior to and outside of social forces, then it ought to evolve in natural ways; that is, men and women should evolve naturally in their attraction to one another, leading ultimately to love and procreation-based intercourse. That is the traditional script, in any case, and despite whatever progressive tendencies we may hold, it is the script into which the vast majority of us are first socialized. To a great extent, all variations of the theme depart from this central starting place.

Janine Montero, whom we first met in chapter 3, learned early on that "getting the right script" is extremely important. The tomboy part she played throughout elementary school earned her little acknowledgment except for the fights she occasionally won in response to being called nasty words, the meaning of which she did not comprehend. She knew they were nasty, though, because of the way they were said and because of the vulgar gestures that accompanied them. When Janine finally "got it"—got that there were better ways to win attention—and started drinking and hanging out with older boys when she was in the ninth grade, she learned to play her role exceedingly well. She developed a keen sense of reading her cues, knowing when guys were interested in her and learning what they wanted her to do if they were to stay interested.

To a certain extent, Janine was getting a secondhand education in human sexuality. She was learning to play roles taught largely by older boys who had learned their craft through the usual media education outlets of magazines and videos. To carry out the scripts they were taught, the boys had to direct their leading ladies to perform accordingly. One of the boys was a particularly good teacher, from Janine's perspective. He was gentle, polite, and encouraging without being forceful. Though her relationship with him lasted only a short time, Janine learned a lot about what felt good, to her and to her partner. She thought about this boy often over the years, wondering why their relationship didn't work out.

At other times Janine couldn't feel anything. These were the times she had had too much to drink and found herself in scary situations, twice ending up with guys she had just met that night, guys who, because they had to share what they knew quickly, tried to turn Janine into a fast learner. These were painful times that, thankfully, she didn't remember very well, due to the combination of excessive drinking and the ability to turn her attention somewhere else in those moments. But even though she couldn't remember them well, these were the times Janine worked hardest to forget.

By the time she started seeing Julian Thomas at the end of the tenth grade, Janine had learned a lot about herself. And Julian knew a lot about her as well. This would lead to many conversations over time, conversations that kept coming back to the pieces left behind. Those conversations, helpful and painful as they were, had every bit as much to do with Julian and his questions about himself as they did with Janine and her efforts to pull it all together and move on with things.

Traditional romantic tales of heterosexual love are as much gender scripting as they are sexuality myths. Such tales provide the gender roles within which "healthy" sexual interactions are expected to develop. These roles are designed to play out in the happy ending of romantic bliss, marriage, and eventually children. In this story, sex is not sex for its own sake but for the sake of one's own and another's enduring happiness. Janine was aware of the traditional script before she became sexually active, and to a certain extent she thought she was following it, even if the route seemed highly circuitous. The traditional script also captures the vague notion of sexuality of which Jerry had some glimmering sense prior to that afternoon in the fourth grade. He had heard that sex and marriage were linked, and his mother had frequently talked with him about someday falling in love with the right girl and having children of his own. But, as with most of Janine's early experiences, this is not what he had seen on the DVD. What he witnessed bore no relationship to how he had conceived of romantic love, to the extent that he had conceived of it at all. The movie, and the many others that followed over the years, only created confusion around the relationship between sex and love. What he saw and what he heard his mother talk about seemed contradictory. But how would he know? He was ten years old when he saw that first film, and things didn't get any clearer over the next few years despite his obsessive attention to each movie he watched and each scene he virtually committed to memory.

Sapon-Shevin and Goodman highlight the *code of silence* that accompanies sexual scripting. One is allowed to watch and even participate, but asking questions is off limits. You figure out on your own or, if you're lucky, with the help of your partner, just how you get to "first base" and even what and where first base is. The same goes for the rest of the diamond. You figure it out base by base until you finally score. At least that is how the script is supposed to play out, according to the authors. And if it does not, one is supposed to figure it out on one's own, which is exactly how Jerry approached things. He could not ask his mother for clarification on the distinctions between her depictions of love and the "intimate" acts he was viewing onscreen. And he could not ask Pat or Ben either. They would either roll on the ground laughing at him or, if he got too serious about the questions, call him a pervert. They might even tell someone about him, tell someone that he has all these sick questions. Going it alone seemed like the only route available. So go it alone he did.

> Unlike many boys, when Jerry had his first wet dream in the sixth grade, he had a clear idea how it came to be. He went to sleep thinking about scenes from a recent movie clip he had watched. He dreamed of the two men he had watched having sex with a female partner, and what each man was doing to her. He could not tell in the dream whether the woman liked what was happening or whether she wanted to participate at all. He could not even tell whether the men liked what was happening or, if they did like it, what it was that they liked. He just heard them yelling and getting excited. When Jerry woke up all sweaty, with his sheets all sticky, he was thinking about the two men. He had done what they had done. He sweated like them and even ejaculated like them. He was now one of them in some remote way. That is what he thought that morning, and as with that first DVD, he could not get the thought of these two men out of his mind.

Clearly, experiences like Jerry's wet dream are not to be talked about, at least not truthfully. Yet dreams like his raise so many questions. Why was he thinking so intensely about the men? Did this mean he was gay? Did it mean he wanted to be like them? Did it mean he wanted to understand them and what they had to teach about being a man? What did they think about the woman they were with? What did they think about each other? Early adolescents are filled with such questions without quite being able to formulate them and, typically, without any safe spaces and available adults with whom to work the questions out. Although students like Jerry bring these semiformulated questions to school every day and frequently daydream or obsess over them from one classroom hour to another, schools also exercise the code of silence. It is okay to have private thoughts; just don't let them intrude into the public sphere. The message again is that sex is a private matter to be learned and worked through on one's own.

This is a mixed message, however, as sociologist Janice Irvine has argued poignantly, reflected in the public attention paid to such issues as former President Bill Clinton's impeachment resulting from his affair with

White House intern Monica Lewinsky.[2] He was not impeached for the affair per se but for lying about it under oath, which heightened public debate over what should be kept private and what should be made public. On one hand, everyone wants to talk about sex and know all there is to know, according to Irvine, but at the same time we are expected to keep our own sexual business private. If that message is confusing to adults, it is all the more bewildering to adolescents who are trying to figure out the very basics.

The Clinton-Lewinsky story classically pulls together at least four common scripts or types of scripting that get played out in much of human sexuality: desire, morality, power, and privacy. Was it morally wrong for President Clinton, a married man, to use his extraordinary power to act on his sexual desire for an intern who worked for him? Or is this a private matter between the two parties, and perhaps the president's wife, in which they hold the right to determine the morality for themselves? The scripting could not be much thicker. But the themes underlying much of adolescent sexuality are not always scripted so clearly, even though they may be no less complex.

In Janine's early sexual history, desire is enacted in ways that are difficult to identify on the surface. More than anything, she desired peer acceptance. She had grown tired of being teased as a tomboy in her earlier years, and her sexual behavior at least kept her getting invited to parties where she felt accepted, particularly after she had a couple of beers. She experienced some semblance of sexual pleasure through her experience with the older boy she found to be a particularly good "teacher," but it would take time for her to access that feeling consistently. In fact, as Janine and Julian got more deeply involved, she found a peculiar distinction between desire and pleasure. She gained an intense desire to be with Julian sexually but often felt little sexual pleasure in their interactions. Janine admired Julian for all she was learning about him through their relationship, and she enjoyed bringing him pleasure, but for her there was an impediment of some sort that would take her a while to figure out.

As Julian and Janine grew closer and began to talk about themselves more openly, Julian progressively asked more questions about Janine's "rep." He was aware that she had a more extensive sexual history than he did, and while he liked the experience she brought to their relationship, he felt a bit disempowered as well. The script was being reversed to a cer-

tain extent, with Janine now the teacher, even if her lessons were delivered subtly. Julian began to worry about how he compared to the other
guys she had been with. Plus, their relationship was not necessarily
monogamous, and Janine continued to attend parties without Julian at
times. Julian went out with his friends as well, but he was not interested
in other girls at the moment. Given Janine's rep, he simply was not sure
she felt the same way. They were fairly new in their relationship, and no
commitments were implied. What each of them did on their own was
their business; that's what Julian told himself. But despite putting up a
good front, he still felt insecure, which in turn made him feel weaker. He
was falling for Janine, his "litt dawgg" companion, but this was not playing out quite in the way he always imagined. This was not the script his
friends were enacting, from what he could tell, although he didn't know
for sure since he and his friends never talked with one another about
what was actually going on in their relationships—what they were feeling and what they were dealing with.

Janine and Julian's budding relationship is rife with the interacting
scripts of desire, morality, power, and privacy. Drawing further from Irvine's
work on scripting theory, and consistent with developmental models presented throughout this book, we can think of these scripts as being organized at three levels of experience: intrapsychic, interpersonal, and cultural. At
the intrapsychic level, we see Janine and Julian struggling with their individual issues. Janine is grappling with the very nature of her own desire, just as
Julian is struggling to cope with feelings of disempowerment and insecurity.
These intrapsychic challenges play out interpersonally through their sexual
interactions, in which Janine is working to integrate her admiration for Julian
with her capacity to experience sexual pleasure through their relationship.
Julian, on the other hand, is coping with his own insecurities in a manner
that he hopes will not interfere with his relationship with Janine, but that is
proving to be a struggle that borders on moral grounds. While he tries not
to judge the morality of Janine's sexual history and, perhaps, her ongoing
sexual behavior outside their relationship, he finds himself at fault for not
being able to handle it better. He feels guilty that despite his efforts not to
be morally judgmental, he still feels privately angry toward Janine for not
being "loyal" to him, even though they do not have a committed relationship. He feels guilty because he recognizes that his anger is irrational and

stems from his own feelings of insecurity, exacerbated by the gender scripts that presuppose the man as the sexual leader.

Perhaps the most complex aspect of Janine and Julian's relationship exists at the cultural level. As a Haitian American young man who has struggled for acceptance with his African American peers, Julian's dating of a White girl adds extra pressure. His friend Antwon, for example, has intermittently chided him for "wasting it on" and applauded him for "giving it to" that White girl. And Janine's parents, who sent her to Central High to get a fresh start in the tenth grade after she got pregnant at the end of the ninth grade, felt mixed about Julian at best. They were grateful to him and Ms. Petersen for pulling Janine out of the academic slump she had been in through the literary project for the yearbook. And it is clear to them that Julian is an exceptional young man in obvious ways. But he is an exceptional young man with very dark-Brown skin, and that complicates things for them. It complicates things for Julian as well. It's so complicated for him at times that he's not sure anymore what his questions are. But he's sure of one thing: he's falling for Janine. If only he were sure this was a two-way street.

The scripting described in existing sociological and psychological theory, some of which is presented in the cases above, is merely a sample of the many common scripts that play out in the minds and through the actions of the students we see in our schools. The point here is not to name the specific scripts per se but to alert educators to the general nature of sexual scripting, including the sources of script development. In addition to the media, family, and larger society, sexual scripts are cultivated within our religious communities, youth centers, friendship networks, and anywhere else that people congregate. Common to all these settings are the roles of power, modeling, reinforcement, and reward. Sexual scripting is generally guided by those who have or seek power of various kinds and use it to enhance their sexual possibilities. Such power is used to model sexual behavior that is then reinforced and rewarded through pleasure, access, status, safety, or any number of desirable outcomes. Sexual scripts are adopted for good reasons. But good reasons are not necessarily associated with healthy development. How might educators inform the sexual scripting of students in a manner that is respectful of boundaries and individual expression while simultaneously being cognizant of the larger influences against which our contributions may be competing?

TEACHING SEX IN SCHOOL: WHAT SHOULD SEX EDUCATION BE?

Most parents would not want their children to learn about sexuality under the influence of alcohol or pornography, as Janine and Jerry did. Yet that is the venue of choice for youth who attend schools without a formal sexuality curriculum, or for those who receive a curriculum that is simply far too limited, particularly in comparison to what can be learned at parties or in the neighborhood. A host of sociologists and psychologists have studied the nature of sexuality education in schools, and virtually all of them conclude that the formal curriculum is extremely narrow.[3] James Sears summarizes five issues in sexuality education that are consistent with findings across a range of studies: extensiveness, relevance, the hidden curriculum, rationalism versus eroticism, and the overemphasis on the technocratic (how it works) approach. In considering whether to develop or revamp the sexuality curriculum, each of these issues serves as an important guide or organizing theme.

All five issues are highly interrelated and are best understood in relationship with one another. How extensive must the curriculum be in order to be relevant? The simplest approaches are grounded exclusively in biology, teaching about sperm and eggs and the ways in which they work in tandem to produce children. One argument is that teaching only "the basics" leaves the more complex issues like sexual values and preferences up to the parents or the individual students. But what are the basics? Do we, for example, depict how the sperm makes it to the egg, and do we discuss the fact that most sexual activity is not oriented toward pregnancy? Isn't the role of pleasure in sexual behavior quite basic? Not according to most middle- and high-school sex-ed curricula, in which the anatomical existence, much less the *function*, of the clitoris and frenulum, for example, are rarely included. Getting to pleasure is going beyond the basics from this perspective. Discussions of pleasure can take us in a host of directions that have little to do with sperm and eggs.

But these are the directions in which we must go, according to Michelle Fine, if our curriculum is to have any meaningful impact at all.[4] Focusing primarily on sexuality education for girls, Fine has found that most meaning-based discussions, versus those that focus purely on biology or basic behaviors, emphasize three primary topics: violence, victimization, and individual morality. While each of these issues is critically important, the general lack of a *discourse of desire*, as Fine describes it, leaves the larger picture frameless. Proactive sexuality, for most people, stems from human desire, whether erotic desire, the desire for relational closeness, or the desire to be socially accepted, as in Janine's case above. To leave it out of the curriculum is to render sexuality education irrelevant at best and borders on being irresponsible. Fine argues that for low-income girls of color, in particular, the lack of discussion of female desire can be particularly dangerous, placing them at heightened risk for victimization. Her argument is rooted in the reality that in many poor and low-income families, particularly those with young children at home, adolescent girls experience pressure to grow up fast, either to help care for younger siblings or to more fully care for themselves as their mothers contend with the combined pressures of economic stress and child care. For a girl, growing up fast means becoming a woman. And in many cases, the external recognition of womanhood dramatically exceeds the inner capacity to manage it.

By beginning with desire as the starting point of most sexual behavior, we could get down to basics, from Fine's perspective—the basics, not only of what girls of color need for their sexual growth and safety, but the basics of what all youth need for a relevant understanding of sexuality. Fine's critique of the missing discourse of desire is consistent with Sears's contention that sexuality is taught primarily from a rationalist orientation rather than one rooted in eroticism. Rationalist teaching focuses on decisionmaking. It is strategic and well organized, with an emphasis on thinking things through before acting. All this makes a great deal of sense, to a degree. We need to teach our children and our students to be smart when it comes to sexual decisionmaking, to avoid decisions that carry heavy and long-lasting implications. At the same time, however, such thinking is irrelevant outside of an appreciation for the intense feelings that lead to such decisions in the first place. If we do not make space for the erotic in the formal curriculum, we must assume that those lessons will be taught elsewhere. But to return to the central problem posed here: presenting sexual thought without sexual feeling leaves the entire issue decontextualized. It is like teaching math skills without a conception of quantity.

In some forms of the basic sexuality curriculum, biology is joined with technology, or the basic ways in which we "do it." Such technocratic teaching, as Sears describes it, can be as minimalist as showing outlines of human bodies that depict the penis entering the vagina. Replete with diagrams of external body parts and internal organs, including action photos of sperm swimming upstream toward the egg, such depictions provide the full biotechno overview. This is the CliffsNotes version of sex ed, and not far from the curriculum that most students experience. Models that go one step beyond tend to focus on prevention of pregnancy and sexually transmitted diseases. Irvine has described this step as the *medicalization of adolescent sexuality*. Building from what she referred to as the twin epidemics of teenage pregnancy in the 1970s and AIDS in the 1980s and 1990s, sexuality educators were armed to prevent such life-altering concerns. The prevention strategy of choice became abstinence, which served to shut down the sexuality discourse in schools rather than opening it up for further understanding. As Fine and many others have argued, while the abstinence approach works for some youth, it places others at greater risk because it is not consistent with their lived experience.[5]

Whatever approach is taken formally, there is a hidden curriculum to all of sexuality education, according to Sears, and its pedagogy can be as varied as its content. In almost all cases, either spoken or unspoken values guide the hidden curriculum. Abstinence approaches to sexuality education, for example, tend to be associated with Christian religious values that espouse saving sexual behavior for marriage, leading some critics of the "abstinence movement" to proclaim this approach an implicit violation of church and state.[6] Sears, Irvine, and others argue that teaching the basic curriculum, by most definitions of the term, perpetuates the status quo of socially constructed gender and sexual identity hierarchies in that they teach the biology and technology of heterosexual relations without expanding outward toward a fuller array of the sexual realities existing in any given classroom. Formally teaching only one form of sexual expression—heterosexual intercourse—implies that other forms do not exist or are not authentic, legitimate expressions.

SEXUAL ORIENTATION: MYTHS AND CONFUSION

In the vast majority of cases, sexual orientation is not formally addressed in school. In an even greater majority of cases, it is not taught or even remotely addressed at home. If it is addressed in church, synagogue, or temple, it is presented as something to be accepted, perhaps, but also at times as something abhorrent, as something to seek help for, perhaps even as divine intervention. How does one learn about sexual orientation—whether one is straight, gay, or bisexual? The common assumption is that these orientations take care of themselves, but is that assumption accurate? It is a convenient assumption in many ways, in that it holds no one responsible for venturing into this complex and often anxiety-arousing territory. But with no one to turn to to work out questions of sexual orientation, this is yet one more arena in which young people are left to figure things out on their own. Whether handed down by nature (or God, if that is one's belief) or evolving through complex human experiences, the assumption that sexual orientation will suddenly become clear without any teaching or guidance on the matter suggests a belief in a convenient myth: one just comes to be sexually orient- ed, with an innate capacity to conceive of what that means. This myth con- tributes to a great deal of confusion.

> When Jerry awoke from his wet dream as a sixth grader, he was aware of being sexually aroused, yet he was anything but sexually oriented. His first waking images were of men's erect penises, and those images stayed with him for years, blending with similar images and provoking questions about his own "manhood" on a multitude of levels. At some point during the sev- enth grade, Jerry saw the first "real" erect penis that was not his own, or at least part of one. His friend Pat had stayed over at his house one night. As the two friends were lying around in their underwear looking at a maga- zine Pat brought over in his backpack, Jerry could see the tip of Pat's penis poking out of his briefs. As speechless as when he saw that first DVD, he caught himself staring at Pat. "What are you looking at, you faggot?" Pat responded teasingly. Catching his breath and just enough of his composure, Jerry shot back, "Nothing . . . nothing to look at little man!" After Pat play- fully jumped on top of him, pretending to "hump him" with intermittent shouts of "take that bitch!" and "take that, faggot!" the two friends laughed off their mini-escapade and went to sleep in their separate bunks.

Harry Stack Sullivan, whose work on interpersonal development was discussed in chapter 5, was perhaps the first mainstream psychiatrist and clin- ical theorist to begin clarifying developmental pathways toward sexual orien- tation. At the time of Sullivan's work in the 1940s, homosexuality was viewed as a form of psychopathology. Although Sullivan did not counter that view fully, he began to weaken it by presenting preadolescent and early-ado- lescent same-sex experimentation as an important form of preparation for later heterosexual relations. Just as importantly, Sullivan made no claims of universality with respect to same-sex experimentation; he simply noted through clinical observations that early friend-to-friend sexual experiences, particularly mutual masturbation, were fairly common in the sexual histories of adult heterosexuals. This step toward "normalizing" more diverse developmental processes helped open the door for subsequent clinical observations and developmental research. Although Sullivan's original contributions in this area are more than 60 years old now and are quite widely accepted within the professions of psychiatry and psychology, the lessons learned from his studies and those that followed rarely make it into everyday discourse. Early-adolescent boys and girls continue to worry that their same-sex experimentation means they are gay, lesbian, or bisexual. And educators of all sorts continue to lack the knowledge to confidently engage with their questions.

Sullivan made a second important contribution that also contributes to our understanding of sexual identity development. He argued compellingly for the initial separation and eventual integration of "love" and "lust." Starting with the traditional romantic script of heterosexual love and marriage described above, Sullivan depicted the psychological problems inherent in confusing the two *dynamisms*, as he referred to them. He depicted lust as a biologically or instinctually dynamic phenomenon primarily, but one that requires practiced socialization to be useful in subsequent human relations. The trust required for safe-enough experimentation is precisely why he viewed close same-sex early-adolescent friendships as a viable practice ground. As we discussed in chapter 5, Sullivan viewed love as the capacity to care for another nearly as much as one cares for oneself, and the love dynamism reflects the dynamic interactions that revolve, in the best-case scenarios, around mutual care of this depth. Human suffering, akin to the angst Julian is feeling in his relationship with Janine, is largely rooted in the challenging task of bringing the love and lust dynamisms together in a singular relationship, according to Sullivan. Each dynamism on its own is enormously complex; in combination that complexity is magnified many times over.[7]

> Over the course of their middle-school years together, it is fair to say that Jerry, Pat, and Ben came to love one another in much the way Sullivan described. The three boys certainly seemed more focused on one another most of the time than on the girls they talked about. And they certainly cared more about one another than they did their schoolwork. Maybe because they were not the most popular boys, they were particularly important to one another. In any case, they grew inseparable and, to a certain extent, began to break the code of silence. If they were going to learn anything about becoming a man, it was going to be from one

another. Ben's brothers just were not around as much as they got older, and they didn't talk seriously to him about this stuff anyway.

"Man, you seem obsessed with those damn DVDs," Ben said to Jerry one day at lunch in the ninth grade.

"What do ya mean, dude? You tellin' me you don't like watchin' 'em?"

"Yeah, they're cool . . . but not all the time. Seems like every time we can't find you, you're at home doin' your thing, if you know what I mean!"

As usual, Pat started laughing hysterically, perhaps as a way to manage his anxiety around the issue. Bumping shoulders with Jerry, he chimed in, "Yeah, dude, remember that one time at your house when I caught you staring at my gigantic thang when we were watching that movie?!"

"What??!! . . . you never told me about that, dude! What the hell were you guys doin' anyway?" It was clear from Ben's tone that he felt he missed a pivotal event in their relationship.

"How could I not check it out, man . . . you were stickin' that little bitty thing out of your damn shorts."

Just after Jerry made this comment, he noticed that Maggie Lang, one of the school counselors, seemed to have overheard him. Miss Lang was sitting two tables over, having just finished an informal conversation with Lisa Prescott, who was talking with her about how she's held up in the weeks since she was ostracized by her friends. Lisa had learned to trust Miss Lang and value her input regarding popularity issues and how to attract dates without giving up on being academically successful. Jerry also liked Miss Lang, having gotten to know her a little because of his problems concentrating in school. He was asked to talk with her after one particularly challenging afternoon when he just couldn't keep his mind on math work.

"Yo, Miss Lang," Jerry called out to her, somewhat embarrassed and trying to save face. "What are you listening in on our conversation for?"

Seeing Jerry's friends laughing giddily, Miss Lang walked over to their table and sat down. She had overheard the boys making playful but sexually derogatory comments about some of the girls in the school previously, and she had considered saying something then but didn't quite have the right opening. She knew these were generally respectful boys, that they pretty much stayed to themselves, but that they were struggling a bit as well, particularly with gender-related issues of fitting in.

"What's so funny, you guys? What's cracking you three up today?"

"Did you hear what he said?" Ben asked Miss Lang, holding his sides to keep the laughter from spilling out and overtaking him.

"I heard something, that's for sure. So what's the topic of conversation here? You guys aren't joking about those girls in Ms. Petersen's class again are you?"

"I wish . . ." Pat blurted out, playfully. "I wish we were talking about those girls instead of this pervert looking at my you-know-what . . ."

"These dudes are crazy, Miss Lang, you know that, right?"

"You're the crazy one, you perv," Ben shot back, still holding his sides.

"You guys are all crazy, in the best way," Miss Lang said. "But now you have me curious. What were you guys really talking about?"

At that point the assistant principal waved everyone on to class. "Okay, to be continued guys," Miss Lang said. "Promise?" As the boys walked to class continuing to laugh and more quietly poke fun at one another, Jerry knew he would go talk to Miss Lang alone later in the week. He had a sense that he could trust her. And he had a sense that he needed to talk seriously to someone about his questions.

Jerry was fortunate to have a breakthrough in the scripted silencing around sexual questioning. Ironically, his crazy friends "outed" him for his "perverted" behavior, which provided an opportunity to reach out to Miss Lang, whom he eventually trusted with his most private questions. Over the course of his high-school years Jerry would check in with her sporadically. In a certain way one might say he fell in love with Miss Lang. He cried in her office over the loneliness and inadequacy he felt when he just could not get a date, which was particularly painful when Pat and Ben started dating. And he sat with her practically paralyzed when he broached the possibility that he might be gay. His deepest fear in bringing up the question of sexual orientation was that Miss Lang might have the answer. But although she did not provide the answer, she had many useful suggestions. And she provided ample space for the questions Jerry needed to ask.

"Thank god those fools called me out that day in the cafeteria," Jerry said to Miss Lang half-jokingly toward the end of his senior year. "I would never have gotten to know you."

"Thank god, indeed, Jerry," Miss Lang responded somewhat teary-eyed, thinking back on all they had discussed over the past four years. "Thank god, indeed."

The counseling relationship Maggie Lang developed with Jerry was as important to her as it was for him. She learned through Jerry that as a female counselor working in a large urban high school, she could be helpful to the boys who were questioning their sexual identities just as she could help the girls work through their questions and stand up to the sexist taunts they confronted on a near-daily basis. Helping Jerry break the code of silence, at least in her office, helped her reach out more actively as an advocate for those students, male and female, who needed to give voice to the questions that previously could not be asked.

COMMON STEPS IN THE DEVELOPMENT OF SEXUAL IDENTITY

Jerry's counseling relationship with Miss Lang was essential to working through critical issues related to his larger sexual identity, rather than just getting clear on his sexual orientation. Similar to the processes of gender, race, and ethnic identity development described in previous chapters, sexual identity development evolves as adolescents attempt to meet particular aspects of their psychological needs within the complex interplay of social expectations or competing sexual scripts. Sexual orientation, like other aspects of sexual identity, is an ongoing negotiation between internal and external forces in one's life. How to make sense of those forces and construct developmental models that explain them, however, is no simple matter. Since the 1940s, when Kinsey first began exploring sexual behavior in humans, psychologists, sociologists, and anthropologists have been investigating how people understand themselves as sexual beings and how that understanding develops over time and across contexts. For example, how do gay Christian men resolve tensions between their faith and their sexuality? How do Latina lesbians negotiate their romantic relationships and their ethnicity? How do gay, lesbian, or transgender (being of one gender but experiencing oneself as the other) youth understand themselves when they are "out" as opposed to when they are "in the closet"? To answer questions such as these, theorists have constructed literally dozens of stage- and status-based models, each claiming a certain level of descriptive validity or accuracy with regard to the population researched.

In an effort to explain common developmental patterns or progressions in sexual identity resolutions, researchers have surveyed large groups of people with specific questions related to understanding sexual thoughts, feelings, beliefs, and decisionmaking. In response to these studies, the field of sexual identity development has expanded and subdivided due to the multiplicity of findings and political agendas that have emerged. Influenced by insights from feminist scholars, many theorists resist stagelike developmental models due to the ways in which they generalize and therefore limit awareness of individual variation and agency. Consistent with the approaches to race and ethnic identity development, for example, sexuality researchers are vigilant in cautioning against such statements as "this is the gay male experience" or "lesbians develop like this." For example, could a model ever adequately generalize the experiences of both Jewish gay adolescents in Philadelphia versus Pentecostal African American gay youth in Atlanta? What about middle-class lesbian middle schoolers in rural Indiana versus wealthy lesbian teens in San Francisco? To say that context is everything and generalizations are dangerous is to understate the point.

With these cautions in mind, it is useful for educators to be aware of the general themes emerging from developmental studies of sexual identity that might inform our work. Specifically, these studies are most helpful in familiarizing ourselves with the terrain gay, lesbian, and bisexual youth navigate as they try to reconcile what society expects of them with what their internal needs demand. Although the field is contentious and the acceptance of generalizations rare, common themes do run through many of the most widely referenced models, many of which echo the Eriksonian and Marcian frameworks outlined in previous chapters. The models proposed by Cass, Troiden, and Coleman are perhaps most used by educators who seek to understand the gay and lesbian youth with whom they work.[8] Each describes a series of stages or statuses, including:

- an initial lack of in-depth consideration of one's sexuality

- a growing awareness of one's sexual proclivities

- a recognition of one's "difference" and its incongruity with the hetero-normative mainstream

- a denial of one's attractions and desires and concerted efforts to "pass" or change one's orientation

- acceptance of one's orientation and the identification of safe spaces in which it can be explored

- the cultivation of alliances and romantic relationships in which one can grow

- experimentation with sexual expression in various contexts

- an eventual resolution of internal and external forces such that private and public expressions of one's sexuality become congruent

Again, context determines how and when the individual progresses from one stage or status to the next (or regresses to previous ones), which is why some gay, lesbian, and bisexual individuals "come out" in middle school and others not until their 50s, if ever. Some may recognize they are gay and claim that identity publicly before ever having had a homosexual experience, while others engage in extensive same-sex sexual behavior and deny a gay identity altogether. To label one person's particular resolution healthier or more developmentally sophisticated than another is questionable to say the least. Accordingly, it is important that we not use developmental theory and research of this type to determine what stage someone is in, but rather that we draw from this knowledge base as a way of orienting ourselves to what *might* be going on for each individual. For educators, the key is to comprehend and engage with the ways in which students are making meaning of their sexual identities and, ideally, to help them cultivate contexts within and outside of school for supportively nurturing its development.

GAY-STRAIGHT ALLIANCES: HOMESPACES FOR SEXUAL IDENTITY DEVELOPMENT

In chapter 6, we discussed Ward's notion of homespaces, which students and educators design in schools to find support for addressing the real issues in the lives of students that do not find space in the classroom. These are relational and political spaces, as Ward describes them, spaces for taking on the relational politics often rooted in race and gender dynamics that can undermine students' safety and success. As noted throughout this chapter, the realm of sexual identity development is replete with relational politics as well, politics typically rooted in issues of homophobia, patriarchy, and the violence and victimization that can accompany them. In response to such issues, gay-straight alliance groups have cropped up in high schools over the past 15–20 years. These groups work to provide relational support both for students who are "coming out" and for those who, already out, face threats to their safety and personal integrity. Gay-straight alliance groups might be considered a particular form of homespace for students who care deeply about sexual identity issues, whether they apply to themselves or others.

Gay-straight alliance groups tend to be particularly effective in providing support when they have the open and strong advocacy of teachers and other educators, including counselors and school administrators. When the school principal sends a clear message verbally and through active participation, gay-straight alliances are more likely to become empowered to be more public with their activities and more diverse in their representation. For such groups to be vibrant contributors to school communities, it is essential that they experience healthy participation from straight students who may not be struggling with sexual orientation issues but who feel strongly that such issues need a place for discussion in the school.

For educators who are wondering how they might contribute to the promotion of healthy sexual identity development for all students, getting active in the development of a gay-straight alliance group could serve as a tangible step. Such work does not come without risks, however, as homophobia runs deep in our society. Some negative reaction from students and families is likely to occur in response to alliance activity, but getting those reactions out into the open is, in the long run, much safer and healthier for gay and lesbian students than keeping them hidden and enacted outside of public awareness.

A relatively small number of students in our schools experience transgender and transsexual issues. Transgender students are those who feel a powerful identity affinity to the gender of the "opposite" sex. That is, some male students feel like females and at times may choose to dress up in girls' or women's clothing and experience either a sense of personal comfort or sexual arousal by doing so. Similarly, some female students may feel more like boys or men and take on heightened male characteristics in order to feel a sense of inner comfort. It is important to note that transgender issues—issues of powerful identification with the opposite sex—are not the same as sexual orientation. The male and female students who take on characteristics of their opposite-sex peers are not necessarily gay or lesbian; this is more a gender orientation than a sexual orientation. We are addressing the issue here, however, because gay-straight alliance groups tend to serve as homespaces for such students to come out, even if to a small, trusted community.

Transsexual students are those who deeply believe they are of the other sex. Sara Herwig, an eloquent lecturer on the topic, describes transsexualism as being born with the body parts of one gender and the brain of the other.[9] It is, she says, as though one were simply born into the wrong body. The intensity of transsexual experiences can be profound enough to lead some adolescents and adults to ultimately pursue "sex changes," or surgery that aligns the body with the brain, as Herwig puts it. Obviously, when such issues confront our students, they tend to be exceptionally conflictual and extremely difficult to discuss. Again, gay-straight alliances can serve an important function in helping such students gain support and in helping the larger school community better understand the wide range of sexual identities that exist in any given setting.

FROM SEXUAL ORIENTATION TO "IDENTITY ORIENTATION"

Sexual orientation is generally defined as one's primary preference for the gender of one's sexual interests and sexual partners. But clarifying the gender of one's preferences only begins to define the nature of one's sexuality, as the section above suggests. Because of the profound impact of homophobia, an overemphasis on gender preferences dominates sexual discourse. But how does one learn to treat another sexually? How is one's personality related to and reflected in one's larger sexual preferences? These are the questions that extend beyond mere gender preferences, and around which deeper experiences of pleasure and mutual growth are developed.

To reiterate our claim at the top of this chapter, identity is persistent in circling back on itself to pull together the loose ends. Over the course of his middle- and high-school years, Jerry so badly wanted to eradicate the impact of watching that first video with his boyhood friends. But try as he might, that experience kept him coming back and, ultimately, led him to Miss Lang. What could have appeared at the time to be a chance occurrence of minimal significance—three elementary school buddies seeking a little mischief on a lazy afternoon—turned into an organizing touchstone for one of them. But the questions raised for Jerry extended far beyond sexual gender preferences. They were questions of how people treat one another sexually and what that says about who those people are and how one ought to be.

Freudian developmental theory places a great deal of emphasis on the notion of *sublimation*, arguing that healthy individual growth and the collective work of creating civil societies is largely a matter of transforming raw sexual drives and impulses into civilized human interactions. Sexual energy is at the core of human functioning in this model. The rest of life is about transforming that energy into constructive rather than destructive ends. Approximating the accomplishment of such a feat reaches far beyond individual identity, however; it requires the collective will and capacity to meet one another where we stand. It requires the courage of committing to struggles like we see in Julian, who questions why he cannot more securely accept his status in his relationship with Janine.

Rather than orienting exclusively to himself and heeding the call of the patriarchal messages that surround him, Julian also is oriented toward understanding Janine for who she is and who she wants to be. Through this process—and all the racial, ethnic, and moral complexity that surrounds it— Julian is oriented toward genuinely understanding and reciprocally constructing the roles he and his new girlfriend perform in each other's lives at the moment. Most impressively, he is doing so without a mutual relational commitment; rather, he is doing it out of what might be deemed a moral sense of responsibility and care. He is struggling with a sense of responsibility to himself and Janine to be fair and reasonable within the larger scheme of their budding relationship, despite the insecurities he feels, and with a sense of genuine care and affection for Janine regardless of the potential outcome of their relationship in the end.

Among all the struggles he must confront, Julian is working particularly hard at taking on the one that will organize the rest of them to a large extent: how to orient oneself in deep, intimate relationships with others. It is that orientation, arguably, that will most intimately come to define his larger identity and, in time, to serve as the binding core around which the remaining strands will find their home.

CHAPTER TEN

Faith and the Development of Ultimate Meaning

As adolescents construct their identities and develop in their capacity to think abstractly, they often confront the big questions: How should I live? Is there a higher meaning to existence, and if so, what is it? If there isn't, from what do I derive purpose and truth? How am I to understand suffering? How does one maintain hope? What is the meaning of death? Who/where/what is "God"? Teens are prone to asking such questions precisely because adolescence is the first developmental era in which they can entertain them with acuity. In this chapter, we examine the extent to which adolescents grow in their capacity to address existential and metaphysical issues and how religious, spiritual, and moral ways of knowing provide core schemas within which youth organize their identities and understand their actions. We outline various ways in which adolescent faith experiences may be understood developmentally, and we illustrate how the evolution of adolescents' "ultimate concerns" affects their understanding of themselves relative to the universe. In exploring these issues as educators, a question we must ask is, How do we address adolescents' spiritual growth in developmentally appropriate ways without violating the beliefs of families and the separation of church and state?

Perhaps more than any other developmental issues, religion and spirituality tend to be avoided in educational discussions—and for good reason. To address the myriad ways in which members of our communities understand questions of religious significance is to confront institutions, belief systems, traditions, cultures, and symbols that often do not yield to developmental analysis. Consequently, some assertions found within this chapter may be met with varying levels of acceptance and rejection, belief and disbelief, depending on one's religious outlook. Our purpose is not to privilege any religious expression or tradition over another, nor is it to advocate for any particular way of thinking about the divine; rather, our goal is to explore how a developmental approach can illuminate adolescents' understanding of religion, faith, or ultimate meaning. Adolescents bring to school (be it a public, ostensibly secular school or a private, religiously affiliated one) their whole selves, including the parts of them that connect to religious and/or spiritual ways of knowing and being. Making oneself aware of how teens may be asking and answering questions about the universe in theological or moral terms is an essential part of meeting their developmental needs. The theological and developmental scholar Sharon Parks says it well: "Faith—the activity of seeking, composing, and being composed by a meaning both ultimate and intimate—cannot, of course, be reduced to psychological processes, but the recognition and understanding of such processes can enhance our appreciation and respect for what concerns human beings most intimately and ultimately."[1]

DEVELOPMENTAL FOUNDATIONS

Faith development is rooted in core components of the cognitive and moral domains of human development. According to Piaget, if a young person dwells in a context that encourages it, the early-adolescent years mark the emergence of reflective thought and the capacity to perceive and manipulate abstract systems of meaning independent of the concrete checks that were previously necessary. As a result, entirely new patterns of reality unfold during the transition from concrete operational to formal operational thinking (see chapter 3 for a more thorough introduction to these concepts). For the first time, one is able to think about thinking itself, to abstract the self and one's perceptions, to begin to discern what is to be considered truth from what one understands to be internal apprehension. As discussed in chapter 3, formal operational thought makes possible the capacity for "third-person perspective-taking"—the ability to hold both one's own perceptions and the perceptions of another at the same time.[2] This powerful new mode of awareness permits much deeper connections with others, with one's self, and with such core concerns as meaning, purpose, faith, and God. As the developmental theorist James Fowler puts it, "In the formal operational stage, thought takes wings."[3]

Newly endowed with the capacity to take as object one's own thinking and relativize it in comparison with others', adolescents are capable of going beyond the meanings and symbols they receive, transcending them through their creativity and criticism. This process is undertaken through the use of language and imagery. The human capacity for symbol-using and symbol-making perhaps finds its most powerful expression in the words and images used to convey what we understand to be God, divinity, the nature of the universe, truth, or any other "imaginative construction" we might employ to describe an "ultimate concern" or the divine. For these reasons, adolescents are often filled with questions, arguments, and feelings about how to orient themselves toward what they perceive to be ultimate—which, in many cases, is understood to be God.

> Steve Chang is beginning to pose these sorts of questions. When we last met Steve in chapter 8, he was struggling to construct an ethnic identity that would feel authentic across multiple contexts and relationships. Committed to maintaining the Korean parts of his identity that were most embraced at home and in his evangelical Korean church, Steve had always enjoyed church as a place where folks who talked and looked like him gathered to discuss the meaning of their lives and its relation to Christian scripture. Being a part of his family meant attending church on Sunday mornings and Bible studies on most Wednesday nights, praying before meals, abstaining from "sins of the flesh," and obeying the "word of God." As a child, Steve always experienced Sunday school as a sort of homelike space where he could be fully Korean, safe and understood. As he grew older and started attending his own youth Bible-study meetings, church became the one social space where he did not have to worry about "being somebody someone else wanted me to be." He knew that God loved him and wanted him to be well and do good, and in those moments where he retreated into isolation to escape the pressures of school and competing relationships, he felt held by God, safe and understood.
>
> Things started to change, however, as Steve began to experiment with different aspects of his identity. His weightlifting and video-gaming friends introduced him to ideas and behaviors from which his parents had tried their best to shield him, and he suddenly found himself doing things he would have labeled as "sin" only months before. He knew his tobacco and marijuana use, his sexual thoughts about Lisa Prescott, his

bullying, and even his homophobic remarks to others all threatened his relationship with God, and this worried him. Deeply conflicted about this, he considered sharing such concerns with his parents, but he feared the punishments and scorn that might result. For a moment after school one day, he considered asking Mr. Harrison, his favorite teacher and a youth leader in a church across town, about his thoughts on sin, but Steve decided against it because he didn't want his peers to hear him asking about such things in school, since being Christian at Central was by no means a ticket to popularity.

As Steve's identity exploration continued, so too did his questioning of the religious teachings he'd received as a child. Examining those questions in Sunday school and Bible study was helpful, but since that part of his life was now isolated from the parts of him that were experiencing the most struggle and change (i.e., his identity as a male Korean student at Central), he felt that not much could be accomplished there. Steve wanted to "go deep" with his friends and not worry about being labeled as a sinner or being prayed for by the youth pastor as he did so. Sure, he wanted to talk about his understanding of "God's plan," but he wanted to talk more about why the real world he saw on the news too often fearfully resembled the apocalyptic video games he loved to play, why his feelings about Lisa Prescott weren't in some ways a good thing, why some of his "bad" friends seemed to be doing so well in life even as they sinned so freely, and how to make a life that had meaning above and beyond just working hard at school and a career. The images of a bearded, fatherly, and sometimes vengeful God watching over him no longer meshed with his understanding of the world. As those symbols faded and new questions about exactly what/who God might be rushed in to displace them, Steve craved discussions that probed for meaning and purpose, right and wrong.

For adolescents such as Steve, immersed as they are in the expansion of cognitive capacity as represented in Piagetian theory, the language and symbols used to describe God or anything of ultimate concern take on immense importance since they function as signifiers of purpose, markers of community, and evaluators of ethical action. With competing versions of reality and a diverse range of possibilities vying for adherence in the public sphere, adolescents (and adults alike) often struggle to organize their experience into what we might call a coherent *frame of orientation*. In concrete operations, this frame of orientation relies on a strict apprehension of the physical world-as-it-is such that possibility is understood to be a subset of reality, not something that can transcend it. As we discussed in chapter 3, the formal operational stage shifts the relationship between possibility and reality. Reality, for many adolescents, becomes a subset of possibility. This new mode of cognition carries with it the potential for an expansion of ethical decisionmaking, empathy, considerations of justice, and comprehensions of ultimate meaning, but it also ushers in waves of doubt, threats of meaninglessness, and struggles with the multiplicity of religious expression and meaning. It is easy to see, then, why many adolescents are so eager to engage in conversations about truth, reality, and the nature of life itself. They want to because they can now grasp such concerns with a level of sophistication that newly defines the world and their place in it.

According to Erikson, a central feature of adolescence is becoming aware that one is creating a sense of identity with every thought, decision, and action, and that this self-creating process is within one's control. This suggests that adolescents are conscious of taking responsibility for choices that can either align with or contradict the preferences of their mentors and peers. When adolescents express unpopular opinions, revolutionary ideas, anti-establishment positions, and stylistic choices that fly in the face of dominant culture, they are, according to Erikson, likely trying on identities as part of their psychosocial moratorium or identity exploration phase. They want to be themselves both in relation and reaction to others. They seek expression that is uniquely theirs yet want to be embraced by their surrounding peers and family.

Just as adolescents seek a "true self," they also yearn for a true orientation, an authentic way to live with meaning and purpose that informs their developing worldview. If examined carefully, Erikson's work underscores the primary role that faith can play in the identity versus role confusion stage. In fact, if we understand identity as a projection of one's self into the world, taking into account past experiences as well as future hopes and expectations, it makes perfect sense to take into consideration the ways in which the adolescent situates that identity within her understanding of the universe. Linked by beliefs, actions, morals, and community, identity and faith are inseparable. To illustrate this, note how the words *faith* and *identity* can be interchanged in the following sentences:

- First, faith/identity provides the structure for understanding who we are as we transcend ourselves in third-person perspective-taking.

- Second, faith/identity is the foundation that furnishes meaning and direction through construction of, surrender to, or immersion within a perceived reality.

- Third, faith/identity enables a person to make hard but hopeful choices from multiple alternatives, thereby providing a sense of personal control, or free will.

- Fourth, faith/identity functions to provide a wholeness, an integration, or a consistency between values, beliefs, and commitments that can too often be experienced as disparate and contradictory.

- And finally, faith/identity enables a person to realize her unique gifts and her potential, providing a personal sense of future goals.[4]

As faith anchors us and provides meaning, it gives shape to our identity. This is especially important to adolescents who are newly able to conceive of multiple and sometimes competing roles within themselves and strive to locate a consistent "me" within varying and demanding allegiances. Erikson himself noted the importance of faith considerations in the identity versus identity confusion stage and linked it to the infant's need for trust in the primary caregiver. "If the earliest stage bequeathed to the identity crisis is an important need for trust in oneself and in others, then clearly the adolescent looks most fervently for [people] and ideas to have *faith* in."[5] Elements of trust, identity, and expression are therefore fundamental to a developmental understanding of faith.

> As the symbols of God that had shaped his childhood began to wane, Steve looked for other things and people in which to have faith. His parents served him well in that capacity for a while, but their inability to understand the social forces that impinged on his identity made it difficult for him to trust that they would be able to entertain deeper existential questions, Steve's answers to which they might not want to hear. Mr. Harrison, however, was the sort of figure Steve could believe in: confident, competent, and charismatic. As a chemistry teacher, Steve had always wanted the Friday "matters that matter" or "matter that matters" discussions to go for hours. In those classroom conversations, Mr. Harrison would take a key concept from chemistry learned in the previous week and apply it to a specific issue, problem, or question relevant to the world today. In those con-

versations, whole worlds opened up to Steve and his classmates as they considered the implications of half-lives and nuclear decay, the chemistry of our sun and other stars, the impact of heavy metals on cell reproduction and mutation, the types of post-petroleum plastics we'll need to produce in order to preserve our way of life someday, and precisely how covalent bonds work at the subatomic level. Although these conversations were ostensibly about chemistry and invariably led to thoughtfully considered essays on subsequent tests, by and large they pertained more to questions of meaning and purpose, to the decisions we make with the knowledge we have and how to make them with a reverence for life. Often, in the absence of a specific topic to explore, Mr. Harrison would simply ask, "Tell me what you think is going on here and why it's a matter that matters," then follow their answers with a fascinating demonstration that would bring the students alive with applause, questions, hypotheses, and pleas to "Do it again! Do it again!" The class period would pass in a flash, and Steve would find himself even hungrier for those conversations than he had been before. To Steve, Mr. Harrison was so clearly in love with the universe and in love with his job that all Steve and many of his friends wanted to do was join him in wondering what it all meant.

In situations like these, the boundaries between what is cognitive, emotional, academic, or moral in one's developmental experiences basically disappear. Meaning and purpose are apprehended in all these domains. Kohlberg linked moral development in adolescence to the emergence of new reflective faculties (from concrete to formal operational thinking) occurring at the same time. He categorized the functional approaches a person takes when determining a moral action into three distinct levels. These levels, which he termed the *preconventional*, *conventional*, and *postconventional*, reflect an expansion of the person's moral sphere from the individual, to a societal, to a universal frame of reference.

In order to make clearer the cognitive subtleties occurring within and between levels, Kohlberg subdivided each of the levels into two stages. For a young child, moral decisions are based on the concrete physical effects of a behavior. If punished, the behavior is deemed bad, and if rewarded, the action is believed to be good (e.g., "Going to church is good because you'll go to heaven if you do"). Kohlberg calls this first stage within the preconventional level *heteronomous morality*. For an older child entering the second stage, moral viewpoints are marked less by the physical effects of behavior and more by the psychological impact. Things are judged good or bad depending on whether they meet the emotional needs of the individual. (e.g., "Going to church is good because then God won't be mad at me"). Adolescence typically begins as one transitions out of this stage.

When a person begins taking in the perspectives and needs of others and can occasionally delay or dismiss personal gratification when doing so, Kohlberg recognizes this as movement into the conventional level and the third stage of moral development, which is called *mutual interpersonal relations.* In this stage, moral behavior is anything that pleases, assists, or meets the approval of others. With the advent of third-person perspective-taking, the adolescent is able to incorporate the needs of others into his cognitive framework and can conceive of the effects of actions in a sphere larger than himself (e.g., "If I go to church, God will be pleased, and so will my family and my community").

When such considerations begin to include allegiance to societal constructs of behavior, such as laws, respect for authority, and maintaining the social order, the adolescent has demonstrated a move to the fourth or *social system and conscience* stage (e.g., "Going to church is my moral duty as a member of this community and as a loyal servant of God"). It is only when the individual begins to define morality and principles for herself, even if this personal definition differs from the law, that the adolescent can be said to have moved into the postconventional level and into stage five, which Kohlberg named the *social contract and individual rights* stage. In this stage, often experienced in middle to late adolescence (but sometimes never achieved), the individual determines what is right based upon internally constructed values and opinions that are held as true regardless of society's philosophical standards (e.g., "Whether or not I go to church is immaterial. What is at issue is my faith and how I choose to live according to that faith").

If it is our hope to address the cognitive/moral developmental issues in adolescents and help them move from stage two to three and from three to four, we must recognize the centrality of faith to such meaning-making constructions. As adolescents develop their moral sensibilities, they require a compass to guide them and a community that embraces them in order to construct a foundation for their worldview. Making appeals to the moral codes generated by faith systems, which are analyzed and applied within communities of shared interpretations, can help anchor the adolescent's developing moral self within a supportive and engaging collective.

Notwithstanding Kohlberg's insights, it should be noted that his work has been critiqued on the basis of its gender and individualistic bias. Carol Gilligan has argued convincingly that Kohlberg's model misses the differences in how girls and women structure their moral reasoning relative to boys and men due to the ways in which they are socialized in our patriarchal society. In Kohlberg's scheme, "conventional morality, or the equation of right and good with the maintenance of existing social norms and values, is always the point of departure."[6] She highlights how Kohlberg frames preconventional judgment egocentrically, as if morality emerges solely from one's individual needs, whereas conventional judgment is based more on the commonalities shared by families, groups, and communities. Gilligan points out that Kohlberg's postconventional level depends on moral principles supposedly universal in their application. Gilligan's work, however, suggests that girls and women often make moral decisions based on foundations different from boys and men, ones that are more defined by relational constructs than abstract principled allegiances. Boys and men tend to appeal to logically constructed notions of justice, whereas girls and women tend to express morality in terms of an ethic of care informed by a logic of relationships. Gilligan's studies underscore the importance of considering voice and interrelatedness in individuals' experiences, and they expand how we might understand adolescent faith formation as a moral endeavor.

Each of the above theorists, whether their focus is cognitive, moral, inter/intrapersonal, or a combination thereof, positions adolescence as a decisive era in a person's life, as an era of unfolding, pervaded by fresh capacities to receive, compose, and be in the world. This passage is an enormous achievement at all levels of an adolescent's being, especially at the deepest ones pertaining to faith. New powers of heart and spirit emerge concurrently with the new powers of mind and new constructions of the self detailed in previous chapters. Such intensification undeniably involves deeper relations with others, with one's self, and with what one perceives to be God.

FAITH DEVELOPMENT

How does an adolescent's faith progress? And precisely what do we mean when we use the word *faith*? In this section, we offer a definition of the term and place it in a developmental context in order to investigate the operations and stages that organize it. This will require some contextualizing of faith first, followed by an exploration into how current theorists have charted its development in adolescence. This section will then conclude with specific suggestions as to how we may assist adolescents in their faith development within public secondary-school settings.

A working definition of "faith"

Fixing a definition of faith is no easy task. As one of the most contentious concepts in any pluralistic society, faith is a tricky term to capture without offending or ignoring significant portions of the population. It has been variously defined as belief, as trust in a higher power, as an acceptance of or adherence to religious tradition, as the apprehension of certain eternal and divine truths, and as security in or loyalty to doctrine. Of all the possible definitions one might employ to probe the developmental significances of faith, theologian Paul Tillich offers perhaps the most succinct and accessible one: "Faith is the state of being ultimately concerned. The content matters infinitely for the life of the believer, but it does not matter for the formal definition of faith."[7] This definition of faith is expressly religious in that it captures the core orientation believers experience and profess in their spiritual practice. However, Tillich's definition does not have to be representative of a single religion per se. For example, one might have as one's ultimate concern a notion of success such that one's life proceeds according to a devotion to it. Life decisions, orientations, activities, beliefs, and relationships might all proceed from that ultimate concern with success. As another example, nationalistic sentiments can grow to be ultimate concerns, and one might hypothesize that allegiances to professional sports teams or rock bands could grow to the level of an ultimate concern as well (consider the ways in which people orient their identities, relationships, activities, and perspectives toward the game or tour schedule of a team or band). One's ultimate concern may be informed by a particular religious tradition, but this is not a requirement for it to be rightfully called faith, as a Marxist and an atheist can both be said to have a faith in an ultimate concern and are thus included in this definition.

The theologian Gordon Kaufman understands faith as a "symbolic frame of orientation," and he contends "it is in terms of these [frames] that persons and communities come to understand themselves and to shape and guide their activities."[8] Whether a frame—a faith—is understood to be imagined, discovered, revealed, or given, it functions "as a kind of map." Without this map, we become lost. Our identities lose their foundation, our relationships lose critical bonds, and the purposes for our actions become meaningless. Kaufman maintains that we cannot do without the map faith provides because to act we need some larger sense of the direction of our movements and the social and moral terrain on which we live. The need for a map is especially pronounced for adolescents, filled as they are with the vulnerabilities and possibilities recently revealed in the expansion of their minds and the formation of their identities.

Implied in Tillich's definition is the notion of commitment: that people do not just possess an ultimate concern but are indeed committed to it in some fundamental personal way. "I believe" statements are often expressions more of commitment than they are of opinion. As such, they are intertwined with the person's identity. For example, when a student discloses that he "believes in the Prophet Muhammed, peace be upon Him," he is not making the statement that he is of the opinion that Muhammed's prophetic statements are true but that he is committed to living according to the divine truths they represent as best he can and that he therefore identifies as a Muslim. The statement is an acknowledgment of the person's truth and a commitment to it, not a statement of belief that may be beyond empirical proof.

When we understand faith as a commitment not only to a particular map but the identity one possesses or inhabits on that map, it is easy to see how personal one's faith can be. Given that it encompasses our ultimate concern, it necessarily directs much of our psychic energy. While one's faith may be composed in moments of silence and isolation in order to attend to the interiority it may require, it carries a strong relational element as well. An adolescent's faith (like an adult's) is often manifest in those with whom she chooses to associate. Indeed, churches, synagogues, and temples are all communal spaces for worship specifically designed to bring people together. Identity, especially in the context of faith, is always constructed at least in part through self-other relations. This is especially true for adolescents, since their newly acquired third-person perspective-taking and immersion within peer groups become so critical to their identity and faith development.

Taking all of the above into account, we shall use the term *faith* to describe *the dynamic and symbolic frame of orientation or the ultimate concern to which a person is committed and from which she derives purpose in life.* Despite the risks of offending people by fixing a definition of faith, to proceed into an analysis of adolescent faith development, we must assume that faith itself undergoes change and complexification over time, and this too may be experienced as a threat to some religious doctrines. It is important to realize that understanding faith developmentally does not necessarily betray the notion that it is received in totality. There is room in the definition above for those who view faith as a given entity—as "revelation"—just as there is room for those who view it as something constructed. Our definition of faith resists the temptation to confine our understanding to "religious" experiences and the meaning made of them in order to make room for so-called secular frames of orientation and sources of meaning that function in the same way and may be as developmentally significant as ostensibly religious ones. As we shall see, this assertion is common in faith development theory.

Models of faith development

Although many theorists have produced stage-based explanations of how humans develop faith over the life journey, James Fowler is perhaps the most well known. Drawing from interviews with over 400 people, from young children to the elderly, Fowler and his associates examined research participants' attitudes and values in life as well as the life experiences that helped shape them. After years of analysis, he discerned six stages to the faith development process and published them in his book *Stages of Faith*.[9] In Fowler's theory, adolescents typically encounter changes in faith development between the second and fourth stages. Thus, it makes sense to briefly examine what the theory says about children's faith before they progress into adolescence.

In infancy, a child possesses a prelinguistic orientation toward his primary caregiver(s) built on experiences of trust, consistency, mutuality, and the satisfaction of basic bodily needs. The basic rituals of care form the foundations on which this faith develops. Experiences of mistrust, deprivation, separation, or pain during this stage may undermine later development. Clearly drawing on the work of Freud and Erikson, Fowler understands infant faith or what he calls *undifferentiated faith* as the orientation that enables a child to overcome the anxiety that occurs when mommy or daddy leaves the child's immediate presence. Since such a faith comes before language or the use of symbols, it is beyond empirical research, which is why Fowler refers to undifferentiated faith as a "pre-stage." If the infant is in an environment where basic trust and care is the norm, the child will develop a faith that affirms she will be okay, that she will be taken care of, and that if her caregiver is not present, they will return shortly.

As the child begins to use language and other symbols, he enters what Fowler calls the *intuitive-projective* stage of faith development. Typically found in children ages three to seven, the intuitive-projective stage is marked by "fantasy filled, imitative" thoughts and behavior "in which the child can be powerfully and permanently influenced by examples, moods, actions, and stories" of trusted adults.[10] Notions of God may be understood as similar to comprehension of superheroes, wizards, or witches, since the childhood penchant for magical explanations of the world is most pronounced in this stage. Children at this stage are confronting for the first time the existence and importance of the sacred, the profane, death, and sex, a development that underscores how one's culture, church/temple/mosque, family, and school can produce lasting effects on the child as s/he grows into adolescence and adulthood and attempts to build on the meaning made of these concepts in childhood. Strongly influenced by experiences of safety and peril, faith images during this stage often represent both the protective and threatening powers in the environment around the child, and stories become the primary means to absorb and convey these images. When the child emerges into concrete operational thinking and exhibits a growing concern to distinguish between what is real and imagined, he or she is understood to be transitioning into the second stage.

If you work in middle schools, Fowler's theory predicts that you will often encounter adolescents in the second stage of faith development, what he calls *mythic-literal faith.* Typically occurring in the early elementary years through early adolescence, this stage is marked by the development of the ability to think logically. In this stage, fantasy-based thinking fades as reality begins to take root in the child's perceptions. Questions about magic morph into inquiries about hierarchy, fairness, and the nature of relationships among individuals and between humans and the universe. Children in the mythic-literal stage begin to figure out such questions for themselves and, in doing so, are able for the first time to consider the perspectives of others. Stories become powerful tools both to receive and explain the wealth of information about how the world (apparently) works, with logical versions receiving the most favor.

Although mythic-literal children rely almost exclusively on stories as the means of organizing meaning and typically understand reciprocity as the central principle in governing divine-human relations and in determining what is just, they do not yet possess the capacity to be reflective about their experience or actions. Stories and myths may give meaning to the child or adolescent's experience in this stage, but that meaning is literal and one-dimensional and seldom open for interpretation. When literalism gives way to a more metaphoric understanding of narrative, when the individual confronts contradictions in or between the stories previously understood as absolute, and when the advent of formal operational thought makes reflection on such stories both possible and necessary, the individual is understood to be transitioning into the third stage.

To transition into stage three, the adolescent often experiences a clash or contradiction that leads to a deeper reflection on meaning, purpose, and identity. The concurrent transition to formal operational thought makes such reflection possible and desirable, but it does not make it easy. Literalism breaks down as the conflicts between stories (e.g., Genesis vs. evolution) are confronted, and relationships are either strengthened or threatened depending on how closely associated they are with what is understood to be authority. During this developmental era, many adolescents begin to recognize competing points of view and start playing with the relativity of perspectives. This is a precious moment in a person's life, one as delicate as it is powerful. The extent to which adolescents experience safety and encouragement within this major transformation of consciousness and faith is equal to the depth of reflection and philosophical risk-taking they will entertain. As the various contents of their faith are deemed incompatible with their lived experience, adolescents must transform their faith itself in order to adapt to new ways of conceiving themselves, the world, and their relationship with what is ultimate. This is why Fowler calls this third stage *synthetic-conventional faith*.

As adolescents emerge into the synthetic-conventional stage, they begin to require more of their faith. Their life, which is so pervaded by change, seeks foundations of meaning, purpose, and identity on which to rest. Family, school, work, athletics, music, peers, fashion, street culture, the media, biological changes, and religion all exert complex and sometimes competing demands. With the advent of formal operational thinking, adolescents have the capacity to reflect on their thoughts, to think about their thinking. Adolescents respond to this maelstrom of potential identities and outlooks by constructing a personal myth of themselves. As the adolescent's past, present, and anticipated future are examined for meaning and a consistent purpose, an ultimate environment is constructed (or revealed) within which the self is placed. "Who am I?" becomes also "What is my purpose?"

and "How shall I live?" Decisions about "what I want to be when I grow up" become more solid, as do visions about what the best way to live should be and how the world ought to operate.

When adolescents form such images contrary to the prevailing symbols presented to them by family, community, and society, they are often perceived to be rebellious or even disrespectful. While this is true some of the time, a developmental understanding of this synthetic-conventional stage helps us see adolescents' statements of earnest righteousness as provisional and experimental, as part of faith's moratorium. With values, ultimate concerns, and frames of orientation suddenly open to interpretation and the new faculties of mind inviting critique at every turn, it is no wonder adolescents often express such passionate commitments to ideals and beliefs as intense as they are fleeting. Even as young adults appear to have chosen rigid and idealistic conceptions of themselves and the way they will relate to the world, the mind and spirit are perhaps more open to possibility at this point than they ever will be. The more the adolescent experiences her environment as being unsafe for experimentation, the more she will retreat into rigid constructions of self and world. Indeed, if fear is allowed to trump trust, and if dogmatic restrictions overpower the ability to craft and explore ultimate questions, what could be experienced as an Eden-like garden of possibility may devolve into a thicket of intolerance, self-loathing, and isolation.

One's ideology and personal myth are constructed precariously in this stage, and it is the adolescent's faith that largely determines how the transition will manifest itself. As they attend to their idealism, adolescents invest authority in their vision, the result being an often rapidly formed and rigidly adhered-to personal ideology. In the classroom, good teaching can capitalize on these newly formed ideal perspectives and challenge them to incorporate greater complexity. The adolescent's fledgling idealism coupled with the advent of third-person perspective-taking may generate a reimagining of God, if God remains or becomes salient in a person's faith at this stage. As adolescents struggle to understand the depths of themselves, God is often conceived as the ultimate embodiment of the inexhaustible depths of understanding, an entity capable of knowing personally every individual as well as the mysteries not yet known or ever knowable about them. Desiring to be known and understood amid such emerging complexity, adolescents often derive meaning and safety from constructions of God that imply a radical acceptance and a sense of being known and loved despite experiences that may suggest otherwise.

The dualistic experiences of finding and being found by meaning, or composing and being composed by God in this case, are at the core of an adolescent's faith development. If stories were accepted at face value in the mythic-literal stage, symbols become the predominant conveyor of meaning for the adolescent during the synthetic-conventional stage. Teens align themselves with popular icons, styles, cliques, fads, teams, musicians, movie stars, athletes, and any number of positive or negative role models, all in an attempt to ascertain symbols that define them. Ultimate symbols regarding meaning, purpose, and identity are also either constructed or accepted at this time. But even as these symbols are recognized as being other than "real," the fact that they are expressive of and attendant to one's deepest yearnings effectively means that the symbols are inseparable from what they symbolize. To critically deconstruct the images that give definition to another's faith is to question the participation of the symbol in the symbolized, and this likely will be experienced as sacrilege, a threat to what the adolescent holds sacred. In this stage, at least, there is simply too much invested in symbols for the adolescent to allow for any demythologization. The symbols are not just something youth use; symbols comprise who they *are*.

If the adolescent experiences a trivialization of their symbols, as our culture so often does when it devalues and pathologizes the various meanings adolescents construct for themselves in order to make sense of their world, the sacred itself is emptied of value. It is a tragic experience for young adults to present their ideologies to family, teachers, spiritual leaders, and their community for approval, only to have them labeled simply as something "cute" or "naïve and idealistic." It is critical in this third stage for adolescents to have the opportunity to show and say to those around them, "This is me. This is how I see the world and what I think is important. This is how I want the world to be. *This is my faith. This is God.*" Schools are too often guilty of either completely ignoring the critical function of symbols in adolescent faith development or are careless with their trivialization and outright emptying of their value. The results for a disillusioned and foundationless young person can be tragic.

Janine Montero's pregnancy in ninth grade had everything to do with a "lack of a moral compass," according to her father. "Without God, you're just wandering lost from one temptation to the next," he once told her. To Janine, however, the pregnancy was accidental only in that she didn't mean to get pregnant. The truth was that she meant to have sex. How to rectify Christian teachings that mark her sexual experimentation as sin with her desire to "get with" some of the boys she liked remained a mystery to her. It was as if she had God and her parents on one shoulder and Julian and her friends on the other. These competing symbols of power and love, safety and exhilaration confused her. After all, the feelings of profound connection, joy, and release she sometimes had in church mirrored those she was now beginning to experience in her sexual relationship with Julian. "What's up with THAT?!" she asked her friend one day. "I mean, why do my friends and boyfriend show me how to feel good but church and my folks only tell me to feel bad?" As if such questions weren't enough, Janine also faced inconsistencies in the symbols of Jesus presented to her at school and in church. There was the "Jesus of Nazareth" in her ninth-grade world history class who was a leader of a Jewish sect and a political dissident executed by the Romans; and then there was the other Jesus, the son of God who died to forgive humanity's sins. "Two symbols, same guy? So who is the *real* Jesus, and what does that mean for me?" Janine wondered.

Moving from one school to the next and having to endure her parents' raised suspicions and restrictions made Janine feel isolated from her old friends, but her church made her feel welcome and valued, and it offered a place to ponder some of these conundrums. Trouble was, when the youth pastor encouraged her to think religiously when asking questions she found difficult to answer, Janine didn't like the implication that she would go to hell if she didn't change her ways and accept Jesus into her heart. It was hard enough to accept into her heart what she perceived as her worried and overbearing parents and her loving but naïvely insecure boyfriend, much less some son of God who died for her long ago. It was as if everyone she met had a different idea about what God wanted for her and from her, and moving back and forth between school, home, church, friends, and all the other places where she spent time only made her more confused. In moments when she sat alone with her thoughts about all this, one question kept creeping into her mind: "How am I supposed to live?"

Both Fowler and Parks recognize that dealing with the multiplicity of potential symbols in the synthetic-conventional stage involves facing the difficult concept of relativism as well. Janine's experience is a perfect example of this. Relativism can present an affront to the durable categories the adolescent constructed as a child in concrete operational thinking. Parks posits that as adolescents move from childlike manners of constructing meaning to adult ones, they move from an *unqualified relativism* to a *commitment in relativism*. Unqualified relativism occurs when a person can no longer avoid the awareness that we construct meaning (rather than simply "receive it as it is"). When this realization occurs, the adolescent must recognize that even "the most trusted adults and the most venerable disciplines of knowledge (even the natural sciences) must each compose reality in a pluralistic and relativized world, now perceived as a universe in which every perception leads to a different 'truth,' and, therefore, every opinion and judgment may be as worthy as another."[11] Parks notes that the position of unqualified relativism is difficult to sustain over time as differences emerge between everyday opinions and those grounded in one's faith. Careful reflection yields discriminations between external truths and those aligned with one's grounded meaning, purpose, and identity. Adolescents accommodate their faith to match new truths if the truths are deemed important to their experience or, if the truths are understood as irrelevant, simply reject them. As this sorting process picks up speed and sophistication, the transition into the next stage looms.

> As students in Mr. Campbell's tenth-grade world history class, both Janine Montero and Steve Chang confront material that shakes their perspectives and generates doubts, the kind that cut to the core of their worldviews. The thing is, they loved that stuff. They wanted the doubts and the questions and the "well, it depends . . ." sort of discussions because they were real. They weren't some "candy-coated Pilgrims and Indians at Thanksgiving all lovey-dovey kinda bull——," as Steve called it. "Mr. Campbell's class tells it like it is." Using history as a field of inquiry to ask deeper questions about how human societies have decided to live and what it means for us today, Mr. Campbell rarely told his students what to think (unless it was that they would indeed do their homework and do it well); instead, he showed them what happened "back in the day" and had the students figure out for themselves what to think about it and what it meant for their lives and the world. In doing so, Mr. Campbell often exposed the dark side of human decisionmaking as expressed in territoriality, battles over resources, struggles for power, religious differences, and the like. Studying the Crusades, for example, Mr.

Campbell made frequent and nuanced allusions to the United States' current military operations in the Middle East, asking students to compare the Holy Wars of the Middle Ages with the holy wars of today. While such issues were sometimes "a downer," Steve and Janine found plenty of opportunities to make meaning and discern purpose in Mr. Campbell's approach to teaching history. In the struggles for freedom by various peoples across the ages, for example, they found inspiration and hope.

All this inspired in Steve and Janine a desire to be part of something big, something that made the world better, something that their pastor might say would "bring the Kingdom of God back to earth." Mr. Campbell, however, never framed things in such terms. He is, after all, a public school teacher. He simply asked, repeatedly, "Why did this happen?" and "What does it mean for us?" Knowing that Mr. Campbell wouldn't accept "it's God's plan" sort of answers, students like Janine and Steve had to learn to frame their understanding in the language of a social scientist. During "Back to School Night," both the Changs and the Monteros expressed concern that his course might challenge the Christian values they were imparting at home. Prepared for this concern, Mr. Campbell explained, "I am committed to caring for my students who find such transitions difficult, and my aim is never to displace your religion with my humanities. My goal is to help my students—your kids—enter into such conversations bilingually, able to use the language of humanities to make sense of something they understand to be a deeply religious issue. I trust them to do that work because that's how smart they are and that's what the world needs."

Educators such as Mr. Campbell must be cautious as they work with adolescents struggling with the relativism of a complex world, and they must be even more careful in dealing with parents who may prefer that such relativism never be revealed. But caution should not lead to an abandonment of big questions or to a disengagement with tough issues. If history becomes only names and dates, English only diagrammed sentences, science only Bunsen burners and test tubes, and math only numbers and variables, schools will only squelch the spirits of youth eager to "get real."

Getting real is not without its trials and tribulations, however. Adolescents frustrated with the moratorium that unqualified relativism represents often voice hopeless objections to a world newly revealed to them to be (for now) nothing more than constructions and perspectives. They may ask, "If thinking doesn't lead us to certainty, why think?" How adults answer such questions has enormous implications for the way in which adolescents' conceptions of prayer, meditation, devotion, and faith may be deepened. The difficulty for educators and the pastors/priests/rabbis/imams who work with adolescents is that they are caught between giving an answer that positions them as the authority (just as adolescents are attempting to discern their own) and not giving an answer, which may produce a paralysis of frustration in the adolescent searching for truth. In such situations, educators are wise to remember the simple beauty of the well-reversed inquiry: "Well, I have some ideas there, but what do *you* think?"

If we open spaces for adolescents to begin to answer existential questions in ways that make sense to them, we help them to develop intellectual and spiritual pathways out of unqualified relativism and into greater clarity. Typically, as adolescents reach the limits of unqualified relativism and tire of its groundlessness, they search for a place to stand. This often will not occur until the young adult has left home and gone off into the working world or to college, but it can happen in the midteens if the environment encourages it. Parks calls this place a *commitment in relativism*. This commitment occurs when the adolescent begins "to take self-conscious responsibility for one's own knowing . . . discerning what is adequate, worthy, valuable—while aware of the finite nature of all judgments . . . a form of world coherence that is formed in a desire to make explicit the meaning of life as best one can."[12] This process rejuvenates the adolescent's faith, since it reestablishes the dynamic and symbolic frame of orientation or the ultimate concern to which the person is committed. However, it is not without its dangers. Parks points out that "it is precisely the awareness that all perspectives are relative that may energize a fierce, and sometimes tenacious, bid for a place to stand within the anxiety of that reality." When faced with competing values and life orientations "such as personal fulfillment vs. communal commitments, work vs. play, tradition vs. innovation, social action vs. academic study or any number of other possible polarities," the adolescent is "in a premature bid for confidence" and is therefore "vulnerable to collapsing the tensions of felt dichotomies."[13] Allowing adolescents to explore their fears of and hopes for such polarity and relativism in an open and supportive atmosphere—one that gives plenty of space for them to frame answers for themselves while keeping tensions alive—can help avoid this collapse.

Where Parks diverges from Fowler is in how much attention she pays to the subtleties within the commitment in relativism stage. She sees the shifting in the locus of authority from without to within as best described not by a single movement but through a two-step process. Parks therefore subdivides the commitment in relativism stage into a *probing commitment* and *tested commitment* to indicate the subtle but critical transformation that transpires within it. When adolescents are in the probing commitment phase, they are often perceived by adults to be ambivalent toward both self and society. As they grapple with the irretrievable loss of trust in a universe now revealed to be relativized, the adolescent may become skeptical—even jaded—about nearly everything. This is the stage in which "whatever" and "it doesn't matter anyway" can be delivered like mantras. But it is important to realize that this skepticism may only be a coping strategy closely linked to the development of their faith and should be viewed, not as simple ambivalence, but as a brave quest and a healthy alternative to the despair that threatens to consume them were it not for their hopeful doubt driving them to press on.

Although the same period is marked by the promise of a new self and a new relationship to meaning as well as intense ideological perspectives that seek to make the world into what it should be, the adolescent is caught between two great human yearnings—to be distinct and to be connected. Attending to these yearnings in order to locate meaning, purpose, and identity somewhere in between can be overwhelming at times, since undergoing the loss of assumed certainty and having to reorder what can be trusted as true and real at the level of one's faith involves emotion as well as cognition. Clinical-developmental psychologist Robert Kegan puts it simply: "A change in how we are composed may be experienced as a change in our composure."[14] When adolescents go through swift mood swings or feel the need to withdraw on occasion, this may be what they are experiencing.

What is important to realize about the ambivalence in the probing commitment stage, however, is that it is not simply a glum retreat but really a phase characterized by what Parks calls a "dynamic stability with integrity and structural power."[15] A commitment to one's faith initially takes on the form of a tentative but intentional exploration of possible truths and their suitability to one's experience of self and world. The content of that commitment and one's relationship to it are sorted out, risked, tested, and retained over time, eventually yielding a faith with a more deeply felt affirmation. Parks locates this exploration (which results in the transition into a tested commitment) primarily in college-aged young adults, but such a transformation may occur or at least begin in middle school.

When an adolescent's faith becomes more cohesive than it is conflicted, when he finds comfort in more consistent expressions of ultimacy rather than in explorations of varied possibilities, it is then that the person arrives at an adult faith, one that Parks calls a *tested commitment*. This stage occurs when one's "form of knowing and being takes on a tested quality, a sense of fittingness, that one is willing to make one's peace with and to affirm (although not uncritically)."[16] This is the era in which individuals become centered in their faith, no longer ambivalent nor divided in their understanding, at times even experiencing a sense of peace in looking back at the struggles that brought them to this stage.

IMPLICATIONS FOR PRACTICE

Exploring the dynamics of faith as they may play out in the adolescents we teach and counsel is important work. Precisely because such territory is fraught with contention, we need to target our practices in ethical, professional, and developmentally appropriate ways. No doubt, this is tricky business within public education. It may be as harmful to adolescents' growth to proselytize as it is to focus on their faith solely as a component of the ego, but we must "go there" even if it means leaning up against the free-exercise clause of the First Amendment. As the "ancient and abiding human quest for connectedness with something larger and more trustworthy than our egos,"[17] faith development transcends the psychological process of reconciling the id and superego tension precisely because it involves the most important questions we can ask about one another and the universe we all inhabit. Schools devoid of such questions risk becoming hollow spaces where facts are dispensed at the expense of meaning and information is relayed without wisdom. When we speak of faith as the dynamic and symbolic frame of orientation or the ultimate concern to which a person is committed and from which one derives purpose in life, it is clear how critical it is that we prepare ourselves to work with adolescents as they develop in this domain. Highlighted briefly below are five ways in which theorists such as Rachael Kessler and Parker Palmer have constructed practices to promote adolescent faith development in public school contexts.[18]

Providing opportunities for deep connection

School can be an alienating experience. Traveling away from one's neighborhood, negotiating hallways crowded with competing peer groups, shuffling from one mandatory class to another, encountering multiple adults often too busy with their full schedules and rosters to make meaningful contact—experiences such as these can make deep connection difficult. But if we are to promote adolescent faith development, we must seek out and enhance opportunities for youth to feel as if they are truly being seen and known and to practice seeing and knowing others, for it is only through connection that we can reclaim our students from anonymity. Teachers accomplish this in many ways, from community-building exercises to cooperative grouping, from self-driven project-based learning to frequent opportunities for sharing perspectives and accomplishments. Even simple things like greeting students by name and getting in the practice of doing impromptu check-ins as simple as "How are you doing today?" or "What did you think of that game last night?" or "I heard something great about you" can go a long way toward making an adolescent feel as though they can and should connect.

Providing opportunities for deep connection means more than just doing it for adolescents. It also means opening ourselves to the possibility of being moved and changed by our relationships with youth. To really create a sense of belonging, *we* must belong, and that means bringing our full selves into reciprocal relationships with youth. This may produce anxiety in those of us accustomed to a more removed manner of relating to our students. When we risk ourselves in our work with youth, especially when issues of faith are on the table, we often bring to the surface the "issues or wounds not yet examined by [ourselves that] show up in neon in the mirror of adolescent search and struggle."[19] This is why it is important for adults in schools to connect with other adults, to provide regular opportunities for reflection and collegial analysis of practice. After all, it is not just adolescents who are searching for identity, community, coherence, purpose, and meaning; struggling with the polarities of relativism and objectivism; and finding little solace in dogma and even less in indeterminacy. Many adults are experiencing these struggles too. This points to the potential for cross-age partnerships, in which people of all ages struggle together to make meaning of one anothers' ultimate concerns.

Providing opportunities for silence and solitude

Many of our students move through their days without ever experiencing quiet, much less silence. They live in households where the TV is always on, walk streets where car horns and jackhammers assault their ears, and inhabit schools where voices are forever raised in an effort to be heard above the din. The ubiquity of MP3 players, iPods, Walkmen, and cellphones among today's youth may be their attempt to take control of at least some of the noise entering their ears. The same is true for seclusion. The adolescents we serve may share their bedroom with a sibling, ride shoulder-to-shoulder on crowded buses, and get lost in the anonymity of school hallways and brimming classrooms. It is no wonder teens sometime take a *long* time in the bathroom—it may be the only time and space in their lives where they can be alone.

To cultivate the deepening capacity for interiority that occurs as the adolescent develops in his faith, it is important to create quiet spaces and safeguard opportunities for seclusion. One need only search the nurse's office for the feigned sick, the tree on the school lawn for the reading recluse, or the library after school for the daydreaming loner to realize how resourceful adolescents are at carving out these spaces for themselves. In the primary grades, nap time often served such a purpose, but this practice is nonexistent in middle and high school. As a result, children and adolescents "are so underexposed to silence and solitude that some have come to be afraid of any experience of emptiness,"[20] making the development of interiority that much more difficult. Trained to respond primarily to the voices and presence of others, adolescents may fail to develop in their capacity to respond to the voices and presence of what emerges from within.

What would it look like if educators provided opportunities for silence and solitude? Structuring time for students to be free from peer stimulation or pressure effectively allows them to be alone even when they are in a busy classroom. As Kessler argues, this "allows students easier access to their own values, beliefs, priorities, goals, and sense of purpose. In academic classes that encourage students to link subject themes to their own lives, quiet reflection will enrich 'journaling' exercises, essays, or discussions that allow students to express these connections."[21] Adolescents often love being able to examine and clarify their own thoughts before being asked to write, read, or react in some way. Given the enormity of developmental tasks facing adolescents, opportunities to slow down and focus are relished. While they may giggle or take their time quieting down, the relief you see on their faces as they settle into silence and their own solitude is often palpable.

Opening space for the exploration of big questions

When adolescents ask, "Who am I?" "Where is truth?" or "What is the meaning and purpose of it all?" such questions are often perceived by adults as impractical and romantic, or they are deemed threatening and defiant, since posing them exposes the answers to doubt or attack. Rather than approaching such questions with reverence, care, and developmental sensitivity, adults in schools (understandably leery of straying into curricular areas precluded by First Amendment protections) often turn away in hopes that teens will seek answers elsewhere or simply drop the questions altogether. Often as a response to classroom lessons and community or world events, adolescents persistently seek out conversations and pose questions about the most profound issues of one's existence. Confronting these questions with urgency and exploring how foundational they are for our relationships, institutions, and communities is a preoccupation for many teens. When the big questions are ignored or dismissed, either because of legal dictates or a lack of preparedness to address them, adolescents may rightfully reject school and the adults within it as legitimate sources of learning and growth. The result is that adolescents are often left alone to face the spiritual vulnerability they experience as their perspectives open and their ideas flourish.

This chapter began with a series of big questions asked as much by philosophers and theologians as by adolescents. When teens ask questions such as these, it suggests the existence of strong and turbulent undercurrents of a developing faith. When we expose our unwillingness to entertain answers to such questions in school, they know we are being hypocritical. Our youth are well aware of the fact that public schools can never claim to stand on faith-less and value-free foundations. Teens know school is always already rife with implicit and explicit faiths. Palmer exposes this fact when he asks and answers the following:

> Why does a good historian care about the "dead" past? To show us that it is not dead at all, that we are profoundly connected to the past in ways we may not even understand. Why does a good biologist care about "mute" nature? To show us that nature has a voice that calls us to honor our connection to the natural world. Why does a good literary scholar

care about the "fictional" worlds? To show us that our deepest connection with reality comes not merely by mastering the facts but by engaging them with the imagination.[22]

Being transparent about the ultimate concerns that undergird our curricula, policies, pedagogies, and assumptions will help adolescents formulate powerful questions of their own and begin to invent answers that contribute to the betterment of our communities.

Approaching adolescents from a developmental perspective helps us pull back and refrain from answering their big questions when they are posed. More often than not, adolescents do not want "fixes or formulas" but simply want to be heard, to be given "compassion and companionship on the demanding journey called life."[23] Adolescents may be justifiably reluctant to articulate such questions in classrooms, and teachers, too, may be hesitant to engage them. After all, why would a student pose a big, meaningful question—one whose answer she may be wrapping her life around—to anyone who may try to dictate the answer for her or ignore that it was asked at all? At some point, adolescents need to discover the answers for themselves, and when adults in schools choose either to invade students' meaning-making by proselytizing or by dismissing the question altogether, a powerful developmental moment is squandered. Even though a teacher's authority is typically predicated on her or his ability to "know the answer" and deliver it in a comprehensible manner, teaching toward adolescent faith development requires a different approach. We must resist the didactic impulse when we are fortunate enough to be in the presence of an adolescent who trusts us to pose the question in the first place. This may mean challenging our own fears of questions that have no empirical answers or allowing curious and passionate kids to suggest that our answers may not work for the questions they need to ask. If we have helped an adolescent find a question he feels is worth asking and orienting his life around, we have done our job. All we must do then is encourage him to go further, to seek out others, and to revel in the excitement of probing the depths of the human experience.

Encouraging experiences of joy

The faith experiences of adolescents are frequently ecstatic, intense, and sometimes overwhelming, just as they are for adults. Epiphanies occur in predictable situations as well as in moments of graceful randomness. To play, celebrate, express gratitude, behold beauty, feel love, encounter wonder, experience justice, or serve another can usher in profound experiences of joy difficult to explain with mere words. The high we and our students experience in such moments may stimulate new frames of orientation or new foundations of ultimacy. We are different after such peak experiences because they cause us to revisit our biggest questions and our deepest motivations in an effort to feel that way again. Educators who provide opportunities for youth to experience joy and who model the sort of abandonment required to achieve it give to their students a reverence for wonder and a taste of what some might call the sacred. This can be as simple as asking, "Did you see that incredible sunset last night?" or as complex and involved as an open-ended unit on cosmology, Mahatma Gandhi, Euclidean geometry, or romantic poetry. It can be as serious as a successful letter-writing campaign to get the state to fix the school's gymnasium floor or as silly as having a cupcake party for the student who accidentally sunk a basket for the other team at last night's basketball game. The point is not to define or contain the experience but to open the possibility that it might occur and then accompany youth as they make meaning of it.

Losing oneself (and thereby finding oneself) in play, beholding a piece of music or a work of art that confirms one's faith, confronting an essential truth underlying an intellectual argument, finding a person in history or literature to whom one feels a pronounced affinity, connecting to another person's worldview in a way that seems more cosmic than conversational, feeling consumed by love for another or for God, apprehending mystery in a manner that inspires awe rather than befuddlement—these are the moments in which teens (and adults alike) feel larger than life. Something profoundly clicks in those extraordinary moments, so much so that many of us find ourselves referring to them as the sort of chapter titles in the story of our lives. "It was when _____ happened that I knew _____ about the universe/myself." Finding ways to inspire such experiences in adolescents is essential to the development of a robust and invigorating faith, and watching them happen is perhaps one of the ultimate rewards in teaching and counseling.

Acknowledging the need for initiation

The poet Michael Meade once wrote that "If the fires that innately burn inside youths are not intentionally and lovingly added to the hearth of community, they will burn down the structures of culture, just to feel the warmth."[24] While possibly overstated in his threatening tone, Meade rightly suggests the need for initiation. Rites of passage confirm the adolescent's place in the community and provide symbols through which ultimate concerns are expressed and reinforced. Initiations anchor adolescents' belonging and ritualize their purpose in life. Without meaningful, generative rites of passage cocreated by adults and youth, adolescents may construct "their own badges of adulthood—from the relatively benign driver's licenses, proms, and graduation ceremonies, to the more dangerous extremes of binge drinking, first baby, first jail sentence, or first murder."[25] Left to ponder why their momentous biological, intellectual, emotional, and spiritual changes are going unnoticed by the significant adults around them, adolescents rightfully look for ways to honor it themselves by incorporating countercultural, antiauthoritarian modes of initiation.

There is no shortage of models from which we may derive inspiration. Numerous cultures around the globe offer meaningful celebrations of adolescents' emergence into new roles, new eras, and new relationships with elders. In tribal cultures of the Americas, Europe, Asia, Africa, New Zealand, and Australia, it is common for boys and girls to undergo lengthy ordeals or take part in long periods of study and celebration to commemorate their transition into adulthood, their ability to hunt, their first menses, their inclusion in the decisionmaking apparatus of the village, and so forth. Protestant and Catholic churches have confirmations, Jewish temples have bar and bat mitzvahs, Chicano communities have quinceañeras, and European-descended aristocrats have debutante balls. For most of our youth today, however, there are few rites of passage that mark the often lonely and confusing journey from childhood to adulthood.

Educators attentive to the faith-development needs of their students will look for ways to honor the profound passages that occur in the years between childhood and adulthood. Opportunities to acknowledge the changes occurring in their lives and underscore the irrevocable transitions they represent are everywhere. For example, being able to go unaccompanied to rated-R movies, voting for the first time, getting one's first savings account or vehicle, registering (or refusing to register) for the selective service, being allowed to stay at home without a parent or babysitter, being permitted to go on a date without a chaperone—all these so-called little transitions in adolescence merit the attention of elders. Although debates rage about the best ways to attend to the biological transformations at puberty, it is clear in our sex-obsessed society we do little to prepare youth for the power of desire, the joy of consensual age-appropriate sexual touch, and the possibility of creating life. When it comes to the transition from middle school to high school, countless communities have designed comprehensive programs of orientation and celebration to make students' initiation as seamless, trouble-free, and exciting as possible. The same is true for the big transition from high school into college or the working world. Much has been done to create rites of passage that highlight such thresholds and to provide tools for making the transitions and separations within them.

In the end, adolescent faith development is like all other forms of development: it is powerful and fragile, fervent and cautious, and it depends on meaningful connection with significant trusted adults. To be one of those adults, we must trust adolescents' capacity to articulate the questions *they* most need to ask. Trusting that we as school-based professionals are not only capable of but actually ought to be engaging those deep undercurrents of adolescent meaning-making sometimes requires us to take what we may fear most—a leap of faith.

CHAPTER ELEVEN

School-to-Career Transitions

Although progressive educators and educational theorists frown on explicit within-school tracking, our educational system is highly tracked implicitly by socioeconomic status. Economically privileged students are largely segregated from their less privileged peers by virtue of family residence as well as attendance at private schools. As a result, most large, urban school systems cater primarily to poor, low-income, and working-class students and their families. The same holds for many working- and middle-class suburban school systems, where wealthier families tend to send their children to private schools. This reality has enormous implications for the meaning of education and the relationship between education and work in that our large, comprehensive public high schools tend to be educating a segregated class of students in preparation, theoretically, for subsequent interactions with the remainder of their peers in the workplace and in college. For many students in large public high schools, however, the links between school and work or career seem irrelevant, disconnected from the realities they see around them. In this chapter we provide strategies for making school more relevant to work and career aspirations, particularly for lower-income and working-class students.

By drawing on approaches used in our own work and those emerging through urban education programs around the country, we show how educators make the links between education and career explicit for their students. We do so, in part, through presentations of "the rules of the game" as they apply to accessing opportunities for economic advancement. While low-income and working-class students certainly hear the rhetoric of a college education in the public schools, many are underexposed to a more explicit representation of the pathways that lead from school to work and career, including multiple pathways to and through higher education. Our goal in this chapter is to help teachers and student-support staff develop strategies for integrating career-development education into all aspects of the curriculum. "Learning for its own sake" is not enough for students whose economic well-being hangs tenuously in the balance.

To complicate matters, many low-income and working-class students who succeed in high school and are prepared to take on the challenges of higher education face complexities that transcend the classroom. At times there are economic pressures at home that require attention. At other times there are concerns about "college" as an alien world, a world capable of alienating first-generation college-goers from their families. For those students who succeed in college and channel those successes into well-paying careers, the effective jumping of social-class strata presents developmental challenges across the board. A person can become economically similar to others in a new socioeconomic status while remaining socially different. Similarly, the economic differentiation from extended family members can manifest real and perceived social differences. From an educational perspective, while our hope may be to promote upward mobility via educational accomplishment, it is important to recognize that such movement is by no means a panacea for personal happiness. In fact, it may bring with it a similar degree of stress as that experienced by those students who remain situated in working-class occupations, albeit stress of a different kind.

> Over the prior chapters we saw Lorena Chávez grow from elementary school academic ace to middle- and early-high-school fighter (chapter 4) to late-high-school rower and science collaborator (chapters 5, 8). Growing up for Lorena was fraught with varying challenges to her identity. Even as she gained confidence in herself through the rowing program and began transferring her accomplishments from that arena into the classroom, the challenges continued. As a Chicana from a close-knit ethnic family, the majority of whom lived in her local community, the prospects of moving on from high school to college filled her with mixed emotions. This was particularly the case given that she was contemplating college matriculation halfway across the country. The idea was fueled by anything but the common adolescent desire to strike out on one's own through gaining some distance from family. Rather, it was sparked by the

offer of a rowing scholarship to a competitive college in a part of the country she had barely heard of, a part of the country that she didn't think even had rivers until she learned of it through one of the girls she competed against in a national competition. She then learned that one of her coaches also attended that college, and so the exploration began.

On the surface, Lorena's story sounds like the American dream. A low-income student from an immigrant family, with no resources for college tuition, earns a scholarship to a competitive university through the combination of her athletic accomplishments and consistently improving academic performance. But that surface only begins to tell the story.

"I know I don't have a reason to complain, no right to complain," Lorena told her coach, Colby. "I'm so lucky to be getting this scholarship and have a chance to go to such a good college. I never dreamed of something like this."

"You earned every bit of this, Lorena," her coach replied. "Over just a couple of years you've become the best rower on the team. And you kicked butt in school too."

"I know. I believe you when you tell me I've come a long way. But now I'm feeling like I have to go away, you know what I mean? Like I can't pass up this opportunity. And that's hard on me and my family."

"But your mom told me she's really proud of you, of everything you've accomplished."

"Yeah, that's true, but she don't tell you everything. She's kinda worried about me going away to college, kinda worried that I'll become somebody different and stop being like the family. She's worried that I won't come home any more after a while. She's seen one of her friends' kids do that."

"She doesn't have to worry about that with you," replied Colby. "She knows you better than that."

"That's easy for you to say, coach. I bet all your family went to college. It's different for people like us. We're supposed to stay close to home and take care of each other. Especially the girls."

Lorena's dilemma presents a challenge for teachers, counselors, coaches, and educational mentors of every stripe. The intersections of academic achievement with social-class status and other identity influences such as ethnicity and gender must be understood in order for us to optimally counsel and guide our students. Certainly, we would not hold back on providing options for all of our students to grow and change, even when that might create the sorts of tensions apparent in Lorena's case. At the same time, however, we must understand and anticipate the many challenges faced by our students as they push the boundaries of their family and cultural backgrounds. Hearing them out and taking these concerns seriously, rather than minimizing them as irrational adolescent anxieties, can be precisely the support they need as they venture into the opportunities that await them in the transition from high school to all that follows. In addition to listening, however, it is essential for educators to present career-development training proactively throughout the primary and secondary school curriculum.

WHAT IS CAREER-DEVELOPMENT EDUCATION?

Career counseling is commonly understood as the working through of career difficulties or uncertainties. People typically seek career counseling when they are struggling with some aspect of their work life. Perhaps it is that they feel ungratified in their current work or that they simply are having a difficult time finding an adequately paying job. Or it may be that promotions are proving impossible within their current profession. All these scenarios can lead to varying degrees of life stress, from mild to debilitating. People who are unhappy at work tend to take that unhappiness into other realms of their lives as well, including family life and other personal relationships. The classic role of the career counselor is to help people work through these struggles and find peace, either through career change, professional-skill development training, or through an examination of underlying issues involved in the workplace.

Career-development education, on the other hand, is not problem-based. It is, rather, a proactive approach to helping people understand the relationship between who they are and the type of work and career for which they are well suited. In a comprehensive overview of career-development education across the primary- and secondary-school grades, Richard Lapan provides numerous examples of how even kindergarten students begin preparing for careers through such activities as drawing and storytelling.[1] Barely decipherable scribbles depicting doctors, truck drivers, teachers, and superheroes mark the early career work of kindergarten and early-elementary-school children. By the late-primary-school years, as students move into what Erikson called the Industry versus Inferiority stage of psychosocial development (see chapter 2), the nature of work begins to take on more traditional forms, including challenging task accomplishments, earning rewards for one's contributions (allowances, for example), and thinking consciously about one's unique productivity strengths and weaknesses. By the middle- and high-school years, most students are thinking actively about how they want to make a living both presently and in the future. Unfortunately, according to Lapan and other promoters of career-development education, such thinking is often limited by the immediate opportunity structure when schools fail to play a helpful role in broadening the information needed for effective career planning and preparation.[2]

The Massachusetts Department of Education (MDOE) has taken on the ambitious task of articulating a basic structure for career-development education from kindergarten through high school. In a document aptly titled *Relevance, the Missing Link*, the MDOE has created a comprehensive matrix that highlights key aspects of career-development education that can be implemented across the curriculum at each grade level.[3] It provides examples for linking math concepts with occupational needs associated with those concepts. It does the same for English or the language arts and for the humanities or social studies. The intent is to encourage teachers from each content area to explicitly link what is being taught with the needs of career development. While it may seem obvious to adults that the entire educational curriculum is designed to prepare students for their eventual careers, it is not obvious to all or even most students, which is one of the reasons so many of them become alienated from formal education. The formal curriculum comes to be viewed as irrelevant to "real life" for such students. School smarts and street smarts become separated, with school smarts viewed as disconnected from their longer-term goals.

In her poignant book *School-Smart and Mother-Wise*, Wendy Luttrell captures varying definitions of knowledge held by working-class girls and women.[4] The participants in Luttrell's study depict the importance of school to conceptions of the self, even when school lessons pale in comparison to the reality of what is learned through such experiences as mothering, working, and everyday being in the world. Unfortunately, however, the perceived disconnection between schooling and life's demands leaves many working-class girls and women seeking knowledge in more immediately relevant contexts, only to later regret the loss of formal education and the opportunities that go with it.

The strategy behind the MDOE document is to connect with students like those depicted in Luttrell's study by approaching them from a multitude of directions, with each approach intended to tap into a different aspect of their educational and larger life experiences. The MDOE document organizes its approach to career-development education within three domains: academic/technical, workplace readiness, and personal/social. Within each domain it outlines benchmarks and competencies for early through late elementary school, middle school, and high school and provides examples for building these competencies in each academic content area. In the academic/technical domain, the goal is to find meaningful connections between the academic material being taught and career development. In the workplace readiness domain, such skills as being clear, assertive, supportive, and collegial are emphasized. And in the personal/social domain, recognition of personal and social strengths results when they are explored for their fit with particular career requirements. Between these three domains, there is ample room across the curriculum to address one or more sets of age-specific benchmarks and competencies.

A teacher reviewing the MDOE document and selecting an example for her high-school history course might focus on the second benchmark in the workplace readiness domain: "Learners will develop and demonstrate an exploratory approach toward self, life, and the world of work," with an emphasis on the first competency associated with that benchmark: students will develop "Exploratory attitudes and skills essential to an identity as a life-long learner."[5] We selected history for this example because students often view it as a course that has little relevance to their future careers, even if they might find it interesting. But by creating a history lesson that asks students to examine how they might have responded to the stresses of the Great Depression or the Civil War, for example, the door is opened to considering how lessons from history, when applied to ourselves, might help us better understand the challenges we currently confront. By helping students explore and constructively debate various sides of historical issues, we are helping them to be more critical and flexible thinkers and, ultimately, more thoughtful workers. Students, however, need the scaffolding of educators to see the connections between debates in history and critical judgments that must be made in the workplace; by making these links more transparent, we potentially help our students better understand how seemingly abstract classroom lessons hold a multitude of real-world implications.

An important aspect of career-development education relative to career counseling is that it is deemed a priority for all educators, not just school counselors. Similarly, it is viewed as educational content that should be taught across the curriculum on a regular basis rather than as an extracurricular activity either after school or through annual career days or fairs. It is especially important that career education be taught explicitly across the curriculum so that educators can work collaboratively to create as comprehensive an approach as possible. This is particularly the case for students from low-income and working-class backgrounds for whom exposure to career opportunities may be restricted. And the need is compounded even further when social class intersects with race, ethnicity, and sexual orientation. Low-income gay students of color are less likely to have had exposure to adults from a range of careers who share their key identity characteristics.

Career-development educator Roger Herring has synthesized a broad range of theory and research addressing the multifaceted implications of human diversity in career-development education.[6] He summarizes research on the socializing influences of gender in career preparation and provides helpful examples of how educators can counter gender bias in their career-based work with students. The key is simply being aware that such biases exist and working diligently to counter that trend in our own efforts. Herring also outlines the impact of racial and ethnic influences in career development, including the dearth of racially and ethnically diverse professional models to which many students are exposed. Among the many strategies he reviews are the inclusion of internships and job-shadowing opportunities for students within settings that feature women and people of color in a wide range of professional roles. Such strategies allow students of color, for example, to move beyond their immediate environment in their exposure to a world of work that includes professionals of their racial and ethnic background.

An important and frequently overlooked aspect of diversity reviewed by Herring is the impact of homophobia on career development. He shows how many gay and lesbian students are particularly sensitive to the culture of work environments to which they are exposed, and even to the attitudes of educators preparing students for those environments. It is critical, according to Herring, that gay and lesbian students have an opportunity to ask honest questions about the receptivity of sexual diversity within particular career contexts. Without the opportunity to ask such questions, they are likely to assume that certain careers will be less welcoming and thereby track themselves within those pathways leading to opportunities that appear to be more welcoming. Appearance is the key here. According to Herring, people create occupational myths when they lack adequate information. Adolescents who have not had family members or other people they have known participate in certain occupations often fill in their knowledge gaps with imagined realities. For gay, lesbian, and transgender youth, these imagined realities are likely to be unfriendly. At times the myths might match reality, at other times not. But without adequate information about occupational realities, youth exposed to sexuality prejudices are less likely to explore their opportunities; they are more likely to go where they perceive acceptance and support, even if such careers are not well-matched with their deeper professional interests.

Educators can address two primary areas, according to Herring, to reduce the constraining effects of occupational myths: promote increased self-knowledge and increased occupational knowledge, then examine the intersection of these two knowledge bases. He refers to the approach of exploring the intersections of self and occupational knowledge as *synergetic theory*, arguing that it provides what should be viewed as the focal point of diversity-based career-development education and, in fact, of career-development education in general. As the term implies, synergetic career development is always moving, always evolving. As we learn more about ourselves in relation to specific career options, our choices are likely to shift; perhaps the career direction itself will remain intact, but our roles within that career may be focused differently or become more complex. A similar shifting is likely to occur as we continue to gain a more refined understanding of certain aspects within particular career options; with enhanced occupational knowledge, certain jobs and career types may seem either better or more poorly matched with aspects of our personalities and interests. Matching self and career is but one synergetic puzzle, however; another equally complex one is the matching of oneself with other people in and around the world of work.

LOVE AND WORK REVISITED

Individually and together, Janine and Julian reflect Freud's insight that healthy human functioning is a matter of working and loving well, or at least well enough. As their relationship grew over the course of their senior year in high school, they became a source of both relational and academic support for one another, although in distinctly different ways. As Janine grew closer to Julian and felt progressively less need to party heavily and date others as a means of gaining social acceptance, she was also able to benefit from his intellectual gifts. By helping her with the calculus course he encouraged her to take, Julian modeled a way of thinking and of being a student. And through their work together he experienced a level of acceptance for his academic self that previously had only come from adults. This intensity of appreciation allowed him to lower his guard socially and stop trying so hard to be "the man" Antwon and others wanted him to be. Julian became more comfortable showing a strong academic self in public and, as a result, started thinking seriously about his plans for college . . . and his plans for Janine.

"Yo, we gotta stop playing, you know. College applications are due in a month and we haven't even started yet. We gotta figure out where we're gonna go."

"Whaddya mean, where 'we' gonna go? You're the man with the options, dude. I'll be lucky if I get in anywhere . . . but I don't even know if I wanna go next year. I might wait a year and figure it out . . . get a little work experience before I think about college."

"What are you, crazy? You're my litt dawgg! You showed everybody you can write. And that's why you took that calculus class, to show you can do math too. With your madd writing skills alone, you be fine. Let's figure out the places we wanna apply to and see where we get in. There's no waitin' till next year, yo."

"Who says I'm going where you go even if I do apply? Maybe we should have some freedom when we go to college. Ain't that what college is s'posed to be about?"

"Yo, hold up . . . what are you talkin' about?! I don't plan on bein' your daddy! You can have your freedom. Hell, I want mine too. But I ain't ready to go away without you after all we been through."

Hearing Julian talk like this brought Janine full circle. She could hardly believe the two of them were talking about going away together to college. It seemed like yesterday when she thought her education was over after the pregnancy scare and change of schools following the ninth grade. She thought about her struggles for acceptance and realized how little she actually thought about anything like a career in the face of her ongoing social challenges. And here was Julian, star student and patient boyfriend, nearly pleading to stand by her and guiding her to take this next step in her life with him. Julian, with the dark-Brown skin that made her parents so anxious, was playing such a central role in her life. The magnitude of it all made her dizzy. Once more she'd need some time. Once more she'd ask Julian to wait while she figured some things out. In the meantime, he began pursuing his options more aggressively, seeking out schools that would fit with his unique combination of interests in art, math and science, and writing. He'd wait for Janine, but he couldn't delay for himself. Not at this point. He'd come too far.

Career development is as much a relational construct as other aspects of identity. As much as we tend to think in terms of "my career," we build our careers with people. We consider who works in what fields and whether we would want to work with them and to be like them professionally. Although Janine and Julian's case demonstrates educational and career development within a close romantic relationship, the reciprocal support they provide each other happens in all types of close relationships. In chapters 3 and 4 we presented Vygotsky's notion of interpsychological development: our minds grow through connections with other people's minds. Thinking about our careers is no exception. Our career cognitions or ideas for how we would like to live out our work lives are enhanced through connections with others' career thinking and general work activity. We can learn about career options abstractly through reading about them, but we learn more meaningfully by experiencing career possibilities through connection with people in their own planning and working processes. Extending Freud's notion of love to relational closeness more broadly, close working relationships are an essential aspect of healthy human functioning: in many respects, we can only work well to the extent that we can relate well on the job.

Internships or apprenticeships have long been staples of vocational development. They provide opportunities to learn not only about work but also how to work together. Frequently, however, they have been associated with extremes along the educational continuum. Academically lower-achieving students often are exposed to apprenticeships through vocational education programming designed to prepare them for such trades or semiprofessional careers as carpentry, auto mechanics, cosmetology, and entry-level clerical work. At the other end of the spectrum, academically high-achieving students in late high school and college historically have been exposed to internships that introduce them to such competitive professions as law, medicine, and engineering. The connection between these two groups of students is that the hands-on experiences were designed for students showing particular academic strengths or weaknesses—specialized opportunities for "special" students.

Today, however, internships and apprenticeships are being reframed as vital learning opportunities for all students. Why should the "middle class" be left out—those students who are neither struggling academically nor scoring near the top of their class. It is these students, in particular, who may benefit most from exploring a range of options that could help determine how to invest their academic time and energy. The Met School in Providence, Rhode Island, has become a pioneer in building apprenticeship opportunities for all its students. Students at the Met rotate through internships during each year of high school, learning firsthand what it means to be a nurse or electrical engineer, for example. Programs like the Met that feature apprenticeship opportunities are most effective when such experiences are integrated within the academic curriculum. If students "do school" for part of the day and do their internships during another part, without the structure to integrate them, the two components of their education and training remain isolated. Conversely, when structures exist for discussing the nature of internship experiences with fellow students and teachers and writing critical analyses of these experiences for class credit, the benefits tend to be deeper. Most importantly, bringing the "work" of internships into the classroom helps build the bridge from school to career. It allows teachers to point out and reinforce the academic skills needed for particular careers, and it challenges them to make their lessons transparently useful to their students' career interests.

The Met School's website provides a clear example of the emphasis on integrating school, career, and relationships that many schools today are seeking.[7] The "Met Intro" page of the website features the logo "Learning: Succeeding Together at the Met." The first two links to other pages are entitled "Sustained Relationships" and "Real-World Learning." On the "Sustained Relationships" page, the introduction reads:

> Relationships undergird all learning at The Met. Keeping adults and other students at bay is not an option. Met students must build close relationships with an advisor, community mentors, and other Met faculty, if they

are to fulfill their personal learning plans. They must also commit to an advisory group made up of peers, plus substantial give-and-take with the larger school community. Perhaps hardest of all, The Met requires that its adolescent students accept their parents as learning "partners." The personal connections that result are at once trusting and complex. "It's a lot harder here," explains one Met student. "The teachers . . . they see all of your strong points, all your weak points, everything."

The "Real-World Learning" page of the Met's website builds on this relational approach by depicting how internship-based learning is brought into the academic curriculum through individualized learning plans and public presentations of lessons gleaned from work-based projects. It also shows how teachers serve as advisers who work with the students to recognize and cultivate the academic skills needed to prepare for the types of careers modeled through their internships; at the core of this preparation is college readiness. In summary, the Met approach integrates work, learning, and healthy relating at every step; their philosophy suggests that success in any one of these domains is rendered more difficult without a balanced emphasis on all three.

We emphasize the Met approach here in part because it has had an enormous influence nationally as a counter to what its founders call "test-based accountability." They refer to their approach as "one student at a time accountability," and have used this approach in their development of a rapidly expanding network of schools under the umbrella of the Big Picture Company, an educational nonprofit that is part of the small-schools movement endorsed by such educational reformers as Ted Sizer and his Coalition for Essential Schools and influential foundations such as the Bill and Melinda Gates Foundation, which has invested millions of dollars supporting the development of innovative small-school approaches to educational reform.[8] The collective goal of these institutions, whether independent small schools, education-reform nonprofits, or philanthropic foundations, is to model the benefits of real-world, relationship-based education. The ultimate goal is not to create niche schools but to encourage all schools to adopt the principles they model. How realistic is such a goal? Can large urban schools manifest the benefits of small schools?

In his book about the Met School, *One Kid at a Time: Big Lessons from a Small School*, Elliott Levine argues convincingly for the merits of smaller schools for all students and presents compelling evidence of the dramatic changes that can happen when teachers have the time to forge meaningful relationships with students.[9] At the core of his argument, however, is the interconnecting of close educator-student relationships and real-world opportunities to build essential work and career skills via apprenticeships. Such principles can be practiced in all schools, but the challenges to doing so are exponentially harder the larger the school and the teacher-student ratio. Dennis Littky, one of the founders of the Met School and the Big Picture Company, makes similar claims in his book with Samantha Grabelle.[10] He argues that the commitment to build smaller, more innovative learning communities ought to be a national priority for everyone, given what is at stake for the country and that it is difficult to envision broad-based, successful outcomes for students through large, overcrowded, comprehensive high schools. So where does that leave those of us who work in such schools?

It leaves us, we argue, faced with the reality that, to prepare our students for the world of work and career, we must commit to knowing them as people, not just as learners with particular aptitudes and skill sets. We must strive to know them as Ms. Petersen persisted in reaching Janine in chapter 3 by recruiting her for the yearbook project. By tapping into Janine's writing skills and helping to forge a working relationship between Janine and Julian, Ms. Petersen helped make learning and educational productivity more real for her struggling student. Although Ms. Petersen did not have the luxury of a better teacher-student ratio nor a formal internship program, she created her own internship possibility through the yearbook project. This allowed Janine to work with the larger editorial team and to both learn from them and contribute meaningfully. Like other positive internship opportunities, this one was made richer by connecting the yearbook project to the larger academic community through public discussions and displays and by connecting the writing project to material learned in Janine and Julian's history class. Whether in specific, targeted projects like this one or larger, more formalized internship possibilities like those sponsored by the Met School, connected learning—learning connected to the world of work and to supportive educators and mentors—is critical to facilitating the school-to-career transition.

FROM HIGH SCHOOL TO COLLEGE

In our work with middle-school students, we find that even those who are struggling to pass their classes typically have aspirations for attending college. The feeling is that things will change in high school, that the earlier grades in school are not relevant to college. This perception, of course, could not be farther from the truth. Academic skill building is a cumulative process, with the elementary and middle-school grades being fundamental to later high-school and college success. But while the student-perceived disconnect between middle school and college is understandable—albeit troubling as a predictor of future academic success and failure—the actual disconnect between high-school and college experiences is even more worrisome. Many low-income and working-class students who perform well in high school ultimately flounder in college, with large percentages of them eventually dropping out. There are a number of leading explanations for this clear and distressing pattern.

Some of the explanations are obvious to even the casual observer: large under-resourced high schools cannot prepare their students well enough to succeed in college; low-income and working-class students often do not have models for college success in their immediate or extended families; lower-income students need to work long hours while they are enrolled in college, making academic success a lower priority or at least probability. Such findings have been documented time and again by a host of scholars.[11] In addition to these explanations, however, others have pointed to fundamental disconnects between the structures of high-school and college learning. Some of the distinctions between the two learning environments include the nature of classroom structure and functioning, the types of assignments expected of students in high school and college, and the levels of both independence and collaboration expected in the two environments. Differences along these lines do not exist across all high school–college comparisons, of course, and they are most pronounced when comparing the structure and functioning of large comprehensive high schools relative to smaller, competitive colleges.

Regarding distinctions in the nature of classroom structure and functioning, many large high schools require students to sit in assigned seats and respond to teacher questions in much the same manner as had been the norm throughout elementary and middle school. Classroom disciplinary practices also can look quite similar to those of earlier grades. This, of course, does not prepare students for the more open seating and discussion formats that exist in most colleges. Accordingly, students who come from schools that functioned most dissimilarly from the nature of their college classrooms are most likely to feel out of place and ill prepared. Motivation, in turn, is reduced, and the likelihood of eventual college dropout is increased.

The nature of classroom work can differ markedly from high school to college, with many large high schools needing to resort to multiple-choice and short-answer tests to cope with large teacher-student ratios. For colleges that rely more heavily on essays and longer-answer assessment practices, students not exposed to a strong writing curriculum in high school are at an enormous disadvantage. Even when written assignments, such as independent research papers, are required for high-school students in large schools, teachers often do not have ample time to provide thorough-enough feedback to enhance critical thinking and writing skills. These are just some of the many disconnects that often exist between high-school and college learning and which educational reform initiatives are beginning to address more aggressively.

Michael Kirst and Andrea Venezia have documented educational policy initiatives that are designed to pave the way for smoother transitions from high school to college.[12] These initiatives, drawn from states across the country, are built around the recognition that lower-income and working-class students who attend large comprehensive high schools, and who may be succeeding in those schools, are being misled in their preparation for college. Because the gaps between college expectations and high-school functioning are at times so large, success at the high-school level can be rendered virtually meaningless to college success. Only by creating an educational system that systematically embraces K–16 curriculum planning and institutional structuring, the authors argue, can we expect to reduce the enormous college dropout rates experienced by successful low-income and working-class students from large comprehensive high schools.

The Bill & Melinda Gates Foundation, which has been so instrumental in funding and helping to envision the small-schools movement, has initiated a model that explicitly addresses the high school-to-college crisis. The Early College High Schools (ECHS) Initiative was designed and sponsored by the Gates Foundation in collaboration with such key partners as Jobs for the Future,[13] an educational and economic development nonprofit organization, to create small schools that explicitly focus on preparing students for college completion. At the center of this initiative are partnerships between high schools and colleges that allow the high-school students to take a wide range of college courses while completing their high-school diplomas. In fact, a goal for the initiative is to encourage students to complete an associates degree while they are in high school, even if this requires taking an extra year to graduate. The initiative serves several core functions in helping high-school students prepare for college success: it exposes them early on to the nature of college coursework and expectations; it socializes them into the structure and functioning of college classrooms, including interaction styles; it covers costs for a substantial portion of one's college career; and it culti-vates habits of coursework preparation. In essence, the initiative creates one means of making the transition from high school to college more seamless. Although definitive results from the initiative are not yet available, it is clear that many students are benefiting from the model, taking and completing college courses while in high school, and feeling prepared for college in a manner they could not have anticipated in larger comprehensive high schools.[14]

As with all the small-school initiatives, a goal of the ECHS Initiative is to provide models for mainstream schools to emulate. In fact, many large high schools have partnerships with colleges, both community and four-year colleges, which allow students to earn college credit while in high school. But in addition to creating such opportunities, it also would behoove high-school educators to forge informal consulting relationships with colleagues from local colleges and universities. These relationships can result in high-school students sitting in on or auditing college courses to get a feel for the reality of the next step. They can also result in tutoring and mentoring rela-tionships between college and high-school students and in opportunities for all-day workshops on college campuses. The stronger the connections between high schools and local colleges and universities, the greater the like-lihood that the high-school students will gain a more realistic grounding in what is expected of them as they transition to postsecondary education.

A WORKING IDENTITY

Whether gained through internship experiences or paid employment at the corner store, "working" can have a profound influence on overall identity development in adolescence. In fact, such demographic identity markers as race, gender, ethnicity, and social class, while profoundly influential, can be mediated quite dramatically through the world of work. That mediation, of course, can take any number of directions. Take Antwon Saladin, for exam-ple. His feelings of being disrespected by Ms. Petersen in his world history class, based largely on his perception that racial biases influenced her actions toward him, could either be exacerbated or ameliorated through the nature of his early employment experiences. Feeling respected at work for his skills and accomplishments might allow him to gain a deeper sense of self-efficacy and, in turn, self-respect. Depending on the nature of that work, Antwon might come to see himself as someone who is especially good with people, with money, or working with his hands. The feeling of competence in the relevant occupational arena, if reinforced thoroughly enough, may come to be experienced as central to who he is and to his place in the world. If, over time, he perceives being respected by a range of colleagues for his performance, including White men and women, the impact of his interactions with Ms. Petersen is likely to be minimized or even positively transformed. If, on the other hand, his work experiences are marked by interracial tension, the disrespect he felt in Ms. Petersen's class is likely to be magnified.

We are, of course, more than a representation of our work. On the other hand, our work does represent us to varying degrees and in a variety of ways. For youth who have not been well represented by their classroom performance or by highly prized extracurricular activities such as sports or the arts, their ability to earn a paycheck, to begin making their way in the world, can be especially powerful. It can, as Antwon's example suggests, represent them as competent and reliable. The power in paid work can be intoxicating. Suddenly, the 17-year-old girl who could not afford the clothes of her admired peers drives to school in her own car! But there can be a steep price to pay for her working wage. Students who derive inordinate amounts of self-worth from working long hours and earning material rewards not enjoyed by their peers run the risk of losing interest in school and falling behind. Good short-term earnings can lead to the loss of longer-term opportunities that bring much larger rewards.

It is difficult for educators to discourage students from earning money to purchase the things their parents cannot afford, yet it is critical to raise students' awareness around the opportunity costs associated with imbalanced work lives. A key part of career-development education in the mid- to late-high-school years is assessing the value of current employment opportunities against both immediate financial needs and longer-term goals. A hallmark of adolescent thinking, as we pointed out in chapters 3 and 4, is the increased ability to think abstractly, which includes projecting oneself from the present to the future, both the short- and long-term future. But such projection typically requires support. Teachers and counselors can help students see the links between their current employment opportunities and their longer-term financial and larger life goals by presenting scenarios that depict various pathways toward goal attainment, financial and otherwise. Where do current jobs fall along such pathways? What are they helping build toward? What might they be inhibiting? Are there optimal hours that should be worked in order to meet both short- and long-term goals? Short of actively posing such questions to students, it is possible that they will never be asked. And if they go unasked, the default, particularly for our most financially needy students, is that they will work as much as possible, maximizing their earnings and sense of self now only to compromise them down the road.

Inventing the future, a future that can pay the full range of dividends that we want for all our students, requires strategic attention to the present. Such strategy must pay particular attention to the role of work in students' lives and the nature of compensation for that work. Successful school work is compensated by good grades and test scores, calling cards for college and professional careers. Successful employment is compensated by money in the here-and-now and is a calling card for further and more advanced employment opportunities. For poor and low-income students who have these two options, there is little wonder so many of them opt for immediate financial compensation. They are inventing their futures in the most reasonable manner—they are building work histories that will create work futures. And they are building identities as workers, working identities that represent who they are and who they are becoming. But as low-income and working-class students claim their roles as workers, they may be foreclosing on other roles simultaneously.

As career-development educators, it is not our role to judge the evolving work histories we see before us, but it is our responsibility to inform and question. Because identity is such a work in progress during adolescence, the "working identities" of our students must be among our top educational priorities.

CHAPTER TWELVE

The Educational Ecology of Adolescent Development

We close this book with what we call the *educational ecology of adolescent development*. This concept refers to the multitude of ways in which learning and development occur through all facets of schooling: in the links between school and home, in peer relationships, in classroom connections and disconnections, and in interdisciplinary efforts to integrate classrooms with counseling and related support processes. In other words, the educational impact on adolescent development emerges from the intersections that make up the young person's world in and outside of school. Every educator—whether teacher, counselor, school nurse, or athletic coach—plays a role, maybe several roles, within the larger educational ecology. Viewed in isolation, those roles would seem to carry their distinct meanings within the adolescent's life and, perhaps, to make their singular contributions to student development. Viewed in interaction, however, each role holds the capacity to make a much larger contribution. Through interaction with other educational roles in the larger ecology, each individual makes a multiplicative contribution to development—an overall contribution clearly greater than the mere sum of its parts. In this closing chapter, we portray coordinated educational interactions that yield an optimally productive educational ecology, one that holds the greatest capacity to promote constructive and healthy adolescent development.

Ecological approaches such as the one we outline here owe a tremendous debt to the work of Urie Bronfenbrenner, a cultural and developmental scholar whose work has dramatically influenced the fields of psychology, education, and human development.[1] Bronfenbrenner articulated a model of human development that was comprehensively grounded in *contextual inter-actionism*—the infinite ways in which cultural contexts interact to shape human development. His model, originally called an *ecological approach to human development*, focuses on the ways in which each individual is situated within the multiple environmental contexts in which she interacts and is influenced. Specifically, Bronfenbrenner articulated four levels of human ecological systems. The *microlevel* focuses on the immediate contexts in which the individual functions on a daily basis. These include student inter-actions with parents, teachers, peers, community organizations, or any other settings visited on a regular basis. Microsystem influences are those in which the student has direct involvement. The *mesosystem* is composed of combina-tions of microlevel influences. Parent and teacher interactions regarding stu-dent engagement in school would constitute a mesolevel influence, as would parent-friend and teacher-peer interactions. The mesolevel, then, captures the impact of interactions among contexts of influence that are particularly close to home for the individual.

The final two levels of Bronfenbrenner's model are a bit more distant from students but still influential. The *exosystem* is composed of contexts in which important people in the young person's life are involved and which, in turn, affect the young person indirectly. Parents' jobs provide the classic example: youth are influenced by the successes and stresses of their parents' work lives or, for many poor children, by the welfare or public support sys-tems in which their parents might be involved. From an educational perspec-tive, students are influenced indirectly by their teachers' professional training workshops, just as they are by the neighborhood influences that affect their peers, who in turn bring those influences into the school. When looked at comprehensively, exosystemic effects are quite profound. Imagine the myri-ad ways in which parents, teachers, and friends are subjected to their own microsystemic influences and then pass these effects on to those around them. Our students are all absorbers of the daily experience of being in the world, but not just of their own being; they absorb the ups and downs of all those they love and care about most deeply and, to a lesser extent, of those to whom they are exposed through the simple act of being a classmate.

Finally, the *macrosystem* is composed of the larger societal contexts that inform all levels of the human ecology. Our students are influenced by the outcome of national elections; by cultural norms manifested through the media via television, movies, and popular music; by a legal system that sets regulations for educational policy and the punishment of criminal behavior in their neighborhoods. Although macrosystem influences exist at the larger cultural, societal, and even global levels, their perceived distance from everyday interactions does not reduce their impact. The wars a nation wages, for example, as they get played out on television and talked about at home and in school, inform the manner in which students perceive the government, perceive "enemies," and perceive themselves as future contributors to the country. Should I plan to serve in the military? Is that my responsibility as a young person? What would my parents think of that? What are the implications of my service for my future? Is this a cause worth dying for? For many youth and their families today, these questions might seem far removed from their reality, but a few short decades ago, at a time when there was a mandatory draft for males, such macrolevel questions carried tremendous weight for the majority of male youth. As global tensions escalate, questions like these come more into focus. Perhaps they are not exclusively about serving in the military but are more broadly related to one's roles and responsibilities within the context of a changing world. Whatever the specifics of one's questions and decisions in this regard, day-to-day life is framed and influenced by the larger world and its defining challenges.

Taken as a whole, Bronfenbrenner's model shows how human development is anything but an autonomous enterprise. Humans grow in interaction with their worlds, through the multiple interactive layers of cultural influence. To acknowledge the role of individual biology in the human ecology, Bronfenbrenner modified his model and renamed it a *bioecological approach to human development*.[2] This modification explicitly shows how individual differences in cognition, emotion, personality, and physical attributes interact with environmental influences to shape development. The addition of a biological or individual component to the model signals that people are not just passive products of ecological influences; rather, they are active agents in the contextual interactionist process. We contribute uniquely to cultural influences just as we are shaped by them.

Margaret Beale Spencer, a developmental scholar who has long been interested in how Black students perceive cultural influences on them and the impact of those perceptions on their school performance, has modified Bronfenbrenner's model further by using it as a starting point for examining how students experience education and other developmental processes.[3] Similar in some respects to Bronfenbrenner's own addition of biological or individual factors, Spencer is particularly invested in comprehending the different ways in which youth actually experience and interpret cultural influences, rather than simply exploring the structure or "facts" of systemic realities and their interactions. Her research has yielded a number of important findings, two of which are as follows. She found that for African American boys in middle adolescence (14- to 16-year-olds), attitudes toward learning were strongly associated with experienced levels of environmental stress, such as poverty, neighborhood violence, etc.; in fact, the impact of experienced levels of such stress outweighed differences in engagement in risky behaviors or reactive coping styles—such as impulsive acting-out behavior—in predicting attitudes toward learning. It is important to note here that the experience of stress is a perceptual or experiential variable; rather than examining "actual" stressors in the environment, Spencer's study focused on differences in the experiences of stress—how students found particular environmental influences to be stressful. From a microsystems perspective, she argues that such experiences can be mediated by parents, teachers, and friends through the provision of support and suggests that, the more schools can do to provide such support, the more we could expect middle-adolescent African American students' learning attitudes, and subsequent academic performance, to improve.

Spencer's second finding focuses on middle-adolescent African American girls. She found that perceived unpopularity with peers was particularly predictive of their learning attitudes. Girls who felt that they were unpopular tended to have poorer attitudes toward learning. Again, according to Spencer, the popularity index here is a perceptual one; it is not about whether the girls in the study actually were popular or unpopular but about how they perceived their popularity. From Spencer's perspective, educators—both teachers and counselors—hold the capacity to mediate this relationship by helping students see these connections and working with them to modify their popularity perceptions either through group interventions or through pedagogical strategies that facilitate healthy student interactions in the classroom. Although Spencer's research focused on African American students, her findings shed light on the experiences of other students as well.

In previous chapters we presented a number of cases in which student perceptions influenced their school-related attitudes and performance. Janine's efforts to become more popular led her to party more extensively to gain social approval and in turn were associated with a slide in her academic performance. Julian too, for a stretch, became anxious about his friends' perception of him as a good student who would not challenge authority and engaged in social interactions that threatened to compromise his school performance. And Steve Chang, tired of being taunted for his academic prowess, experimented with a "hard enough" social posture that might gain him broader peer approval; this effort, in turn, was associated with temporary academic decline.

In summary, Spencer's work provides a useful way for educators to think practically about the ecological influences *on* their students. Rather than feeling helpless over the layers of influence that exist in all students' lives beyond our awareness, the opportunity created by Spencer's experiential and interpretive approach is for educators to enter the interpretive process *with* their students. In the sections that follow, we present examples of how that might be done.

RERUNS: CRITIQUING THE MEDIA IN OUR CLASSROOMS

Competing and interacting with the impact of parents, friends, and schools, the media exert a profound influence on the adolescent's understanding of herself and the world. Arguably more than any other source, the media provide the dominant images that frame what it means to be a child, a teen, an adult, a man, a woman, an African American, a Latino/a, a Korean, a homosexual, a heterosexual, you name it. If it can sell, it will be represented. While others may be reticent to take on some of these issues, the media profit by doing so, and often by doing so in simplistic, caricatured ways—if that's what sells best. Television, movies, billboards, radio, video games, CDs, DVDs, the Internet, magazines, and newspapers all bombard youth with depictions of the ideal and the reprehensible. With the ubiquity of such images growing exponentially over the past few decades and the production of such media becoming more condensed into large conglomerates, concerted attention must be given to how adolescents organize their identities in response to the media's offerings. The effect of the teen market on movies, advertising, television, and radio is enormous. The fixation in our society with things youthful leads to teen-saturated and often dangerously reductive depictions of what it means to be young and beautiful, alive and vivacious—what it means, in essence, to "have" what it takes to be either at the very center of things or out at the head of the pack leading the way. What effect might the various media have on adolescents reared on a steady diet of its messages?

How might educators accompany youth as they navigate through the media and understand themselves in relationship to it? How can we help adolescents become critical citizens in a media-rich society? What opportunities might we provide for adolescents to *be* the media?

Perhaps the strongest statement of the media's impact on the students presented in the prior chapters can be found in Jerry's case. His initial reaction to and ongoing obsession with hard-core pornography left him confused and rendered captive to a world that was at once foreign and progressively familiar. He came to know sexual intimacy only through DVDs and found himself unable to connect with real-life romantic partners despite his growing desperation to do so. Jerry was fortunate to eventually find support through Maggie Lang, his school counselor, but we wonder how his struggles might have been modified through a critique of pornography's influence on human development as a classroom exercise. Granted, this would constitute a fairly risky endeavor for any teacher. There would be fears of overstimulating students via introduction of the very topic. But most students are hyperexposed to intense media-based sexual imagery already; critiquing it is unlikely to heighten that level of arousal in a dangerous or counterproductive manner.

What might such a classroom critique look like? It might begin with a display of imagery from television commercials and popular magazine covers, images the students have likely seen repeatedly. Students would be asked to analyze their impression of these images, including the extent to which they find the models portrayed attractive and sexy. They would then be asked to venture an opinion on whether there is anything problematic in depicting human beings as sex objects and human interactions in sexually objectified ways for the purpose of selling products. Following some discussion, teachers might ask about additional images commonly seen on the Internet or through other media outlets. There might be a shift from popular sexualized images to pornographic material proper with another discussion on students' perceptions of that topic. It might be valuable to present statistics on the volume of pornography depicted through various media outlets and the amount of money made by the larger pornography industry. That discussion might be followed by a summary of research on the psychological effects of viewing pornography, how it shapes our perceptions of others, of ourselves, and of our attitudes toward intimate relationships.[4] While the progression of this sort of media critique and sexuality education lesson might prove difficult to manage, particularly without adequate preparation, the odds are that students like Jerry would gain valuable insight from such discussions and might be empowered to talk through their personal concerns sooner. Such information helps students recognize that they are not alone in their concerns, that they are not odd or unusual, and that support is available if they choose to access it.

A group of educators and youth developmentalists from Portland, Oregon, initiated a proactive approach to media representations in their community. Take the Time—a youth development and community-change group affiliated with Search Institute's Healthy Communities–Healthy Youth Initiative—recognized that their local newspaper portrayed youth problems at a rate grossly disproportional to their positive contributions and set out to rectify the imbalance by organizing youth contributions to the paper through articles written about and by youth.[5] The group was able to accomplish this feat by approaching the newspaper, as it did other media outlets, and recruit them as participants in their community-wide approach to promoting healthy youth development. The Portland initiative, citing the media tenet "If it bleeds it leads," put the media front and center in their community-change work, arguing that it is virtually impossible to promote healthy shifts in youth development if we cannot shift the dominant representations of young people in the pages of our newspapers and related media outlets. But whether educators reach out to mainstream media outlets or work to create their own media representations of young people within the pages of their school publications, it is critical for students to have an active role in creating and critiquing the representations of youth that come to represent who and how they are and the roles they play in the construction of their communities.

THE ECOLOGY OF RESISTANCE IN LEARNING AND DEVELOPMENT

Student resistance is one of the most frequently cited barriers to learning. In traditional "resistance models," students are understood to resist teachers' efforts to reach them due to the psychological baggage they bring to school. In these models, resistance is viewed as a form of pathological or defensive reaction, a critical impediment to healthy functioning in and outside the classroom. In some cases, it seems clear that student resistance is an unhealthy overreaction to their environment, stemming from a history of abuse or other childhood difficulties. Feminist and other critical psychological researchers, however, have presented alternative versions of resistance models to help explain why this phenomenon is so widespread in our schools. Specifically, they have shown how resistance can be a healthy defensive response to oppressive and potentially abusive relationships. This theory extends not only to the microlevel ecology of family systems but also to the mesolevel classroom and larger educational institutions. From the perspective of this alternative model, it is imperative that educators view student resistance as a form of engagement rather than a form of distancing. That is, resistance should be viewed as a signal of vulnerability, not one of aggression. This signal, in turn, needs to be received as an invitation to reach out, to acknowledge that educational engagement, like other human relationships, must be built on a foundation of trust. For students who have developed healthy resistance to unhealthy circumstances, learning connections need to be developed over time. If teachers give up on this negotiation prematurely, opportunities for trust building and engaged learning are lost. In this section, we present strategies for building trust and fostering engagement in learning relationships with students who have needed to resist in order to survive.

In addition to shifting our view of resistance from pathological to potentially healthy, educators are encouraged to examine their role in resistant processes, to question how they participate in an ecology that produces resistant behaviors in youth. Why might students be resisting our efforts to reach them? What are we, as educators, contributing to the resistant dynamic? Understanding resistance purely as a student phenomenon ignores the educator's role in the dynamic. Reflective education requires that we examine our roles in educational relationships. A relational approach to learning, as we discussed in chapter 5, assumes an educational relationship rather than unilateral teaching and learning processes. From this perspective, resistance cannot be viewed as a response strictly of one relational partner; rather, it must be viewed as a dynamic bred in the relationship itself.

Working with adolescents in schools, as one teacher once put it, "can be a real trip." As anyone who's ever been on such a trip knows, it isn't always a thrill—for all parties involved. Sometimes, despite our best intentions and most carefully considered approaches, youth reject what we have to offer, which can make our work frustrating, if not painful. Our care, teaching, advice, guidance, and all the hours that go into them are sometimes met with resistance, and, despite our most concerted efforts to remain professionally objective, when our students don't want what we have to give, it can hurt. Nobody likes being rebuffed. But in those moments where we are put off by their refusals or offended by what we perceive to be their lack of respect for all we do on their behalf, it is important to remember that resistance can serve a healthy, and even necessary, function for our students. It is one of the most developmentally powerful behaviors available to an adolescent, positioning as it does the sense of self and worldview the individual wants against the identity and circumstances she may be challenging. Seen through a developmental lens, moments of resistance are moments of identity construction. If we are courageous enough to stay engaged with adolescents resisting our work rather than turn away when we feel snubbed, that construction may become collaborative—co-constructive, if you will.

Herbert Kohl has described some of the reasons students resist what we do and why that resistance might be understood as a healthy response.[6] Framing learning and schooling relationally, Kohl characterizes the dynamic of child and adolescent resistance to educators' work as "I won't learn from you." This response emerges as youth confront the fact that what they are being asked to learn sometimes entails a denial of what they may already know. Being required to sit in a certain way, speak in a specific tone, adhere to grammatical standards, refrain from socializing with valued peers, avoid questioning authority, ask before going to the restroom—all these seemingly "normal" school behaviors may differ significantly from the student's family or culture. Without regular opportunities to express one's home-self and have it valued, adolescents may rightfully resist school because it is being experienced as a displacement. Especially for adolescents outside the White-male, middle-class, heteronormative, and Christian mainstream, to agree to learn from an adult who does not display knowledge of nor respect for your integrity can cause a major loss of self. Additionally, as was the case with Lorena, many students experience the trajectory of "success" offered by schools as a severing of the familial and community ties that most energized them during their formative years. If this sort of success is understood as a subtractive process—less as a journey up and away and more as a ticket out and apart—adolescent opposition to school and to the adults charged with its operation makes psychological sense.[7]

In a series of studies over the past two decades, Signithia Fordham and the late John Ogbu have advocated one of the most pervasive theories regarding adolescent resistance to school.[8] Their research explores the causes and representations of *oppositional identities* in what they call "involuntary minorities," or the racial and ethnic populations that have been incorporated into the United States against their will (namely African Americans, Latino/as, and Native Americans). Since these groups' perspectives stem from a shared legacy of oppression in which definitions of success require a comparison with the dominant White majority, school can sometimes be understood as an instrument of indoctrination and exclusion. For youth with this disposition, to do well in school is to cooperate with an institution and with adults who may not be acting in one's best interests. Fordham and Ogbu argue that for some involuntary minorities, to accept and align oneself with a school's curriculum is to "act White." Therefore, to retain their racial or ethnic identity, the adolescent must reject school by opposing its methods and personnel, essentially creating an identity that is opposed to school.

Folk theories about oppositional identities abound in schools. Students from low-income families or involuntary minorities are often said not to recognize the benefits of education as much as more successful students from middle-class or White families who tend to perform better. These "underprivileged" students are sometimes said to possess less motivation and demonstrate diminished engagement due to a lack of appreciation for what school offers. The students "just don't care," and their parents, often either reluctant to enter an institution they experience as unwelcoming or too busy working multiple jobs to make time for school visits, "just don't value education." The implication is that such students arrive at school with a deficit of knowledge and an underdeveloped investment in school. Failure is therefore their fault. Confronting perspectives such as these, it is no wonder that many African American, Latino/a, and Native American students channel their intelligence and energies into resistance rather than compliance. Wanting to feel smart, to be valued, and to experience growth, students rightfully challenge educators who exhibit such deficit-model orientations and may avail themselves of the developmental benefits of resistance.

Many researchers have challenged Fordham and Ogbu's conclusions because of the way in which they suggest a monolithic portrayal of involuntary minorities whose lives are overdetermined by rigid castelike hierarchies. Choosing to focus on the positive aspects of resistance as opposed to the victimhood of an oppositional identity, researchers such as Janie Ward (see chapter 6), Prudence Carter, and L. Janelle Dance present research that shows adolescents as agents in their development. Carter's research shows that urban Latino/a and African American adolescents subscribe to the basic values of mainstream education and a productive work ethic as much as and, in some cases, even more than Whites.[9] These students' resistance to "acting White" stems more from a lack of embedded experiences in school than from a philosophical rejection of education. Rarely made to feel as though they belong and seldom finding homespaces in which they can experiment with their identities and critique social expectations, students may talk back to their teachers, reject the care of counselors, and purposefully neglect academics in order to preserve the parts of them they cannot bring to school. Carter suggests that the most successful students in such schools are not those who adopt a wholly mainstream identity but are instead the ones who become most skilled at moving back and forth between domains, eventually developing the intellectual, cultural, and behavioral resources they need to maintain a multicultural identity.

Dance's research examines similar patterns of adolescent resistance to school by juxtaposing the identities students bring from the street with those they may be required to adopt in order to "do school."[10] She presents three ostensibly resistant identities—"tough fronts," as she calls them—that students often bring to school: the *hardcore*, the *hardcore wannabe*, and the *hard-enough*. The hardcore student is involved in gang activity, has donned hip-hop modes of dress and adopted a tough ready-to-fight demeanor, uses profane and slang-dependent language, and often reacts with violence to perceived threats from others. The hardcore wannabe student, on the other hand, although nearly identical in posture and appearance to the hardcore, is in fact not involved in violent or criminal activity and has assumed the hardcore persona largely to protect herself from neighborhood threats. Whereas the hardcore is ready, willing, and able to "walk the walk" if need be, the hardcore wannabe is more interested in "talking the talk," in making a fashion statement and hoping to avoid situations in which that identity is put to the test. As opposed to the hardcore and hardcore wannabe, being hard-enough means being familiar enough with the culture of the street and linguistically capable of communicating with the hardcores and hardcore wannabes such that one can pass as hard, but all the while attending to academic matters and attempting to succeed in school underneath the scrutiny of one's harder friends.

While the differences between these identities and the types of resistance they present are of enormous consequence to the students in Dance's study, many of the educators with whom her participants work seem unable or unwilling to see how one differs from another. In fact, students in Dance's study consistently lament the paucity of educators who have the ability to distinguish between these three identities and engage students in a way that demonstrates an understanding of the streets. Unable to make distinctions between hardcore and hard-enough, educators often misread student posturing as "disruptive" behavior, even though for many students such conduct is a necessary front for surviving on the streets. When educators lump all street-inspired resistant behaviors into a single gangster category, they not only lose their students' attention and respect but confirm the harder students' suspicion that schooling is irrelevant and the teachers are clueless. The inevitable result is that the student learns to favor the life of the street and reject what educators have to offer, legitimizing the gangster way of life.

Taking adolescent development seriously means sometimes not taking youths' "tough fronts" at face value. Educators who promote healthy resistance in youth will consider their students' stance toward school in the larger ecology of the choices they make as they create lives and identities for themselves. Providing homespaces for relationship-building and belonging, distinguishing between mere postures and actual commitments to gang activity, encouraging resistance for liberation as much as for survival, and extolling and enhancing the assets of flexible and adaptable multicultural identities can go a long way toward reclaiming the developmental benefits of healthy resistance. Humor, patience, and trust are invaluable resources here and are frequently the characteristics students look for in adults they feel possess a certain "with-it-ness," who "get" what it means to be an adolescent today.

To "get" youth, to understand them within the complex realities of their lives, is a critical step toward an effective educational process. As we have suggested in the chapters of this book, however, understanding is one part of a larger developmental dynamic. It stems from committed relationships with our students, just as it provides the foundation for deeper relating and more connected learning. Because development is an ongoing constructive process, efforts to understand our students require the capacity to tolerate misunderstanding as well—to recognize that despite our best efforts, we can only know so much about our students, and as a result often miss the mark in our attempts to reach them where they are. Developmentally, "where they are" is always on the way toward somewhere else. If we understand that, we have a chance to grow with them through our roles in the larger ecology of their lives, whether embraced for our contributions or resisted through our students' need to lead the way.

Notes

1. THE CONSTRUCTION OF ADOLESCENCE

1. All case studies for this book are fictional representations of common challenges faced by students and educators. The cases and characters are composites based on experiences from our work, and as such are not intended to depict actual students or educators. Any matching of characters' names or specific challenges with actual people is purely coincidental.

2. Karen Bartsch, "Adolescents' Theoretical Thinking," in *Early Adolescence: Perspectives on Research, Policy, and Intervention,* ed. R. M. Lerner (Hillsdale, NJ: Lawrence Erlbaum, 1993), 143–57.

3. We use the term *constructionist* here and throughout the book to define our applied developmental approach, which emphasizes the interaction of the adolescent's own meaning-making constructions of reality with those of significant others, including family, friends, and educators. Our constructionist perspective is derived from the assumption that youth (like all people) are the primary authors of their own life stories, the main builders of their identities, relationships, experiences, and the meaning made of them. At the same time, however, this perspective argues that no person is a solo author of her life experiences or narratives; we all have our life stories coauthored by those people who are most meaningful to us. We chose *constructionist* over its more commonly used relative *constructivist*, given that the latter term carries particular implications within the field of developmental psychology that do not necessarily hold here, including, in many cases, an emphasis on developmental stages, levels, or related structural hierarchies.

4. Lev Vygotsky, *Mind in Society* (Cambridge, MA: Harvard University Press, 1978).

5. In addition to Vygotsky's original writing on the zone of proximal development with its implications for scaffolding, see Lev Vygotsky, *Thought and Language* (Cambridge, MA: MIT Press, 1986). For a particularly clear overview of these and related concepts for educators, see Joan Wink and LeAnn Putney, *A Vision of Vygotsky* (Boston: Allyn & Bacon, 2002).

6. Mary Haywood Metz, "Teachers' Ultimate Dependence on Their Students," in *Teachers' Work: Individuals, Colleagues, and Contexts*, ed. Judith Warren Little and Milbrey Wallin McLaughlin (New York: Teachers College Press, 1995), 130.

7.   Metz, "Teachers' Ultimate Dependence," 131.

8.   Michael J. Nakkula and Sharon M. Ravitch, *Matters of Interpretation: Reciprocal Transformation in Therapeutic and Developmental Relationships with Youth*, 1st ed. (San Francisco: Jossey-Bass, 1998).

9.   We have chosen to capitalize the terms "Black" and "White" here and throughout the book, for a variety of reasons. Although *The Chicago Manual of Style* dictates that the terms be left in the lower case, we have chosen to capitalize them in order to maximize the potential that they be understood as specific historical, cultural, and political identifiers. In doing so, we seek to highlight the fact that "Black" and "White" function as designations more than descriptors; that is, the terms denote reified categories that operate in society as social markers, not simply as characterizations of skin color. Because there is relatively little guidance on the matter, we have provided a reasoned explanation of our thinking, one that we subdivide into three main influences: grammatical standards, scholarly precedents, and historical awareness.

Grammatically speaking, Black and White generally should not be understood as adjectives. The terms rarely function in sentences as modifiers of nouns, such as the way "pink" or "brown" might be used to describe the colors of skin. Black and White do not, in fact, refer simply to skin tone (and if they did, their inaccuracy would be obvious); rather, they designate a people and label a set of shared experiences stemming from both a difficult and triumphant historical legacy, one that merits the designation of the terms as proper nouns. Words used to label groups of people according to their race, culture, or ethnicity function as nouns. For example, in the U.S. context, a woman from China is Asian or Chinese. A man from El Salvador is Salvadoran or Latino. A child descended from African slaves or immigrants is African American or Black. Although technically all of the capitalized labels in each of the preceding three sentences are indeed adjectives, they function as *names*—proper nouns we use to describe our origins, associations, and positions in society. As an attempt to establish parity between mono- and multiracial/ethnic markers (e.g., Hawaiian, American Indian, Caribbean American, Scottish), it is important to capitalize both Black and White, since they too refer to distinct groups with specific histories, cultures, privileges, and disadvantages. Therefore, we depart from *The Chicago Manual of Style* and choose instead to look elsewhere for insights into how to think strategically, politically, and with cultural sensitivity about racial and ethnic labels.

In terms of precedent, we draw from standards set by multiple scholars from various fields. From law, we adopt the approach of the legal scholar, Kimberlé Williams Crenshaw (see K. W. Crenshaw, "Race, Reform, and Retrenchment: Transformation and Legitimation in Antidiscrimination Law," *Harvard Law Review* 101, no. 7 [1988]: 1331–87), which is to use "an upper-case 'B' to reflect my view that Blacks, like Asians, Latinos, and other 'minorities,' constitute a specific cultural group and, as such, require denotation as a proper noun" (from footnote 2, p. 1332). Catherine MacKinnon, also a legal scholar (see C. MacKinnon, "Feminism, Marxism, Method, and the State: An Agenda for Theory," *Signs: Journal of Women in Culture and Society* 7, no. 3 [1982]: 515–45), notes that "Black" should not be understood "as merely a color of skin pigmentation, but as a heritage, an experience, a cultural and personal identity, the meaning of which becomes specifically stigmatic and/or glorious and/or ordinary under specific social conditions" (pp. 515–16). In fact, since October 1997, the U.S. government has standardized the capitalization of both Black and White in the research and publications it sponsors on race and ethnicity (for a full description of the Standards for Maintaining, Collecting, and Presenting Federal Data on Race and Ethnicity issued by the Office of Management and Budget, see http://www.census.gov/population/www/socdemo/race/Ombdir15.html). As we assert in chapter 8, there are historical, cultural, and developmental differences suggested by how and when a person self-identifies as, for example, Haitian, African American, and/or Black, and we attempt to highlight those differences in the text where pertinent. As to why we sometimes choose Black over African American in describing more generalized situations, we draw from the insights of feminist ethnographer Wendy Luttrell, who, in her book *Pregnant Bodies, Fertile Minds* (New York: Routledge, 2003), uses the label Black in both upper and lower case to underscore instances when she wants to "draw attention to the persistent force of racial categorization according to skin color" (p. 191) that is sometimes veiled by the use of African American.

Historically, for the better part of the twentieth century, African Americans were labeled "Negroes," a term that was usually capitalized. (Citing W. E. B. Du Bois, however, Crenshaw chronicles how "the 'N' in Negro was always capitalized until, in defense of slavery, the use of the lower case 'n' became the custom in 'recognition' of Blacks' status as property; that the usage was defended as a 'description of the color of a people,' and that the capitalization of other ethnic and national origin designations made the failure to capitalize 'Negro' an insult"; Crenshaw, "Race, Reform, and Retrenchment," p. 1332). In the 1960s and 1970s, Black nationalist groups, activists, scholars, and various public intellectuals in the African American community began to claim Black as the preferred term, in part to reflect the growing racial pride movement. Black subsequently began to displace Negro in publications that were aware of and sensitive to the shifts occurring in the Black community. But as the mainstream media adopted Black, it was interpreted as an adjective instead of a proper noun, and the standard to use lower case was established. In our view, this interpretation is flawed. When the word Black is used synonymously with African American (or what would have been labeled Negro in the past), it should be capitalized. Since White also refers to a socially situated and historically distinct (i.e., privileged) people and not simply to a color, the same standard of capitalization should apply. That said, when these terms are used to describe a *characteristic* of a person (e.g., "Her skin is white" or "His skin is black"), as opposed to designating a person's *identity*, it makes sense to use the lower case.

2. IDENTITY IN CONTEXT

1. This list is adapted from P. M. Miller. "Theories of Adolescent Development," in *The Adolescent as Decision-Maker*, ed. J. Worell and F. Danner (San Diego, CA: Academic Press, 1989), 23–24.

2. The foundation for Erikson's early work on identity development can be found in Erik H. Erikson, *Childhood and Society* (New York: Norton, 1993). Originally published in 1950, this classic text had an enormous impact on the field of child development and human development more broadly.

3. See, for example, Barbara M. Newman and Philip R. Newman, *Development through Life: A Psychosocial Approach*, 9th ed. (Belmont, CA: Thomson Wadsworth, 2006); see also Edwin J. Herr, Stanley, H. Cramer, and Spencer, G. Niles, *Career Guidance and Counseling through the Lifespan: Systematic Approaches*, 6th ed. (Boston: Allyn & Bacon, 2004), 304–07, for an overview of Erikson's impact on the interrelated fields of lifespan development, developmental guidance, and career guidance and counseling.

4. See Erikson, *Childhood and Society*.

5. Erik H. Erikson, *Identity, Youth, and Crisis* (Hillsdale, NJ: W. W. Norton, 1968), 130.

6. Erikson, *Identity, Youth, and Crisis*, 211.

7. Erikson, *Identity, Youth, and Crisis*, 235–36.

8. James E. Marcia, "Identity in Adolescence," in *Handbook of Adolescent Psychology*, ed. J. Adelson (New York: Wiley), 159–87.

3. RISK TAKING AND CREATIVITY

1. Richard Jessor and Shirley L. Jessor, *Problem Behavior and Psychosocial Development: A Psychosocial Study of Youth* (New York: Academic Press, 1977); R. Jessor, "Risky Driving and Adolescent Problem Behavior: An Extension of Problem Behavior Theory," *Alcohol, Drugs, and Driving* no. 3 (1987): 1–11; and Martha R. Burth, Gary Resnick, and Emily R. Novick, *Building Supportive Communities for At-Risk Adolescents: It Takes More Than Services* (Washington, DC: American Psychological Association, 1998).

2. Cynthia Lightfoot, *The Culture of Adolescent Risk-Taking* (New York: Guilford Press, 1997).

3. Lightfoot, *The Culture of Adolescent Risk-Taking*.

4. Karen Bartsch, "Adolescents' Theoretical Thinking," in *Early Adolescence: Perspectives on Research, Policy, and Intervention*, ed. R. M. Lerner (Hillsdale, NJ: Lawrence Erlbaum, 1993), 143–57.

5. See Jean Piaget, *The Language and Thought of the Child* (New York: Meridian Books, 1955); Barbara Inhelder and Jean Piaget, *The Growth of Logical Thinking from Childhood to Adolescence* (New York: Basic Books, 1958).

6. Sharon Parks, *The Critical Years: The Young Adult Search for a Faith to Live By*, 1st ed. (San Francisco: Harper & Row, 1986).

7. Lev Vygotsky, *Mind in Society* (Cambridge, MA: Harvard University Press, 1978).

8. Jessor, *Risky Driving*.

9. Mihaly Csikszentmihalyi and Reed Larson, *Being Adolescent: Conflict and Growth in the Teenage Years* (New York: Basic Books, 1984).

10. Mihaly Csikszentmihalyi, *Finding Flow: The Psychology of Engagement with Everyday Life* (New York: Basic Books, 1997).

11. Jessor and Jessor, *Problem Behavior and Psychosocial Development*.

12. Michael J. Nakkula and Karen M. Foster, "Growth and Growing Pains: Second-Year Findings from a Longitudinal Study of Two Early College High Schools," unpublished research report, Harvard Graduate School of Education and Jobs for the Future, 2005.

4. FLOW AND POSSIBILITY DEVELOPMENT

1. Mihaly Csikszentmihalyi and Reed Larson, *Being Adolescent: Conflict and Growth in the Teenage Years* (New York: Basic Books, 1984).

2. The Project IF strength-based assessment can be found on the following website by clicking on the "Tools" link: *www.gse.harvard.edu/~projectif.*

3. Kurt W. Fischer, "A Theory of Cognitive Development: The Control and Construction of Hierarchies of Skills," *Psychological Review* 87, no. 6 (1980): 477–531; Kurt W. Fischer and Thomas R. Bidell, "Dynamic Development of Psychological Structures in Action and Thought," in *Handbook of Child Psychology: Theoretical Models of Human Development*, 5th ed., series eds. Richard M. Lerner and William Damon (New York: Wiley, 1998), 467–561.

4. Jari E. Nurmi, "Age Difference in Adult Life Goals, Concerns and Their Temporal Extension: A Life Course Approach to Future-Oriented Motivation," *International Journal of Behavior Development* 15, no. 4 (1992): 487–508; Jari E. Nurmi, "Adolescent Development in an Age-Graded Context: The Role of Personal Beliefs, Goals and Strategies," *International Journal of Behavior Development* 16, no. 2 (1993):169–89.

5. Michael J. Nakkula and Sharon M. Ravitch, *Matters of Interpretation: Reciprocal Transformation in Therapeutic and Developmental Relationships with Youth*, 1st ed. (San Francisco: Jossey-Bass, 1998).

6. Susan A. Jackson and Mihaly Csikszentmihalyi, *Flow in Sports: The Keys to Optimal Experiences and Performances* (Champagne, IL: Human Kinetics, 1999); Megan A. Horst, "Organized Sports Participation in the Lives of Adolescent Hispanic Girls: A Mixed-Methods Analysis" (doctoral dissertation, Harvard Graduate School of Education, 2005).

7. Edward Seidman and Sara Pedersen, "Holistic Contextual Perspectives on Risk, Protection, and Competence among Low-Income Urban Adolescence," in *Risk and Vulnerability: Adaptations in the Context of Childhood Adversities*, ed. Suniya S. Luthar (Cambridge, England: Cambridge University Press, 2003), 318–42.

8. Peter C. Scales and Nancy Leffert, *Developmental Assets: A Synthesis of the Scientific Research on Adolescent Development*, 2nd ed. (Minneapolis: Search Institute, 2004).

9. See the Search Institute's website: *http://www.search-institute.org/communities/hchy.html.*

10. Richard M. Lerner and Peter L. Benson, *Developmental Assets and Asset-Building Communities: Implications for Research, Policy, and Practice* (New York: Springer, 2002).

11. Michael J. Nakkula, Karen M. Foster, Marc Mannes, and Shenita Lewis, *Community Collaboration for Positive Youth Development: An Intersection of Psychology and Social Change* (New York: Springer, in press).

5. RELATIONAL IDENTITY AND RELATIONSHIP DEVELOPMENT

1. Harry Stack Sullivan, *The Interpersonal Theory of Psychiatry* (New York: Norton, 1953).

2. Lev Vygotsky, *Mind in Society* (Cambridge, MA: Harvard University Press, 1978).

3. Robert L. Selman, *The Growth of Interpersonal Understanding: Developmental and Clinical Analyses* (New York: Academic Press, 1980); Robert L. Selman and Lynn H. Schultz, *Making a Friend in Youth: Developmental Theory and Pair Therapy* (Chicago:

University of Chicago Press, 1990); Robert L. Selman, Caroline L. Watts, and Lynn H. Schultz, eds., *Fostering Friendship: Pair Therapy for Treatment and Prevention* (Hawthorne, NY: Aldine de Gruyter, 1997).

4. Lawrence Kohlberg, *The Psychology of Moral Development: The Validity of Moral Stages* (San Francisco: Harper & Row, 1984).

5. Selman, *The Growth of Interpersonal Understanding*.

6. Robert L. Selman, *The Promotion of Social Awareness: Powerful Lessons from the Partnership of Developmental Theory and Classroom Practice* (New York: Russell Sage Foundation, 2003).

7. Selman and Schultz, *Making a Friend in Youth*.

8. See chapter 4, "Risk, Relationship, and the Importance of Personal Meaning," in Selman, *The Promotion of Social Awareness*.

9. Carol Gilligan, *In a Different Voice: Psychological Theory and Women's Development* (Cambridge, MA: Harvard University Press, 1993).

10. See Lynn Mykel Brown and Carol Gilligan, *Meeting at the Crossroads: Women's Psychology and Girls' Development* (Cambridge, MA: Harvard University Press, 1992); Carol Gilligan, "The Centrality of Relationship in Human Development: A Puzzle, Some Evidence, and a Theory," in *Development and Vulnerability in Close Relationships*, ed. Gil G. Noam and Kurt W. Fischer, (New York: Erlbaum, 1996), 237–61.

11. Nancy J. Chodorow, *The Reproduction of Mothering: Psychoanalysis and the Sociology of Gender* (Berkeley: University of California Press, 1978).

12. Jean Baker Miller et al., "Some Misconceptions and Reconceptions of a Relational Approach" (paper, Stone Center Colloquium Series, Stone Center for Developmental Services and Studies, Wellesley College, 1990); Judith V. Jordan, Alexandra G. Kaplan, Jean Baker Miller, Janet L. Surrey, and Irene Pierce Stiver, *Women's Growth in Connection: Writings from the Stone Center* (New York: Guilford, 1991); Judith V. Jordan, Linda M. Hartling, and Maureen Walker, *The Complexity of Connection: Writings from the Stone Center's Jean Baker Miller Training Institute* (New York: Guilford, 2004).

13. Jean E. Rhodes, *Stand by Me: The Risks and Rewards of Mentoring Today's Youth* (Cambridge, MA: Harvard University Press, 1992).

14. David L. DuBois and Michael J. Karcher, eds., *The Handbook of Youth Mentoring* (Thousand Oaks, CA: Sage, 2005).

15. Robert C. Pianta and Daniel L. Walsh, *High-Risk Children in Schools: Constructing Sustaining Relationships* (New York: Routledge, 1996).

6. GENDER IDENTITY DEVELOPMENT

1. Lynn Mykel Brown and Carol Gilligan, *Meeting at the Crossroads: Women's Psychology and Girls' Development* (Cambridge, MA: Harvard University Press, 1992).

2. Michael Rutter, "Nature, Nurture, and Development: From Evangelism through Science Towards Policy and Practice," *Child Development* no. 73 (2002): 1–21; Robert Sternberg and Elena L. Grigorenko, *The General Factor of Intelligence: How General Is It?* (Mahwah, NJ: Lawrence Erlbaum, 2002).

3. M. Sapon-Shevin and J. Goodman, "Learning to Be Opposite Sex: Sexuality Education and Scripting in Early Adolescence," in *Sexuality and the Curriculum: The Politics and Practices of Sexuality Education*, ed. James T. Sears (New York: Teachers College Press, 1992).

4. Carol Gilligan, "The Centrality of Relationship in Human Development: A Puzzle, Some Evidence, and a Theory," in *Development and Vulnerability in Close Relationships*, ed. Gil G. Noam and Kurt W. Fischer (Mahwah, NJ: L. Erlbaum, 1996).

5. Carol Gilligan, "Joining the Resistance: Psychology, Politics, Girls and Women," in *Beyond Silenced Voices*, ed. Lois Weis and Michelle Fine (Albany, NY: SUNY Press, 1993).

6. Lisa Machoian, *The Disappearing Girl: Learning the Language of Teenage Depression* (New York: Dutton, 2005).

7. Myra Sadker and David Sadker, *Failing at Fairness: How America's Schools Cheat Girls* (New York: Charles Scribner's Sons, 1994).

8. Russell J. Skiba et al., "The Color of Discipline: Sources of Racial and Gender Disproportionality in School Punishment," *The Urban Review* 34, no. 4 (2002), 320.

9. Ann Arnett Ferguson, *Bad Boys: Public Schools in the Making of Black Masculinity* (Ann Arbor: University of Michigan Press, 2000); R. W. Connell, "Disruptions: Improper Masculinities and Schooling," in *Beyond Silenced Voices: Class, Race, and Gender in United States Schools: Class, Race, and Gender in United States Schools*, ed. Lois Weis and Michelle Fine (Albany, NY: SUNY Press, 1993).

10. U.S. Dept. of Education, *Digest of Education Statistics* (Washington, DC: GPO, 2002).

11. Wendy Luttrell, "'Good Enough' Methods for Ethnographic Research," *Harvard Educational Review* 70, no. 4 (2000).

12. Mary Pipher, *Reviving Ophelia: Saving the Selves of Adolescent Girls* (New York: Putnam, 1994); Rosalind Wiseman, *Queen Bees and Wannabes: Helping Your Daughter Survive Cliques, Gossip, Boyfriends, and Other Realities of Adolescence* (New York: Crown, 2002); Rachel Simmons, *Odd Girl Out: The Hidden Culture of Aggression in Girls* (New York: Harcourt, 2002); James Garbarino, *Lost Boys: Why Our Sons Turn Violent and How We Can Save Them* (New York: Free Press, 1999); Ferguson, *Bad Boys: Public Schools in the Making of Black Masculinity*; William Pollack, *Real Boys: Rescuing Our Sons from the Myths of Boyhood* (New York: Random House, 1998); John J. DiIulio, "The Coming of the Super-Predators," *Weekly Standard*, November 27, 1995.

13. Michelle Fine and Nancie Zane, "Bein' Wrapped Too Tight: When Low Income Women Drop Out of High School," in *Dropouts from Schools: Issues, Dilemmas, and Solutions*, ed. Lois Weis, Eleanor Farrar, and Hugh G. Petrie (Albany, NY: SUNY Press, 1989).

14. Bonnie J. Ross Leadbeater and Niobe Way, *Urban Girls: Resisting Stereotypes, Creating Identities* (New York: New York University Press, 1996).

15. Jennifer Pastor, Jennifer McCormick, and Michelle Fine, "Makin' Homes: An Urban Girl Thing," in *Urban Girls: Resisting Stereotypes, Creating Identities*, ed. Bonnie J. Ross Leadbeater and Niobe Way (New York: New York University Press, 1996).

16. Prudence L. Carter, *Keepin' It Real: School Success Beyond Black and White* (New York: Oxford University Press, 2005); L. Janelle Dance, *Tough Fronts: The Impact of Street Culture on Schooling*, ed. Michael Apple (New York: RoutledgeFalmer, 2002); Angela

Valenzuela, *Subtractive Schooling: U.S.-Mexican Youth and the Politics of Caring* (Albany, NY: SUNY Press, 1999); Janie Ward, "Raising Resisters: The Role of Truth Telling in the Psychological Development of African American Girls," in *Urban Girls: Resisting Stereotypes, Creating Identities*, ed. Bonnie J. Ross Leadbeater and Niobe Way (New York: New York University Press, 1996).

17. Tracie Robinson and Janie V. Ward, "'A Belief in Self Far Greater Than Anyone's Disbelief': Cultivating Resistance in African-American Female Adolescents," in *Women, Girls and Psychotherapy: Reframing Resistance*, ed. Carol Gilligan, Annie Rogers, and Deborah Tolman (New York: Harrington Park Press, 1991), 87–103.

18. Jean Baker Miller et al., "Some Misconceptions and Reconceptions of a Relational Approach" (paper, Stone Center Colloquium series, Stone Center for Developmental Services and Studies, Wellesley College, 1990).

19. Michael S. Kimmel, *The Gendered Society* (New York: Oxford University Press, 2000); Michael S. Kimmel, "Masculinity as Homophobia: Fear, Shame, and Silence in the Construction of Gender Identity," in *Theorizing Masculinities*, ed. Harry Brod and Michael Kaufman (Thousand Oaks, CA: Sage, 1994).

20. Kimmel, "Masculinity as Homophobia," 126, 130.

21. Kimmel, "Masculinity as Homophobia," 133, 132.

22. Kimmel, "Masculinity as Homophobia," 138.

23. bell hooks, *Sisters of the Yam: Black Women and Self Recovery* (Boston: South End Press, 1993).

7. RACIAL IDENTITY DEVELOPMENT

1. Howard Winant, "Dictatorship, Democracy, and Difference: The Historical Construction of Racial Identity," in *The Bubbling Cauldron: Race, Ethnicity, and the Urban Crisis*, ed. M. P. Smith and J. R. Feagin (Minneapolis: University of Minnesota Press, 1995), 31.

2. Stephen Jay Gould, *The Mismeasure of Man* (New York: Norton, 1981).

3. Michael Omi and Howard Winant, "On the Theoretical Status of the Concept of Race," in *Race, Identity, and Representation in Education*, ed. Cameron McCarthy and Warren Crichlow (New York: Routledge, 1993), 6.

4. Joe L. Kincheloe and Shirley R. Steinberg, "Constructing a Pedagogy of Whiteness for Angry White Students," in *Dismantling White Privilege: Pedagogy, Politics, and Whiteness*, ed. Nelson M. Rodriguez and Leila E. Villafuerte (New York: Peter Lang, 2000), 183.

5. Helen A. Neville et al. "Construction and Initial Validation of the Color-Blind Racial Attitudes Scale (Cobras)," *Journal of Counseling Psychology* 47, no. 1 (2000): 59–70.

6. See Nakkula and Ravitch's *Matters of Interpretation* for a more extensive discussion of this concept.

7. Michelle Fine et al., "Before the Bleach Gets Us All," in *Construction Sites: Excavating Race, Class, and Gender among Urban Youth*, ed. Lois Weis and Michelle Fine (New York: Teachers College Press, 2000).

8. Lisa D. Delpit, *Other People's Children: Cultural Conflict in the Classroom* (New York: New Press, 1995), 46.

9. Delpit, *Other People's Children*, 46.

10. Robert T. Carter, "Is White a Race? Expressions of White Racial Identity," in *Off White*, ed. Michelle Fine et al. (New York: Routledge, 1997), 199.

11. Robert L. Selman, *The Growth of Interpersonal Understanding: Developmental and Clinical Analyses* (New York: Academic Press, 1980); Robert L. Selman, M. Levitt, and Lynn Hickey Schultz, "The Friendship Framework," in *Fostering Friendship: Pair Therapy for Treatment and Prevention*, ed. Robert L. Selman, Caroline L. Watts, and Lynn Hickey Schultz (New York: Aldine de Gruyter, 1997).

12. Margaret Beale Spencer and Sanford M. Dornbusch, "Challenges in Studying Minority Youth," in *At the Threshold: The Developing Adolescent*, ed. S. Shirley Feldman and Glen R. Elliott (Cambridge, MA: Harvard University Press, 1990), 131.

13. Spencer and Dornbusch, "Challenges in Studying Minority Youth," 131.

14. See Ann R. Fischer and Bonnie Moradi, "Racial and Ethnic Identity: Recent Developments and Needed Directions," in *Handbook of Multicultural Counseling*, ed. Joseph G. Ponterotto (Thousand Oaks, CA: Sage, 2001).

15. William E. Cross, *Shades of Black: Diversity in African-American Identity* (Philadelphia: Temple University Press, 1991).

16. Fischer and Moradi, "Racial and Ethnic Identity," 347.

17. Cross uses the term *stages* to describe her theory even though, like Marcia's *statuses*, one may proceed in nonlinear fashion through them.

18. Richard Majors and Janet Mancini Billson, *Cool Pose: The Dilemmas of Black Manhood in America* (New York: Simon & Schuster, 1993).

19. Ruth Frankenberg, *White Women, Race Matters: The Social Construction of Whiteness* (Minneapolis: University of Minnesota Press, 1993); Gary R. Howard, *We Can't Teach What We Don't Know: White Teachers, Multiracial Schools* (New York: Teachers College Press, 1999); Tina Q. Richardson and Timothy J. Silvestri, "White Identity Formation: A Developmental Process," in *Racial and Ethnic Identity in School Practices*, ed. R. H. Sheets and E. R. Hollins (Mahwah, NJ: Lawrence Erlbaum, 1999); Wayne Rowe, Sandra K. Bennett, and Donald R. Atkinson, "White Racial Identity Models: A Critique and Alternative Proposal," *Counseling Psychologist* 22, no. 1 (1994): 129–46; Joseph G. Ponterotto, "White Racial Identity and the Counseling Professional," *Counseling Psychologist* 21, no. 2 (1993): 213–17.

20. Carter, "Is White a Race?" 199 (italics added).

21. Erin McNamara Horvat and Carla O'Connor, eds., *Beyond Acting White: Reframing the Debate on Black Student Achievement* (Lanham, MD: Rowan & Littlefield, 2006); Pedro Noguera, "The Role of Research in Challenging Racial Inequality in Education," unpublished paper presented in Technical Report S-520, "Qualitative Research Methods" (Harvard Graduate School of Education, 2001), 24.

22. As quoted in Beverly Daniel Tatum, "Talking About Race, Learning About Racism: The Application of Racial Identity Development Theory in the Classroom," *Harvard Educational Review* 62, no. 1 (1992): 13.

23. Robert T. Carter, "Reimagining Race in Education: A New Paradigm from Psychology," *Teachers College Record* 102, no. 5 (2000): 864–97.

T1. C. A. Arce, "A Reconsideration of Chicano Culture and Identity," *Daedalus* 110 (1981): 177–92; D. R. Atkinson, G. Morten, and D. W. Sue, eds., *Counseling American Minorities: A Cross-Cultural Perspective*, 3rd ed. (Dubuque, IA: William C. Brown, 1989); R. T. Carter, "Reimagining Race in Education: A New Paradigm from Psychology," *Teachers College Record* 102, no. 5 (2000): 864–97; W. E. Cross, *Shades of Black: Diversity in African-American Identity* (Philadelphia: Temple University Press, 1991); J. E. Helms, *Black and White Racial Identity: Theory, Research, and Practice* (Westport, CT: Greenwood Press, 1990); J. Kim, *Processes of Asian-American Identity Development: A Study of Japanese American Women's Perceptions of Their Struggle to Achieve Positive Identities*, unpublished doctoral dissertation, University of Massachusetts, Amherst, 1981; J. E. Marcia, "Identity in Adolescence," in *Handbook of Adolescent Psychology*, ed. J. Adelson (New York: John Wiley, 1980), 159–87; J. S. Phinney, B. T. Lochner, and R. Murphy, "Ethnic Identity Development and Psychological Adjustment in Adolescence," in *Ethnic Issues in Adolescent Mental Health*, ed. A. R. Stiffman and L. E. Davis (Newbury Park, CA: Sage, 1990), 53–72; J. G. Ponterotto and P. Pedersen, *Preventing Prejudice: A Guide for Counselors and Educators* (Newbury Park, CA: Sage, 1993); A. S. Ruiz, "Ethnic Identity: Crisis and Resolution," *Journal of Multicultural Counseling and Development* 18, (1990): 29–40; A. Wilson, "How We Find Ourselves: Identity Development and Two-Spirit People," *Harvard Educational Review* 66, no. 2 (1996): 303–17.

8. ETHNIC IDENTITY DEVELOPMENT

1. Michael J. Nakkula and Claudia Pineda, "Students at Risk," in *Encyclopedia of Human Development and Education,* ed. Stephan J. Farenga and Daniel Ness (Armonk, NY: ME Sharpe Publishers, 2005).

2. Various statistical projections identify the fact that within the next 10–20 years, people of color will outnumber Whites in the United States, making the majority-minority comparison less robust than issues of identity and one's relationship to power. For this reason, the term *minority* makes little sense anymore, and its use may even contribute to the marginalization or "minoritization" of the soon-to-be nonWhite majority.

3. Beverly Daniel Tatum, "Talking About Race, Learning About Racism: The Application of Racial Identity Development Theory in the Classroom," *Harvard Educational Review* 62, no. 1 (1992): 9–10.

4. Pepi Leistyna, "Racenicity: Understanding Racialized Ethnic Identities," in *Multi/Intercultural Conversations*, ed. Shirley R. Steinberg (New York: Peter Lang, 2001).

5. See, for example, Lisa Delpit, *The Skin That We Speak* (New York: New Press, 2002); Margaret A. Gibson and John U. Ogbu, *Minority Status and Schooling: A Comparative Study of Immigrant and Involuntary Minorities* (New York: Garland, 1991); Jonathan Kozol, *Savage Inequalities: Children in America's Schools* (New York: Crown, 1991); Cameron McCarthy and Warren Crichlow, *Race, Identity, and Representation in Education* (New York: Routledge, 1993).

6. Rubén O. Martinez and Richard L. Dukes, "The Effects of Ethnic Identity, Ethnicity, and Gender on Adolescent Well-Being," *Journal of Youth and Adolescence* 26, no. 5 (1997): 514.

7. John Raible and Sonia Nieto, "Beyond Categories: The Complex Identities of Adolescents," in *Adolescents at School*, ed. Michael Sadowski (Cambridge, MA: Harvard Education Press, 2003), 146.

8. Rosa Hernandez Sheets, "Human Development and Ethnic Identity," in *Racial and Ethnic Identity in School Practices: Aspects of Human Development*, ed. Rosa Hernandez Sheets and Etta R. Hollins (Mahwah, NJ: Lawrence Erlbaum, 1999), 94.

9. Ann R. Fischer and Bonnie Moradi, "Racial and Ethnic Identity: Recent Developments and Needed Directions," in *Handbook of Multicultural Counseling*, ed. Joseph G. Ponterotto (Thousand Oaks, CA: Sage, 2001); J. S. Phinney, "Ethnic Identity in Adolescents and Adults: Review of Research," *Psychological Bulletin* 108 (1990): 499–514.

10. Fischer and Moradi, "Racial and Ethnic Identity," 342.

11. Hernandez Sheets, "Human Development and Ethnic Identity," 108.

12. Hernandez Sheets, "Human Development and Ethnic Identity," 108.

13. Hernandez Sheets, "Human Development and Ethnic Identity," 109.

14. Nakkula and Pineda, "Students at Risk."

15. Martinez and Dukes, "The Effects of Ethnic Identity," 513.

16. Hernandez Sheets, "Human Development and Ethnic Identity," 109.

17. Cornel West, "The New Cultural Politics of Difference," in *Beyond a Dream Deferred: Multicultural Education and the Politics of Excellence*, ed. B. Thompson and S. Tyagi (Minneapolis: University of Minnesota Press, 1993), 31.

18. As quoted in Hernandez Sheets, "Human Development and Ethnic Identity," 97.

19. Phinney, "Ethnic Identity," 502.

20. Phinney, "Ethnic Identity," 503.

21. Phinney, "Ethnic Identity," 511.

22. Herbert J. Gans, "Second-Generation Decline: Scenarios for the Economic and Ethnic Futures of the Post-1965 American Immigrants," *Ethnic and Racial Studies* 15, no. 2 (1992): 174.

23. Gans, "Second-Generation Decline," 182.

24. Mary C. Waters, "Ethnic and Racial Identities of Second Generation Black Immigrants in New York City," *International Migration Review* 28, no. 4 (1994): 799.

25. A. Portes and M. Zhou, "The New Second Generation: Segmented Assimilation and Its Variants," *Annals of the American Academy of Political and Social Science* 530 (1993): 74–97.

26. Portes and Zhou, "The New Second Generation," 801.

27. Waters, "Ethnic and Racial Identities," 799–800.

28. Waters, "Ethnic and Racial Identities," 802 (emphasis added).

29. Waters, "Ethnic and Racial Identities," 802.

30. Waters, "Ethnic and Racial Identities," 802.

31. Waters, "Ethnic and Racial Identities," 805, 806.

32. See Gans, "Second-Generation Decline," 173–92; Portes and Zhou, "The New Second Generation," 74–97.

33. Waters, "Ethnic and Racial Identities," 808, 812, 807.

9. DEVELOPING A SEXUAL IDENTITY ORIENTATION

1. M. Sapon-Shevin and J. Goodman, "Learning to Be Opposite Sex: Sexuality Education and Scripting in Early Adolescence," in *Sexuality and the Curriculum: The Politics and Practices of Sexuality Education*, ed. James T. Sears (New York: Teachers College Press, 1992).

2. Janice M. Irvine, *Talk About Sex: The Battles Over Sex Education in the United States* (Berkeley: University of California Press, 2002).

3. Irvine, *Talk About Sex*; Debbie Epstein and James T. Sears, eds., *A Dangerous Knowing: Sexuality, Pedagogy, and Popular Culture* (London: Cassell, 1999); James T. Sears, "School Administrators as Public Intellectuals: Developing a Sexuality Curriculum in a Multicultural Society," in *What School Administrators Should Know*, ed. S. Tonnen (Champaign, IL: Charles Thomas, 2000).

4. Michelle Fine, "Sexuality, Schooling, and Adolescent Females: The Missing Discourse of Desire," *Harvard Educational Review* 58, no. 1 (1988): 29–53.

5. Janie Victoria Ward, *The Skin We're In: Teaching Our Children to Be Emotionally Strong, Socially Smart, and Spiritually Connected* (Boston: Free Press, 2000).

6. Irvine, *Talk about Sex*.

7. Sullivan, *The Interpersonal Theory of Psychiatry*. See pages 274–76 of chapter 17 ("Early Adolescence") for a discussion of the relationship between love and lust.

8. Vivienne Cass, "Homosexual Identity Formation: A Theoretical Model," *Journal of Homosexuality* 4 (1979): 219–35; R. R. Troiden, "The Formation of Homosexual Identities," *Journal of Homosexuality* 17 (1989): 43–73; E. Coleman, "Developmental Stages of the Coming Out Process," *Journal of Homosexuality* 7 (1982): 31–43.

9. Sara Herwig is attempting to become the first openly transgender priest ordained by the Presbyterian Church. She is the director of operations for the International Foundation for Gender Education (www.ifge.org), which publishes the widely subscribed newsletter *Transgender Tapestry*. The comments attributed to Herwig here are derived from her Spring 2006 lectures in Michael Nakkula's course on adolescent development at the Harvard Graduate School of Education.

10. FAITH AND THE DEVELOPMENT OF ULTIMATE MEANING

1. Sharon Parks, *The Critical Years: The Young Adult Search for a Faith to Live By* (San Francisco: Harper & Row, 1986), 42.

2. Parks, *The Critical Years*.

3. James Fowler, *Stages of Faith* (San Francisco: Harper & Row, 1981), 71.

4. Adapted from the cognitive conclusions reached by G. R. Adams et al., "Identity Development," *Adolescent Life Experiences* (Pacific Grove, CA: Brooks/Cole, 1994), 280.

5. Erik H. Erikson, *Identity, Youth, and Crisis* (New York: W. W. Norton, 1968), 129.

6. Carol Gilligan, *In a Different Voice: Psychological Theory and Women's Development* (Cambridge, MA: Harvard University Press, 1993), 73.

7. Paul Tillich, *Dynamics of Faith* (New York: Harper & Row, 1957), 4.

8. Gordon Kaufman, *In Face of Mystery: A Constructive Theology* (Cambridge, MA: Harvard University Press, 1993), 341.

9. Fowler, *Stages of Faith*, 133.

10. Fowler, *Stages of Faith*.

11. Parks, *The Critical Years*, 47.

12. Parks, *The Critical Years*, 50.

13. Parks, *The Critical Years*, 91.

14. As cited in Parks, *The Critical Years*, 52.

15. Parks, *The Critical Years*, 50.

16. Parks, *The Critical Years*, 84.

17. Parker Palmer, "Evoking the Spirit in Public Education," *Educational Leadership* 56, no. 4 (1999): 6.

18. Rachael Kessler, *The Soul of Education* (Alexandria, VA: Association for Supervision and Curriculum Development, 2000); Parker Palmer, "Evoking the Spirit in Public Education."

19. Kessler, *The Soul of Education*, 163.

20. Kessler, *The Soul of Education*, 38.

21. Kessler, *The Soul of Education*, 44.

22. Palmer, "Evoking the Spirit in Public Education," 8–9.

23. Palmer, "Evoking the Spirit in Public Education," 8.

24. Kessler, *The Soul of Education*, 135.

25. Kessler, *The Soul of Education*.

11. SCHOOL-TO-CAREER TRANSITIONS

1. Richard Lapan, *Career Development Across the K–16 Years: Bridging the Present to Satisfying and Successful Futures* (Alexandria, VA: American Counseling Association, 2004).

2. See American School Counselor Association, *The ASCA National Model: A Framework for School Counseling Programs* (Alexandria, VA: Author, 2003); D. L. Bluestein, C. L. Juntunen, and R. L. Worthington, "The School-to-Work Transition: Adjustment Challenges of the Forgotten Half," in *Handbook of Counseling Psychology*, ed. S. D. Brown and R. W. Lent, 3rd ed. (New York: Wiley, 2000), 435–70.

3. "Relevance, the Missing Link: A Guide for Promoting Student Success through Career Development Education, Training, and Counseling," 2005 Massachusetts Career Development Education Guide, *http://www.doe.mass.edu/cd/resources/cdeguide_drft.doc*.

4. Wendy Luttrell, *School-Smart and Mother-Wise: Working-Class Women's Identity and Schooling* (New York: Routledge, 1997).

5. MDOE Career Development Education Guide, 47.

6. Roger Herring, *Career Counseling in Schools: Multicultural and Developmental Perspectives* (Alexandria, VA: American Counseling Association, 1998).

7. Met School's Web address: *http://www.whatkidscando.org/portfoliosmallschools/MET/Metintro.html*.

8. See Theodore R. Sizer, *Horace's Compromise: The Dilemma of the American High School* (Boston: Houghton Mifflin, 1984) and *Horace's School: Redesigning the American High*

School (Boston: Houghton Mifflin, 1992); Coalition for Essential Schools website: *http://www.essentialschools.org*; Bill and Melinda Gates Foundation website: *http://www.gatesfoundation.org/Education.*

9. Elliott Levine, *One Kid at a Time: Big Lessons from a Small School* (New York: Teachers College Press, 2001).

10. Dennis Littky and Samantha Grabelle, *The Big Picture: Education Is Everyone's Business* (Alexandria, VA: Association for Supervision and Curriculum Development, 2004).

11. Vincent Tinto, *Leaving College: Rethinking the Causes and Cures of Student Attrition* (Chicago: University of Chicago Press, 1993); N. Soucy and S. Larose, "Attachment and Control in Family and Mentoring Contexts as Determinants of Adolescent Adjustment in College," *Journal of Family Psychology* no. 14 (2000): 125–43; Georges Vernez, Richard A. Krop, and Peter Rydell, *Closing the Education Gap: Benefits and Costs* (Santa Monica, CA: RAND, 1999).

12. Michael Kirst and Andrea Venezia, *From High School to College: Improving Opportunities for Success in Postsecondary Education* (San Francisco: Jossey-Bass, 2004).

13. Jobs for the Future website: *http://www.jff.org.*

14. See Michael J. Nakkula and Karen Foster, *Growth and Growing Pains: Second-Year Findings from a Longitudinal Study of Two Early College High Schools* (Harvard Graduate School of Education, unpublished research report, 2006); and Ronald A. Wolk, *"It's kind of different": Student Experiences in Two Early College High Schools* (Boston: Jobs for the Future, 2005).

12. THE EDUCATIONAL ECOLOGY OF ADOLESCENT DEVELOPMENT

1. Urie Bronfenbrenner, *The Ecology of Human Development: Experiments by Nature and Design* (Cambridge, MA: Harvard University Press, 1979).

2. Urie Bronfenbrenner, *Making Human Beings Human: Bioecological Perspectives on Human Development* (Thousand Oaks, CA: Sage, 2004).

3. M. B. Spencer, D. Dupree, and T. Hartmann, "A Phenomenological Variant of Ecological Systems Theory (PVEST): A Self-Organization Perspective in Context," *Developmental Psychopathology* 9, no. 4 (1997): 817–33.

4. Diane E. H. Russell, *Dangerous Relationships: Pornography, Misogyny, and Rape* (Thousand Oaks, CA: Safe, 1998); Fitzhugh G. Houston, *Men Let's Talk! Pornography: The Quiet Addiction* (Panorama City, CA: Houston Spectrum, 2003); Gail Dines, Robert Jensen, and Ann Russo, *Pornography: The Production and Consumption of Inequality* (New York: Routledge, 1998).

5. See chapter 4 for a description of the Search Institute's Healthy Communities–Healthy Youth Initiative.

6. Herbert R. Kohl, *I Won't Learn from You: The Role of Assent in Learning* (Minneapolis, MN: Milkweed Editions, 1991).

7. Angela Valenzuela, *Subtractive Schooling: U.S.-Mexican Youth and the Politics of Caring* (Albany, NY: SUNY Press, 1999).

8. S. Fordham and J. U. Ogbu, "Black Students' School Success: Coping with the Burden of 'Acting White,'" *Urban Review* 18, no. 3 (1986): 176–206; Signithia Fordham, "Racelessness as a Factor in Black Students' School Success: Pragmatic Strategy or Pyrrhic Victory?" *Harvard Educational Review* 58, no. 1 (1988): 54–84; John Ogbu, "Class

Stratification, Racial Stratification, and Schooling," in *Race, Class, and Gender in American Education*, ed. L. Weis (Albany, NY: SUNY Press, 1988); John Ogbu, "Minority Status and Literacy in Comparative Perspective," *Daedalus* 119, no. 2 (1990): 141–68; John Ogbu, *Minority Education and Caste: The American System in Cross-Cultural Perspective* (New York: Academic Press, 1978); John Ogbu, "Minority Education in Comparative Perspective," *Journal of Negro Education* 59, no. 1 (1990): 45–57.

9. See Prudence L. Carter's "'Black' Cultural Capital, Status Positioning, and Schooling Conflicts for Low-Income African American Youth," *Social Problems* 50, no. 1 (2003): 136–55; "Intersecting Identities: Gender and Academic Achievement," in *Beyond Acting White*, ed. Eric McNamara Horvat and Carla O'Connor (New York: Rowan & Littlefield, 2006), 111–32; and *Keepin' It Real: School Success Beyond Black and White* (New York: Oxford University Press, 2005).

10. L. Janelle Dance, *Tough Fronts: The Impact of Street Culture on Schooling* (New York: RoutledgeFalmer, 2002).

About the Authors

Michael J. Nakkula is a research associate at the Harvard Graduate School of Education (HGSE), where he has taught courses on counseling, urban education, and adolescent development and helped develop HGSE's Risk and Prevention Program. Nakkula was named HGSE's inaugural holder of the Kargman Assistant Professorship in Human Development and Urban Education, an appointment he held from 1998 to 2004. He is the coauthor, with Sharon Ravitch, of *Matters of Interpretation: Reciprocal Transformation in Therapeutic and Developmental Relationships with Youth* (1998). His current research focuses on the experiences of adolescents as they traverse the challenges of urban educational systems en route to work, college, and careers. Nakkula earned bachelor's degrees in communications and psychology from Michigan State University, a master's degree in counseling from the University of Minnesota–Duluth, and his doctorate in counseling and consulting psychology from HGSE.

Eric Toshalis is an instructor in education and advanced doctoral candidate at HGSE. A former middle and high school educator, he has worked with youth and adults in schools as a coach, mentor teacher, community activist, teachers union president, afterschool group leader, and curriculum writer. Since 2003 he has cotaught the course on adolescent development for preservice teachers in Harvard's teacher education program. As a researcher, Toshalis studies how teachers and students variously resist the tendency of public schools to reproduce social inequality and how such resistance can be promoted in the classroom. He received his bachelor's degree, teaching credential, and master's degree in education from the University of California, Santa Barbara, and his master of theological studies from Harvard Divinity School.

Index

Note: Page numbers followed by *f* or *t* indicate figures or tables, respectively.